The San Juan Islands

Fourth Edition

MARGE & TED
MUELLER

A must-have for anyone setting out to explore the San Juans, whether you are visiting by car or boat...Marge and Ted Mueller are just the people to make sure you don't miss a thing.
—*WaveLength* magazine

If your experience of the San Juans has been limited to Friday Harbor, let the Mueller's guide you to quieter nooks and crannies.
—*Everett Herald*

With sailing season under way, this revised guide to the San Juan archipelago should come in handy.
—*Seattle Times/Post-Intelligencer*

Afoot and Afloat has intriguing island diversions we might otherwise miss. From the water, ferry, car, or footpath—this is the book that will make your San Juan visit better.
—*The Reel News*

THE MOUNTAINEERS BOOKS

Published by
The Mountaineers Books
1001 SW Klickitat Way, Suite 201
Seattle, WA 98134

First edition 1979. Second edition 1988. Third edition 1995. Fourth edition: first printing 2003, second printing 2005, third printing 2006, fourth printing 2008, fifth printing 2010

Distributed in the United Kingdom by Cordee, www.cordee.co.uk

Manufactured in the United States of America

Editor: Christine Clifton-Thornton
Cover design: Mayumi Thompson
Book design and layout: Marge Mueller, Gray Mouse Graphics
Mapmakers: Marge and Ted Mueller, Gray Mouse Graphics
Photographers: All photos by Marge and Ted Mueller, except as noted
Cover photograph: *Anchorage in Active Cove, Patos Island*

Library of Congress Cataloging–in–Publication Data
Mueller, Marge.
  The San Juan Islands : afoot & afloat / Marge & Ted Mueller.—4th ed.
      p. cm.
Includes bibliographical references and index.
  ISBN 0-89886-881-5
  1. San Juan Islands (Wash.)—Guidebooks. I. Mueller, Ted. II. Title.
  F897.S2M79 2004
  917.97'74—dc22
                                        2003026401

Printed on recycled paper
ISBN (paperback): 978-0-89886-881-4
ISBN (ebook): 978-1-59485-181-0

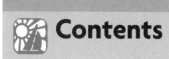

Contents

chapter seven • Orcas Island   173

chapter eight • Moran State Park   203

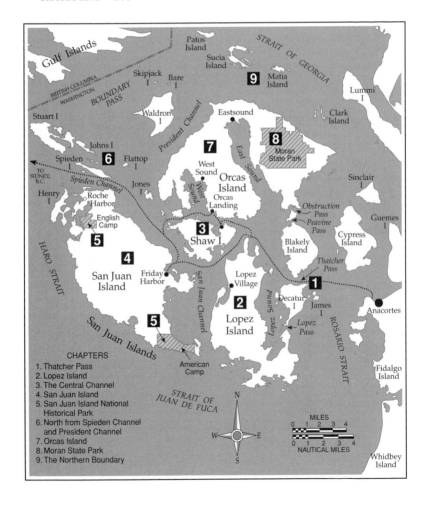

MAP KEY

▬▬▬	major road	lighthouse	
─────	minor road	or literal sketch of lighthouse	
╍╍╍╍	forest service road		
▬·▬·▬·	park boundary	reef	
──┼──	gate	wildlife refuge	
------------	trail	ranger station	
) (	bridge	picnic area	
··········	ferry route	campground	
▭▬┿▬▭	airstrip or airport	primitive campsite	
⚓	anchorage	Cascadia Marine Trail campsite	
●	mooring buoy	* submerged or submerging rock	
♂	oil buoy	lake	
········	lineal mooring	marsh	
▮▮	cemetery		
禾	navigational beacon		

NOTE:

This book's sketch maps are not intended for navigation. Not all hazards, such as rocks or reefs, are shown.

The mileage scale indicates general distances. However, because nearly all the maps are drawn in perspective, as if seen from an airplane, front to back distances are somewhat greater than indicated, due to foreshortening.

Icons for mooring buoys and campsites are placed to show their general location, but the number of icons is not indicative of that item's total number. The number in parentheses (X) next to buoys and campgrounds indicates the number of buoys or campsites at each location.

Flotsam and Jetsam: Lists, Tables, Maps, and Sidebars

Lists, tables, and special maps scattered throughout the text provide a quick summary of information. Sidebars are our digressions of thought into something in the islands we found interesting. We hope you, too, will find them of interest.

Quick Reference to Facilities and Recreation

Some kinds of marine recreation, such as boating and beachcombing, are found throughout the San Juan Islands. Others, however, are more specific to particular areas. The following table provides a quick reference to important facilities and activities. Some facilities listed might be at commercial resorts or marinas; some might close off–season. For detailed information read the descriptions of specific areas in the text.

Marine Services include marine supplies and repair; in some places they might be of a very limited nature.

Moorage refers to marinas that have guest moorage. It also includes public docks and buoys at marine parks.

Launch Facilities includes shore access only for hand-carried boats. Hoists and slings are always at commercial marinas. Ramps might be at either commercial or public facilities.

Groceries/Shopping might be of a very limited nature.

Camping is listed under recreation to avoid duplicating it as a facility. However, it also means that campsites, as a facility, are available.

Point of Interest includes educational displays, museums, and self-guided nature walks.

(•) = Nearby; [•] = Freshwater
Fuel: D = On Dock; S = Service Station
Launch Facilities: R = Ramp; H = Hoist; C = Hand Carry
Restroom or Toilet: S = Shower Also
Camping: M = Cascadia Marine Trail Campsite Also
Hiking/Beach Walking: B = Beach Walk

Fuel	Marine Pumpout	Marine Services	Moorage	Launch Facilities	Restroom or Toilet	Lodging	Groceries/Shopping	Restaurants	Location	Fishing	Shellfish	Paddling	Scuba Diving	Camping	Picnicking	Hiking/Beach Walking	Wildlife Watching	Point of Interest
									1. THATCHER PASS									
D/S	•	•		•/S		•			Blakely Island	•		•						•
			R						Decatur Island		•	•						
		•		•					James Island Marine State Park	•		•	•	•/M	•	•		
									2. LOPEZ ISLAND									
		•	R	•					Odlin County Park	•	•	•	•	•/M	•	•/B	•	•

7

Fuel	Marine Pumpout	Marine Services	Moorage	Launch Facilities	Restroom or Toilet	Lodging	Groceries/Shopping	Restaurants	Location	Fishing	Shellfish	Paddling	Scuba Diving	Camping	Picnicking	Hiking/Beach Walking	Wildlife Watching	Point of Interest
			•		•				Upright Channel State Park		•	•			•	B		
S					•/s	•	•	•	Lopez Village							•	•	•
D	•	•	•	R/H	•/s	•	(•)	•	Fisherman Bay	•	•	•			•		•	
				C					Otis Perkins Park			•			•	B	•	
				[R]	•				Hummel Lake	[•]		[•]				•	•	
			•	C	•/s				Spencer Spit State Park	•	•	•	•	•/M	•	•/B	•	
			•	R					Hunter and Mud Bays	•	•	•				B	•	
					•				Shark Reef Recreation Area						•	•	•	
									Richardson	•		•	•					
				R	•				Mackaye Harbor	•		•	•				•	
				C					Agate Beach Picnic Area			•	•			•	B	
									Hughes Bay County Park						•	B		
									Point Colville and Watmough Bay			•	•			•	•	

3. THE CENTRAL CHANNEL

Fuel	Marine Pumpout	Marine Services	Moorage	Launch Facilities	Restroom or Toilet	Lodging	Groceries/Shopping	Restaurants	Location	Fishing	Shellfish	Paddling	Scuba Diving	Camping	Picnicking	Hiking/Beach Walking	Wildlife Watching	Point of Interest
			•		•		•		Shaw Island and Shaw Landing			•						•
			•		•				Blind Island Marine State Park	•	•	•	•	•/M	•	B	•	
				R	•				South Beach County Park	•	•	•		•/M	•	•/B	•	
									Parks Bay and Tift Rocks			•					•	
									The Wasp Islands	•		•					•	
									Yellow Island Preserve			•				•	•	
			•		•				Jones Island Marine State Park	•	•	•	•	•/M	•	•/B	•	

4. SAN JUAN ISLAND

Fuel	Marine Pumpout	Marine Services	Moorage	Launch Facilities	Restroom or Toilet	Lodging	Groceries/Shopping	Restaurants	Location	Fishing	Shellfish	Paddling	Scuba Diving	Camping	Picnicking	Hiking/Beach Walking	Wildlife Watching	Point of Interest
D/s	•	•	•	H	•/s	•	•	•	Friday Harbor			•			•			•
			•		•				Turn Island Marine State Park	•	•	•	•	•	•	•/B	•	
				C					Turn Point Road Access	•	•	•					•	
				[R]					Sportsman and Egg Lakes	[•]		[•]					•	
				R	•				Jackson Beach Park/Boat Launch			•			•	B	•	
				[C]	•/s	•	•		Lakedale Campground	[•]		[•]		•	•	•	•	

Fuel	Marine Pumpout	Marine Services	Moorage	Launch Facilities	Restroom or Toilet	Lodging	Groceries/Shopping	Restaurants	Location	Fishing	Shellfish	Paddling	Scuba Diving	Camping	Picnicking	Hiking/Beach Walking	Wildlife Watching	Point of Interest
				C	•				Reuben Tarte Picnic Area			•	•		•		•	
									Westcott Bay Nature Reserve and Sculpture Park							•	•	•
•/s	•	•	•	R	•/s	•	•	•	Roche Harbor	•		•	•			•	•	•
					•				Posey Island Marine State Park	•		•	•	•/M	•	B		
									Battleship Island			•	•				•	
									Henry Island and Mosquito Pass	•		•	•					
									Westcott Bay	•	•	•						
D	•	•	•	R	•	•	•	•	Mitchell Bay (Snug Harbor)	•	•	•	•	•	•		•	
				R	•		•		San Juan County Park			•	•	•/M	•		•	•
					•				Lime Kiln Point State Park			•	•		•	•	•	•
									False Bay							B	•	
				C					Eagle Cove Public Access			•	•		•	B		
		•			•				Griffin Bay State Park			•		•/M	•	B	•	
					•				Cattle Beach and Cattle Point	•					•	•/B	•	•
									5. SAN JUAN ISLAND NATIONAL HISTORICAL PARK									
					•				English Camp	•	•	•				•	•/B	•
				C	•				American Camp	•		•	•			•	•/B	•
									6. NORTH FROM SPIEDEN CHANNEL AND PRESIDENT CHANNEL									
									Spieden and Sentinel Islands			•					•	
									Flattop Island, Other Bird Refuges			•					•	
									Stuart Island	•		•	•				•	•
		•	•		•				Stuart Island Marine State Park	•	•	•	•	•/M	•	•	•	
									Waldron Island	•		•	•				•	
									Skipjack and Bare Islands	•		•					•	
									7. ORCAS ISLAND									
D		•			•	•	•	•	Orcas Landing							•	•	•

Fuel	Marine Pumpout	Marine Services	Moorage	Launch Facilities	Restroom or Toilet	Lodging	Groceries/Shopping	Restaurants	Location	Fishing	Shellfish	Paddling	Scuba Diving	Camping	Picnicking	Hiking/Beach Walking	Wildlife Watching	Point of Interest
			[C]						Killebrew Lake	[•]		[•]						
D/S		•	•	R/C	•/S	•	•	•	Deer Harbor			•		[•]			•	•
									Frank Richardson Wildlife Preserve								•	
D		•	•	(•)H	•				West Sound (Marina)	•		•						
									Skull and Victim Islands			•			•			
			•		•		•	•	Olga			•						
D	•	•			•/S	•	•	•	Rosario Resort and Cascade Bay	•		•	•			•	•	•
S		•	•	C	•	•	•	•	Eastsound Village			•			•	•/B	•	
			•	R					North Shore Resorts	•		•	•			B		
•		•	•	R	•/S		•		West Shore Resorts	•		•	•	•		B		
									Point Doughty State Park	•		•	•	•/M	•		•	
									Freeman Island Marine State Park			•	•					
•		•		R		•	•		Obstruction Pass	•		•						
					•				Obstruction Pass Campground	•	•	•	•	•/M	•	•		
			•		•				Doe Island Marine State Park	•		•	•	•/M	•	•		
									Peapod Rocks			•						•
									8. MORAN STATE PARK									
				[R/C]	•/S	•			Moran State Park	[•]		[•]		•	•	•		•
									9. THE NORTHERN BOUNDARY									
			•		•				Patos Island Marine State Park	•	•	•	•	•	•	•/B	•	
			•		•				Sucia Island Marine State Park	•	•	•	•	•	•	•/B	•	•
			•		•				Matia Island Marine State Park	•	•	•	•	•	•	•/B	•	
			•		•				Clark Island Marine State Park	•	•	•	•	•	•	•/B	•	

Using This Book

- This guide is arranged geographically, moving roughly from east to west, as you might travel through the islands. Chapter openings give you a quick overview of the area.
- The matrix table in the front of the book, "Quick Reference to Facilities and Recreation," offers a boiled-down version of the site information, providing a fast way to find your favorite recreation or get an overview of a particular site.
- Most chapters open with an overview map of the area covered and are followed by detail maps. Because the detail maps cover many different sites, they are cross-referenced at the beginning of each site description.
- Attractions, activities, and facilities listed at the beginning of each site description are arranged, in general, with the most important attractions for that site first and lesser ones later. For example, Yellow Island is the place for wildflowers, and Lime Kiln State Park is the place for whale watching; however, there are other nifty things to see and do at either site.
- Below the attractions list, the information blocks give a quick rundown of data pertinent to the site, such as facilities available, park and trail statistics.
- To help you get to each site, access directions are given via car 🚗, boat 🚤, or airplane ✈, as is applicable. However, most sites can be reached from a variety of different points, so the access directions and distances are from the most likely spot, usually the ferry landing.
- This book does not give complete navigational information; however, in a number of places hazards in the vicinity of the sites are described. These comments are marked in the text with a ship's wheel ☸.

Look for orange honeysuckle in the woodland of Yellow Island Preserve.

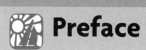# Preface

THE FIRST EDITION OF THIS BOOK was published in 1979 and since then has become the top-selling recreation guide to the San Juan Islands. In this fourth edition, we have set out to make the best even better. In addition to updating all information, we've included:

- Additional maps
- Better driving and boating directions
- New tables on facilities and activities
- Tables on local wildlife and birds
- New sidebars on interesting trivia such as natural history and island tales

Thankfully, the islands themselves haven't changed a great deal in the twenty-five years since this book was first published. The ambiance is still delightfully slow-paced, the villages are just as charming. The county still has no freeways, no stoplights, no railroads, and only one incorporated town. And the islands still have their magnificent beauty.

Some things are different, of course. Today there is less agriculture, fishing, and logging; instead, tourism has become the economic mainstay. The ferry system now has larger boats, more streamlined operations, and better parking. The towns are a bit more urbanized, with such modern trappings as a few latté shops and Internet cafés, and a couple of quite posh hotel.

Population and tourism has grown, and the islands are seeing far greater recreational use. Because of this, some of the natural areas are now protected by federal, state, or county agencies, and new regulations protect wildlife. The people who live here are increasingly aware of what a natural treasure the San Juans are, and are actively working to keep them that way.

About This Book

As its title indicates, this book deals with a broad spectrum of healthy, active, and largely nonpolluting recreation available in the San Juan Islands, either on land or on water. Yet readers thumbing through these pages for their favorite sport will soon see that island recreation does not divide itself into two neat categories of either afoot or afloat, for some hikes and campgrounds are accessible only by boat, fishing can be from either boat or land, scuba diving can be boat or shore based, and many beaches can be reached

Opposite: *Doe Island Marine State Park, only a short distance from Orcas Island, offers a pleasant stay at the dock or at inland campsites.*

either by land or by sea. And, to achieve a catchy title, bicycling was not implied at all, although it certainly is one of the most delightful pastimes in the San Juans, and one that is frequently mentioned here.

In addition to active types of recreation, this book includes take-it-easy, stop-and-smell-the-flowers diversions. The islands aren't very big; one could rush through the three largest ones in a day and claim to have "seen" the San Juans. We urge you to stop and think about the history of the Indians who first arrived here in long dugout canoes, and the Spanish and English explorers who came later in sailing ships. Take time to notice the unique birds, flowers, and animals, and the special quality of the clouds piled high above the long, horizontal reaches of the islands. The more you look, the more there is to see.

This is a guide to recreation rather than facilities, but any visitor to the San Juans needs to have at least a general idea of what to expect in the way of amenities. Commercial facilities listed in this book are mentioned primarily on a "need-to-know" basis, such as where to find food, lodging, fuel, moorage, and other necessities, and if fees are charged for services such as moorage and boat launching. For visitors interested in specifics regarding island commercial facilities, our book, *The Essential San Juan Islands Guide,* fourth edition, published by JASI, provides full information. A number of tourist publications and various websites also give information on businesses in the islands.

The places described in this book were surveyed over a period of several years and rechecked just prior to publication. Changes to facilities do occur, however. We would appreciate knowing of any changes so future editions can be updated. Contact us directly via the Internet at *MargeTed@aol.com,* or comments can be addressed to:

> Marge and Ted Mueller
> c/o The Mountaineers Books
> 1001 SW Klickitat Way, Suite 201
> Seattle, WA 98134

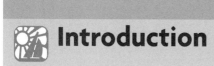 # Introduction

Tucked away in the northwest corner of the state of Washington lie the San Juan Islands—a cluster of emerald gems set in a shimmering azure sea. Their rugged beauty, mild climate, and remoteness make them a true "get-away-from-it-all" destination. But that is only a portion of the islands' draw. Many vacationers come to the islands for the recreation—and there's plenty to be found. It ranges from whale watching and scuba diving to flower finding and beach snoozing. Whatever your reason for visiting, the islands are there for you to enjoy.

The San Juan Islands, tops of mountains and their sedimentary coverings, were sculpted by massive glacial ice sheets that spread over them, rounding

A Washington State ferry travels through Wasp Passage. In the foreground is Broken Point on Shaw Island. On the left lies an unnamed rock. To the right of the ferry is Bell Island, and beyond is Crane Island. Photo: Bob and Ira Spring

off tall peaks, gouging out watery channels and estuaries, and, upon their retreat, depositing monstrous piles of gravelly debris. The bedrock heart of the mountains remains today, still bearing the marks of the glaciers' southward journey. Eroded cliff sides expose layers of sedimentary sandstone and limestone from the ancient sea. Soft glacial till in lowlands has fostered the

San Juan Geology—450 Million Years, Quickly

The jumbled rock of the San Juan Islands presents a challenging puzzle. At least six different terranes (distinctive rock groupings, each framed by fault lines), have been identified here. These terranes have been folded, uplifted, sheared off, and intruded to such an extent that geologists can only speculate about the events that formed and transformed them. San Juan rock is largely sedimentary, with a basement of igneous rocks and an overlayment of glacial deposits. Fossils embedded in the sedimentary rock provide enticing clues.

Some geologists surmise that the islands' oldest rocks, revealed in Turtleback Mountain, on Orcas Island, began as the bottom of an ancient sea, probably in the vicinity of the equator. These rocks have been dated to the Paleozoic era, some 450 million years ago (give or take a few). This ocean floor was covered by sediments containing warm water corals, brachiopods, and other animals; these now comprise the limestone deposits found near Roche Harbor.

It is thought that during the Mesozoic era, some 200 million years ago, hot magma erupted underneath the sea, flowing on top of the ocean-floor sediments, and the hardened magma formed a chain of volcanic cones. Rock from this volcanic activity now is seen on Mount Constitution on Orcas Island. Pillow basalts along the southwest side of San Juan Island show that this basalt was extruded under water, causing it to cool quickly. Sedimentation continued, accumulating atop these mountains, evidenced by the limestone that is found at Limestone Point on San Juan Island.

As the depositing of these successive layers of magma and sediments was occurring, the tectonic plates that make up the ocean floor were shifting. The part of the ocean bottom on which the seamounts rested drifted toward the North American continent at the galloping rate of an inch or so a year. About 90 million years ago it collided with the edge of the continent, which at that time ended about where the Cascade Mountains and British Columbia's Coast Range are. The hard plate subducted (dove under the edge of the continent), and the ocean floor, mountains riding atop it, and layers of sedimentary rock were scraped off. The folded and crunched pile of debris was deposited along the edge of the continent, building it outward. There it remained as the ocean rose, covering the area, and more sediments were deposited. It continued to lift, sink, and be folded as later plates arrived and collided with the continent; one of these plates brought Vancouver Island, and another brought the seamounts that became the Olympic Range. The slightly growth of forests, thickets, and meadows. The buffeting of wind and water on mile upon mile of coastline has formed fascinating shapes, ranging from wide, bay-bottom tide flats and long, curving sand spits to narrow, wave-cut rock benches.

The San Juans generally are accepted as those islands lying north of

different geology of the Sucia Islands group is described in Chapter Nine.

This tectonic activity was followed, about 2 million years ago, by massive glacial ice sheets that several times covered the area, grinding off mountain tops and sculpting the rocks. The last of this glaciation, which occurred between 20,000 years to 14,000 years ago, left behind the coating of glacial till found on the south end of San Juan Island and other places. As the glaciers retreated, the sea poured in, filling troughs and leaving high points exposed.

The final sculpting of the islands came from wind and water that eroded them, carrying away some of the glacial deposits, wearing away hard rock, and depositing sand, gravel, and soil along the shores. This sculpting continues today, as hills, cliffs, beaches, and sandspits continue to be modified by nature into the beautiful forms of the San Juan Islands.

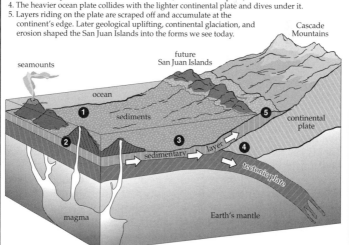

FORMATION OF THE SAN JUAN ISLANDS

1. A layer of sediments accumulates on the ocean floor.
2. Erupting magma flows over the sediments and forms a chain of volcanic seamounts.
3. The tectonic plate drifts toward the continent (itself a tectonic plate).
4. The heavier ocean plate collides with the lighter continental plate and dives under it.
5. Layers riding on the plate are scraped off and accumulate at the continent's edge. Later geological uplifting, continental glaciation, and erosion shaped the San Juan Islands into the forms we see today.

Cascade Mountains

seamounts

future San Juan Islands

ocean

sediments

continental plate

sedimentary layer

tectonic plate

magma

Earth's mantle

Washington's Strait of Juan de Fuca, south and east of the Canadian boundary, and west of—aye, there's the rub! Where do we draw the eastern boundary? San Juan County uses Rosario Strait as its line of demarcation, but islands eastward ache to be called San Juans, too, and with some geological justification. But, holding to bureaucratic boundaries, this book covers those islands lying within San Juan County. Outlying islands are described in a companion volume, *Afoot and Afloat: North Puget Sound.*

The Skagit County islands of Fidalgo, Guemes, and Cypress serve as an entrance to the San Juans. A majority of the people headed for the San Juans passes among them, either as passengers on the ferry from the city of Anacortes or as boaters traveling through Deception Pass or Swinomish Channel.

San Juan County boasts some 375 miles of saltwater shoreline—more than any other county in the United States and nearly as much as the Pacific Ocean shorelines of Washington and Oregon combined. And how many San Juan Islands are there? As difficult as the territory might be to define, it is even harder to catalog. Figures range from 172 to more than 700! If that seems a startling discrepancy, consider: When is an island merely a rock? How many rocks make a reef? Is a reef an island? What about tidal changes that cause rocks and reefs to appear and disappear and split apart or join together? The problems are legion.

The figure of 172 theoretically includes all of those named islands or islets within San Juan County, but don't try to count them—you'll never come out with exactly that number. For now, let's say around 200. Of these, only four—San Juan, Orcas, Lopez, and Shaw—are reached by ferry and have significant populations. Of the smaller islands, around thirty hold a few homes or are marine state parks; they can be reached only by small boat, floatplane, or, in some cases, small airplane.

Welcome to the San Juan Islands

Public-owned lands in the San Juans are a patchwork quilt of county, state, and national parks, lands owned by the state Department of Natural Resources (DNR), lighthouses owned by the U.S. Bureau of Land Management, fishing lakes owned by the state Department of Fish and Wildlife, and wildlife refuges operated by the U.S. Fish and Wildlife Service. San Juan residents recognize the value to the islands of recreational lands, as they bring tourists and their dollars here. At the same time, there is some resentment because these lands are not on the tax rolls and thus do not directly add money to the county coffers.

Not including the wildlife refuges, this public property totals in excess of 12,000 acres, scattered about more than fifty separate locations. The wildlife refuges are an additional 353 acres on eighty-four individual sites. All of these lands are open to public recreation, except for the wildlife refuges (which have two exceptions that will be noted later) and the lighthouse reserves.

Three organizations hold parcels of land on the islands. Although not publicly owned, some of this land is open for public recreation. *The Nature Conservancy*, a private conservation organization supported by memberships and donations, has purchased some environmentally important property in the islands and holds it as nature preserves. A second group, *The San Juan Land Bank*, funded by a 1-percent real estate transfer tax, purchases land or conservation easements to preserve property of environmental, aesthetic, cultural, historic, or recreational value. Purchased property is often open for low-intensity public use; however, easements don't usually include public use. *The San Juan Preservation Trust* is a nonprofit corporation dedicated to preserving scenic spaces, agricultural lands, wetlands, and shorelines. They encourage voluntary conservation easements, gifts of land, or financial donations for the purpose of purchasing property easements.

A family views Shaw Island from the car deck of the ferry.

A few parcels of land around the islands are posted as Open Space. On these, the property owners receive a tax reduction in exchange for allowing public use of the land. However, such use must be compatible with its natural state; in other words, observe posted fire regulations, do not litter, and do not deface or destroy either personal property or natural features.

Some 78 percent of the tidelands in the San Juan Islands are owned by the DNR and are open for public use. For the most part, these are only the lands lying below the mean high water level, and the upland property is privately owned. In some cases, these tidelands are so steep and rocky that they are unapproachable, but some beaches are suitable for recreation.

These sites together offer a rich variety of recreation: boating, paddling, fishing, scuba diving, beach walking, shellfish gathering, hiking, bicycling, birdwatching, camping, sightseeing, and many other activities.

Of "No Trespassing" Signs and Other Aggravations • One of the most negative aspects of the San Juans—and most noticeable to those of us devoted to good, clean public recreation, and lots of it—is the proliferation of "No Trespassing" signs on fence posts and beaches, screaming, "Stay away, this is mine, and I don't want you here!" Under such duress, the meek become paranoid and the feisty grow defiant.

San Juan residents aren't unfriendly—in fact they're some of the nicest folks around, and many of them feel that tourism is a vital asset to their islands. These people are simply tired of boorish boaters who come ashore to relieve themselves and their dogs on private beaches, leaving feces and toilet paper strewn about; they're tired of fences ripped down and campfires built in dry timber and grasslands by campers; they're tired of farm animals shot and children endangered by overzealous hunters; they're tired of ignorant disregard of privacy and outright vandalism and thievery.

The horror stories are plentiful—enough to make fellow tourists ashamed of their breed. But we know we're not all like that—in fact few of us are—so don't take "No Trespassing" signs as a personal affront. Instead, respect the rights of the people who own the property, who keep the islands functioning with their tax money, and who are doing their best to keep them unspoiled for the future. On public tidelands, do not stray onto adjacent private land and uplands.

Even if lands are unposted, do not assume they are public or that no one cares if you trespass. Unless clearly designated as public land, stay off—somebody owns it. The growth of public recreation in the San Juans lies largely in the hands of the residents. More lands are available for development now, and more could become available, but it will take a favorable position by these residents, convinced that tourism is good for their economy, before there is any marked increase in public recreation facilities.

The Fly in the Ointment

Most paradises have their flaws and the San Juans have theirs, for they are loved almost too much. They can be crowded—exasperatingly crowded! In the summer, long ferry lines can mean up to a three-hour wait for car passengers and in extreme cases a four- to five-hour delay. (Foot passengers rarely have extensive waits.)

Is it worth it? You bet it is! But you must be prepared to be patient and relax; that's one of the great secrets of the island magic. If the ferry leaves you at the dock, there's nearly always another one soon, and no matter how many people there are, the scenery is big enough for everyone to share.

So be forewarned—if visiting the islands in summer, expect waits in the ferry line, crowded accommodations, congested marinas, and filled campgrounds. Signs attempt to notify prospective campers of campsite availability before they board the ferry in Anacortes. After Labor Day, the tourist crowds almost magically disappear and, except for an occasional sunny off-season holiday, the islands are returned to their grateful residents.

Does that mean that the San Juans aren't any good off-season? Shhh—that's the best kept secret of all. During the "shoulder" seasons of spring and fall, they're often better. The San Juans receive only half the amount of rain that falls on Seattle and other Puget Sound areas, so the dry climate can make spring and fall delightful. The crowds are gone, and although the weather is cooler and more unpredictable, the beauty remains—and is even enhanced. On a crisp fall day when Indian summer colors the forests, or on a damp spring day when wildflowers brighten hedgerows and lambs cavort in fields, the islands truly show the many subtle nuances of their beauty. On blustery winter days when waves lash furiously at beaches, or drizzly rain encourages you to curl up by a cabin fireplace, the San Juans become a true "getaway" from mundane city life.

Some Economic Facts ● Some visitors to the San Juans have squalled loudly when they discovered that some prices are higher than for comparable goods on the mainland a few miles away. In a few cases prices can run 20 percent higher. Residents are not out to gouge the summer visitor—residents have to pay those prices, too.

The problem is that the islands produce relatively few hard goods, and it is tough to earn a living here. Many of the residents are retired; a few others make a living by commuting to mainland jobs; some are writers, artists, and craftspeople whose jobs are not dependent on local buyers. Unlike earlier times, only a few people in the county are engaged in full-time farming, and the fishing industry is but a shadow of what it once was. Today, only around 2 percent of the islands' work force is engaged in farming, forestry, or fishing. Tourism is the leading industry here, and as such it must pay for itself. The people who live here and provide services for the tourists still have to pay taxes and feed their families all year, even after the tourists have gone home.

The available public lands (especially parks and campgrounds) are heavily used by tourists, and there is a constant cry for more. Unfortunately, the more tourists that arrive, the greater the burden on public utilities such as power, water, and sewer, and public services such as road maintenance, fire protection, and law enforcement—all of which are paid for by local taxes.

Consider also that nearly all goods that are consumed here must be brought in by ferry. Gasoline, for example, is brought by tanker trucks on special night runs after regular passenger runs, due to its hazardous nature. The cost of this special service must be passed on to the consumer. Although this is one of the more extreme examples, it illustrates the reasons some goods and services are more expensive on the San Juan Islands. The people who live year-round on the islands do so because they love it here—but they aren't making a killing on the tourists. With this in mind, don't resent it if residents expect a fair price for their goods and services or expect suitable pay for use of their property.

On the other hand, you can make some excellent purchases in the islands. Locally grown produce items and flowers, offered in stores and summer farmers' markets, are wonderfully fresh and very reasonably priced. And, of course, local seafood is the finest you can buy. Resident artists and craftspeople offer superb works of art for sale at local stores, at galleries, at artist cooperatives, or in their own shops. Pottery, porcelain, fiber arts, wood arts, gallery photographs, and jewelry are among the offerings, as well as paintings, sculpture, and limited-edition art prints. Some people make a point of adding a few pieces of art to their collection each time they visit, and of course island art makes wonderful gifts.

Tread Lightly, Boat Gently

WATER. "Water, water, everywhere, but not a drop to drink" might soon become the theme of the San Juans. At present there's barely enough potable water to go around. Some of the small marine park islands have none at all, and wells at several of the other parks frequently run dry by midsummer. Even in the towns water is at a premium, with new construction of homes and businesses limited in some areas by unavailability of water hookups. Heavy demand on wells and catch basins is causing these water resources to be depleted.

As ridiculous as it might sound, when visiting the San Juans, bring water! Fill up camper and boat water tanks at home or at the last mainland stop, and once you're there, take it easy. There's enough water at present to assure reasonable cleanliness for everyone, but don't let faucets run unnecessarily at campgrounds, don't use a gallon of water when a quart will do. At marinas, washing boats with freshwater might be strictly prohibited and subject to a stiff fine. The Port of Friday Harbor requires that any hoses used to fill boat water tanks must have a shut-off faucet attached so water is not wasted. Whether it is legal or not, unnecessary water use is a sign of disregard for a critical islands resource.

FIRE. Going hand-in-hand with the water problem in the islands is the problem of serious fires. There are few convenient hydrants on street corners (and hardly any street corners). In remote areas, reaching a fire is very difficult and putting it out more so. By late summer, grasses and thickets can be tinder dry, so please be extremely careful with matches, cigarettes, and campfires.

DOGS. It might come as a surprise, but good old Fido is not exactly welcome in the San Juans. In this largely rural county, city dogs and farm animals often do not mix well, and every year there are tragic incidents of domestic animals being killed by dogs roaming free. The perpetrators were not vicious watchdogs, trained to attack, but friendly, sit-by-the-fire family pets. The San Juan County dog ordinance states that any unlicensed dog found at large in rural areas may be shot. This applies to dogs of residents and visitors alike. Leave your pet at home or keep it on a leash at all times. Several boarding kennels are available for those who choose to bring their pet.

Getting Around the Islands is Half the Fun

Ferries • A watery highway system of broad straits and fjordlike channels links the San Juan Islands. Gleaming green and white state ferries cruise the waters, busily "busing" people, cars, motorcycles, bicycles, trailered or car-top boats, and a startling range of other conveyances from island to island. All state ferry routes begin at the terminal on the west side of the city of Anacortes and usually stop at four of the largest islands: Lopez, Shaw, Orcas, and San Juan. Some ferries occasionally continue on to Sidney, British Columbia, on Vancouver Island. Two smaller, private passenger ferries operate from Bellingham and Anacortes. Although Anacortes is on Fidalgo

Island, that island lies so close to the mainland that it is connected by a bridge, so it is considered a mainland city.

On the state ferries, passengers enjoy what is advertised as "the most scenic ferry ride in the world," with views from picture windows in the comfort of the ferry's interior and from breezy open decks resembling balconies above the water. At times, the vista is a broad panorama of sparkling sea and receding layers of gray-green islands backed by distant snowcapped mountains. Other times, rugged rockbound shores seem almost within touching distance as the ferry threads through narrow passages.

Depending on the season, and the luck and sharp eye of the observer, jumping salmon, curious seals, soaring eagles, flocks of migrating waterfowl, or even a group of orca whales might be seen. At each time of day, each change of weather, each advance of season, the islands are painted in infinite variety: the vivid hues of a perfect summer day, the drifting mists of a springtime fog, the blaze of a sunset.

Travel Options, Briefly

The many possible ways to get to the San Juans can be confusing. Basically, unless you have your own boat, you must come in by ferry or airplane: the ferries go only to the four largest islands, and a few others can be reached by plane. Once there, getting around presents another set of choices. The following briefly outlines them.

Traveling TO the San Juans
- Drive, bicycle, or walk onto the state ferry from Anacortes, Washington, or Sidney, B.C.
- Walk onto a private passenger ferry at Bellingham, Anacortes, Seattle, Everett, or Victoria. Most offer service to Friday Harbor or Roche Harbor; some will deliver you to the marine state park islands and pick you up there later.
- Skipper a private boat, or a boat rented or chartered from nearby mainland cities such as Anacortes or Bellingham.
- Fly to the major islands via a scheduled, chartered, or private airplane from Seattle, Anacortes, or other mainland cities; seaplanes go to several islands.

Traveling ON the four large islands by land
- Drive your own vehicle brought from the mainland via ferry.
- Hire a taxi or rent a vehicle on islands where they are available.
- Ride a bicycle or moped, transported via ferry or rented on the islands.
- Walk to nearby facilities, or hike around the island on roads.

Traveling AMONG the many islands by water
- Skipper a private, rented, or chartered boat.
- Hire a skippered charter from within the islands or from a mainland city.
- Paddle a canoe or kayak transported to the four large islands via the ferry, or put in on the mainland, and paddle across Rosario Strait.

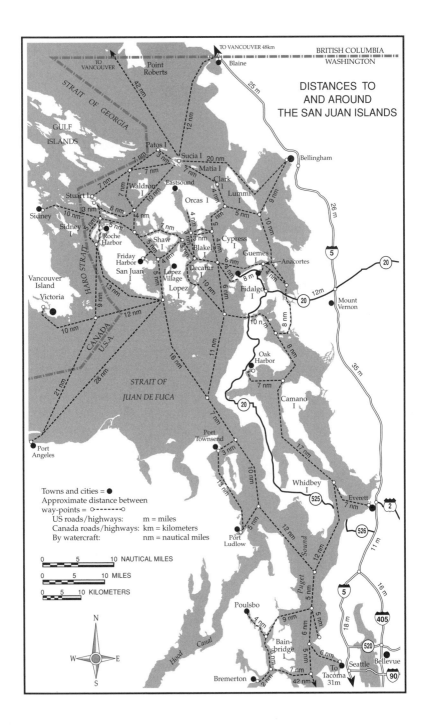

DISTANCES TO
AND AROUND
THE SAN JUAN ISLANDS

Towns and cities = ●
Approximate distance between
way-points = ○- - - - -○
    US roads/highways: m = miles
    Canada roads/highways: km = kilometers
    By watercraft: nm = nautical miles

Airplanes • For a speedier trip to the islands, air flights are available; in good weather this is an especially scenic way to go. San Juan, Orcas, and Lopez Islands have small airports; San Juan Airlines maintains a regular schedule year-round from Seattle's Boeing Field and Anacortes to and from San Juan, Orcas, and Lopez airports, with added flights in the summer. Kenmore Air offers daily scheduled seaplane flights from Seattle to Orcas, San Juan, and Lopez Islands. Other air services based at San Juan Island, Anacortes, and Seattle charter either small planes or seaplanes for flights throughout the islands. Seaplane floats are maintained at Fisherman Bay, Friday Harbor, Roche Harbor, and Rosario Resort. Many of the other islands have single-landing-strip airfields for use by small private planes or charters.

Private boats • Of course, private boats, too, travel these waterways—do they ever! Seeking Nirvana in salt-scrubbed air, crystal water, tranquil anchorages, they arrive, drove upon drove. Unfettered by such things as stodgy ferry schedules, they wander freely, visiting big and little islands, and particularly frequenting the numerous boat-in marine state parks.

But the non-ferry-served islands are not reserved for affluent yacht owners. Even a kayak, canoe, or rowboat will do to reach some, for several of the state parks lie within paddling distance of mainland put-ins. Islands lying across broader channels can be reached by boats brought via the ferry to launching spots on the larger islands. Alternatively, marinas within the San Juans offer a wide variety of boats to be rented for the hour or day, or chartered for extended cruises. Charters are also available at the nearby cities of Anacortes, Bellingham, and Victoria. Skippered charters, which leave the navigation to an experienced captain and the relaxed sightseeing to the guests, are also available. Some specialize in wildlife viewing, fishing, or scuba diving.

Bicycles or Boots • Many tourists leave their automobiles at Anacortes. Unfettered by four wheels, they walk onto the ferry with bicycle or backpack and hiking boots. Roads on the ferry-served islands are gently rolling, traffic is light, and the slow and quiet traveler will see far more wildlife and far more beauty than those who rush from here to there in automobiles.

So You've Decided to Take the State Ferry....

For the novice ferry user, the state ferry system might at times seem bewildering; even experienced ferry commuters accustomed to cross-sound runs will find the procedure in the San Juans is different. In addition, the system can change from season to season and year to year, depending on the demand, operating funds available, and new ideas implemented to streamline the operation. Reservations are available only for vehicles traveling to Sidney, British Columbia, on the international run.

Three types of ferry runs operate through the islands: the *domestic*, the *inter-island*, and the *international*. In the summer, departures are about hourly; however, not all ferries stop at all islands. Confusing? It certainly can be. Just remember: It is up to you to be sure you are on the right ferry for your destination. Read the ferry schedule carefully, and when in doubt ask the ticket agent. Ferries are two- or three-deck ships holding from 75 to 160 vehicles and up to 2500 passengers.

The *domestic* run shuttles between Anacortes and the four major islands of Lopez, Shaw, Orcas, and San Juan. At Anacortes, tickets for this run are sold only as round trips, eliminating the need for collecting fares for the return trip. If you buy a ticket for an early stop, such as Lopez Island, and then later decide to continue west to a different island, an additional fare will be collected.

The *inter-island* run is on a smaller ferry traveling only between the four major islands, with no direct service to the mainland.

The *international* run travels from Anacortes to Sidney, B.C., in spring, summer, and fall. Reservations for vehicles destined for Sidney are accepted on these trips, so space for San Juan-bound vehicles might be very limited on that ferry. Travelers headed to Sidney purchase one-way tickets. If you travel from Anacortes to the San Juans, you do not go through customs, even if you are on the international run; however, if you should happen to catch the international run at Friday Harbor as it is returning

What's the Tab?

To give you a rough idea of what a ferry trip to the islands will cost, the following list is for round-trip fares between Anacortes and Friday Harbor on peak summer days, as of 2006. Vehicle fares for the shorter rides to Lopez, Shaw, and Orcas Islands are slightly less, depending on destination. The list is somewhat abbreviated and does not include all the senior, disabled, or off-days options. Winter rates are less.

- Regular passenger (walk-on or passenger in vehicle): $13.15
- Senior (sixty-five or older) or disabled: 50 percent of regular fare
- Youth (five through eleven): 50 percent of regular fare
- Child (under five): Free
- Vehicle (under 20 feet) and driver: $51.10
- Vehicle (under 20 feet) and senior or disabled driver: $46.05
- Motorcycle and driver: About half the auto rate
- Bicycle walked on: $4.10
- Stowage of canoe or kayak not attached to vehicle: Same as motorcycle fee
- There is a surcharge for vehicles under 20 feet, but more than 7 1/2 feet high (this height maximum includes bicycles or anything else attached to the top of the vehicle)
- Oversized vehicles and combinations are charged on a sliding scale, in 10-foot increments. Vehicles and combinations more than 80 feet long are charged per additional foot. Check the web site at *wsdot.wa.gov/ferries* for current rates

from Sidney on Vancouver Island, you will be slightly delayed by the customs inspection in Anacortes.

Schedules and Fares • Printed ferry schedules (which, by the way, change quarterly) are available at the ferry terminals and at many businesses in ferry-served cities. The ferry website, *www.wsdot.wa.gov/ferries*, offers excellent information, including schedules, fares, and ferry-line cameras that give you a real-time view of traffic backlogs at several terminals. Schedules and other information can also be obtained by writing to Washington State Ferries, Pier 52, Seattle, WA 98104, or by phoning the automated number, (800) 843-3779, or (888) 808-7977 (also automated, but once you work your way through the numbered options you might get to a live person).

Ferry fares increase during the tourist season. During the recent state budget crunch, a new fare schedule was introduced, which recognized the critical needs of residents over the transient needs of tourists. As a result, with the exception of the international and inter-island runs, year-round fares are lower Sunday through Tuesday, when most passengers are residents, and are higher Wednesday through Saturday, when tourist travel strains the system.

Tickets for walk-on passengers or cyclists are sold in the terminal. At Anacortes and Sidney, vehicle tickets are sold at a toll plaza, prior to parking. At other locations, drivers who are westbound to other destinations must park in a loading lane and walk to the ferry landing to purchase tickets. Eastbound travelers do not need to obtain tickets. On the islands, the ticket office might be closed until just shortly before the arrival of a ferry.

Walk-on Passengers • Riding the ferry is a simple matter if traveling by foot: Simply buy a ticket and walk on board when the boat arrives, relax by a window, and enjoy the beautiful ride—no hassle, rarely any wait, and very inexpensive. You cruise through the islands, watching the changing scene from the ferry's breezy decks or large enclosed cabins. Maps posted on one of the main decks show the route. Vending machines and a coffee shop sell snacks, sandwiches, and beverages. Some ferries have beer and wine for sale.

Loudspeakers announce destinations as they are approached. Although foot passengers embark and debark via an overhead ramp at Anacortes, at island destinations they use the car deck.

Disabled Facilities • Facilities for the physically disabled are available on nearly all the San Juan ferries. If this is a concern, you can phone the ferry information line or check their website. At Anacortes, persons in wheelchairs load via the foot passengers' overhead ramp to the observation deck. For debarking at any of the islands, those ferries that are equipped for disabled persons have a small elevator that operates between the upper decks and the car deck. At Friday Harbor, San Juan Island, the facilities of the town are within a few blocks, and streets are reasonably level. On Lopez and Orcas Islands, facilities are some distance away, and the exit roads are quite steep. Taxis are usually on call on these three main islands.

If you are a physically disabled person traveling by car, you might want to leave your vehicle to go to the observation deck. You, or someone traveling with you, should inform the attendant of that when you purchase your ticket. The crew will attempt to see that your vehicle is parked near the elevator and there is room to unload a wheelchair; however, if the ferry is very crowded this might not be possible.

Animals • There is no charge for taking pets on the ferry. Except for service animals, they are not allowed in terminal buildings unless they are in a pet carrier. If on a leash, they can be walked in outside areas of the terminal, on the car deck, or in some cases on the outside upper ferry decks. Dogs that are not people-friendly should be muzzled. Any waste deposited by your animal must be cleaned up immediately.

Bicycles and Hand-Carried Boats • Passengers are responsible for loading and unloading their own equipment, and for its safety and security during the ferry crossing. Bicycles and kayaks are usually loaded and unloaded as a group, ahead of vehicles; follow the directions of the ferry crew. After leaving the boat, cyclists should be aware that a long line of cars is coming right behind you. Stay well to the side so you don't hold them up.

Vehicles • Oh, you want to take your car? Well, that's another matter. The first question is—won't you reconsider? Will you really need it on the island? Call ahead and see what transportation arrangements can be worked out, for there are many alternatives: Taxi service and car, bicycle, or moped rentals are available on Lopez, Orcas, and San Juan Islands. Many resorts and inns and some boat chartering services provide pick-up service at the ferry; inquire when you make reservations.

As of 2006, parking fees in the lots at the Anacortes terminal range from $10 for one day to $40 for a week. For longer-term parking, monthly permits are available. Parking is not permitted on residential streets near the terminal.

However, if you're convinced your vehicle is necessary, remember that ferry travel by vehicle can be a delight or an aggravation—it depends largely on the frame of mind of the traveler. Vehicles are loaded in order of arrival; off-season, arrive at least 20 minutes ahead of the time of departure to allow time for purchasing tickets, obtaining information, and loading.

Peak hours are in the early morning and early evening. Busiest days are Friday through Sunday and, of course, holidays. If possible, avoid these times. During periods of peak traffic, it is advisable to arrive at the terminal at least 90 minutes ahead of departure time. As noted earlier, you might have a wait of 3 hours or more due to heavy traffic.

LANE ASSIGNMENT. To achieve smooth and quick unloading, your car will be assigned to a lane when you purchase your ticket. Lanes at the landing are usually signed by destination; however, if you are uncertain, check with an agent to see that you are correctly parked.

Do not be upset if later-arriving cars are assigned to shorter lanes. Space on the ferries is apportioned according to typical traffic, with more spaces allowed for Orcas and San Juan Islands and fewer for Lopez and Shaw. The system is as fair as possible. At times the ferry will leave the dock with cars still waiting, but open space still obvious. This is done only when it is necessary to save room for cars already waiting on another island.

Most important of all—don't try to crash the line. In addition to being rude it can be injurious to your health. After waiting in line for an hour or more, motorists have been known to become pretty irate at people who do not play by the rules.

The word is relax; be patient and courteous, stay alert, and follow directions. Ferry employees have a monumental task in properly loading cars for the various destinations and assuring that space is fairly allocated to all. Don't hassle them—they know what they're doing. Aside from a genuine medical emergency, they cannot grant special favors to passengers.

ISLAND STOPOVERS. The ferry agent will ask your destination; tell the agent your first stop. If you plan to later continue on to another island, be sure that you are parked in the lane for your *first* destination, not your *final* one.

OVERLOADS. At times there are too many vehicles for a particular ferry to hold, and you must wait for the next ferry, or the one after that, or.... Take along a book to read (this one is highly recommended), a pillow to take a nap, or a deck of cards to play games with the kids. Drain the dog on a leash, and in the nearby bushes, please.

Walk around, but be alert for ferry arrivals and departures; during peak traffic hours an extra ferry might be put into service and can appear without warning. Ferry schedules are often loose during times of heavy traffic, as the vessels hurry to provide maximum service. If you are parked in a loading lane and are not in your car when the ferry begins loading, you can be ticketed and your vehicle impounded and towed.

Anacortes, Friday Harbor, and Orcas Landing have nearby shops to browse and restaurants, cafés, or coffee shops where you can eat while waiting; Lopez has a snack bar usually open during peak hours. If you plan to dine in a restaurant, tell your server what your schedule is, and ask if your service can be hurried along, if necessary.

A reservation system would be the ideal solution to ferry waits; unfortunately, no workable system has yet been devised, taking into account the complexity of loading for multiple destinations.

WHEW! Now that you've made it on board, you can leave your car and go topside to enjoy the scenic boat ride. The loudspeaker will announce when your destination is near, giving you ample time to return to your vehicle.

Recreation in the San Juan Islands

Boating • Boating is such a broad category, indulged in by so many people in so many different ways, that it is difficult to discuss. Cruisers have one point of view, sailors another, anglers another, and paddlers yet another. The authors of this book have been sailors and thus are especially aware of such unpleasant things as scraping keels across rocks, running aground, and encountering strong tidal currents (this perhaps also accounts for our take-it-easy point of view).

The use of personal watercraft (PWCs) such as Jet Skis® is banned on all San Juan County waters, including lakes, due to their negative effect on this delicate, confined environment and on people's nerves and eardrums.

Comments in this book regarding boating are as general as possible, touching on as many situations as possible; however, this book cannot, in any way, take the place of a good nautical chart and boating know-how. Charts covering the San Juans are listed in Appendix B.

There are many hazards, both in the islands and inherent to boating. Before attempting any cruising, boaters are urged to take a boating safety course. The U.S. Power Squadron's classes in small boat handling are excellent; information regarding the course can be obtained through the U.S. Coast Guard.

In many places throughout the text, cautionary comments refer to "small boats," a vague category including dinghies, rubber rafts, canoes, and kayaks, or, in general, any watercraft that is hand powered or has minimal power. These cautions can also apply to boaters in larger boats who have had little experience in handling adverse conditions, whatever the size of the craft.

Many kayak and canoe trips are possible in the San Juans, ranging from quiet paddles around protected bays to extended open-water excursions. Paddlers should have training in ocean traveling before attempting any open water trips, and any boater, before beginning any trip, should check on local weather conditions. Unpredictable winds, strong tidal currents, and tide rips, common in some San Juan waters, can raise havoc.

ROCKS, SHOALS, AND TIDAL RANGE. Most hazardous rocks and shoals lying in well-traveled areas are marked with lights, buoys, or similar navigational devices. In less-frequented places these hazards might be unmarked, although they will be shown on large-scale charts. Local boaters will occasionally mark notorious keel-killers with a vertical pole; these aids are not always maintained and do not show on charts. Another warning of a rock or reef is long streamers of bull kelp floating on the surface; approach any bed of kelp cautiously.

The tidal range in the San Juan Islands is about 14 feet, except for extreme tides. The lowest of low tides run about minus 4 feet, the highest of high about plus 12 feet. During extreme low tides, rocks and shoals that are normally well covered are close enough to the surface to cause grief to unwary skippers. Check a tide table, and during times of minus tides, use special care to consult navigational charts; if mooring, check tide tables to be sure the night will not find you mired on the bottom.

TIDAL CURRENT. Tidal currents in the San Juans vary from one to six knots, with the strongest currents usually occurring in Spieden Channel and the southern entrance to San Juan Channel. The more severe currents can cause small boats serious problems, and a strong beam tide can create difficulties for even larger boats navigating in a dense fog.

Heavy weather sailing in San Juan Channel is a challenge.

Tidal current is not the same as the tide, although one does give rise to the other. Tides measure the vertical distance water rises and falls above the sea floor due to the gravitational attraction of the sun and moon, as well as more obscure forces. Tidal currents represent the horizontal flow of water resulting from this rise and fall of the tide.

Tidal current tables (not tide tables), which are printed annually, are keyed to station points on the small craft portfolio of charts. The approximate time of maximum velocity of the current can be computed by referencing the tidal current tables to the station point. Although many other factors enter into the actual surface velocity and even the direction of the current, general knowledge of the predicted current is invaluable for safe navigation.

TIDE RIPS. Navigational charts typically bear notations of "tide rips" off points of land between channels. Tide rips are caused by either the impact of tidal currents meeting from differing directions or the upwelling of currents as they meet underwater cliffs. In either case the surface appearance is the same: the water appears to dance across an area in small to moderate choppy waves, and appears to swirl like a whirlpool. A boat crossing a tide-rip area might have difficulty maintaining course when erratic currents spin the vessel first one way and then another. Kayakers and persons in small boats might find rips an uncomfortable experience—one that should be avoided. The positive aspect of tide rips is that the upwelling current also brings to

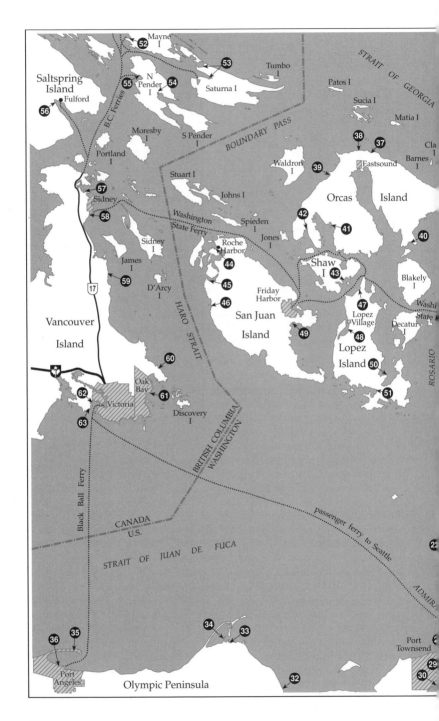

Mayne I
Saltspring Island
Fulford
Portland I
Moresby I
S Pender I
N Pender I
Saturna I
Tumbo I
Patos I
Sucia I
Matia I
Cla I
Barnes I
Waldron I
Eastsound
Orcas Island
B.C. Ferries
BOUNDARY PASS
Sidney
Stuart I
Johns I
Spieden I
Jones I
Roche Harbor
Shaw I
Blakely I
Washington State Ferry
Sidney I
James I
D'Arcy I
Friday Harbor
San Juan Island
Lopez Village
Decatur I
Washi
State
Vancouver Island
HARO STRAIT
Lopez Island
ROSARIO
Oak Bay
Victoria
Discovery I
BRITISH COLUMBIA
WASHINGTON
STRAIT OF GEORGIA
passenger ferry to Seattle
Black Ball Ferry
CANADA
U.S.
STRAIT OF JUAN DE FUCA
ADMIR
Port Townsend
Port Angeles
Olympic Peninsula

52 53 55 54 56 57 58 59 60 61 62 63
38 37 39 42 41 40 44 45 46 43 47 48 49 50 51
34 33 32 36 35 29 30
17

32

disease are destroyed and wastes are broken down, by special bacteria and fungi, to a compost similar to garden soil. *Note:* Boaters and campers should not empty portable toilets into these composting toilets because the addition of other chemicals and water might hinder bacterial growth.

Wildlife Viewing and Birdwatching • If you don't bring binoculars with you to the San Juans, you probably will wish you had. You are almost certain to see some interesting local wildlife. On pilings by the ferry landings you might spot a gull nest or see cormorants spreading their wings to dry. You might note that those rounded brown objects on offshore reefs are not rocks, but basking seals. The islands are on the Pacific Flyway, a major route for migratory waterfowl, and thus host large numbers of nonresident birds. However, the San Juans also have a healthy population of resident species, including bald eagles, which are spotted much of the year. The bird list at the back of the book names a portion of those species you might see.

For insights into the local wild population, go on one of the many wildlife tours; however, with just binoculars, some patience, and a couple of field guides, you can "bag" a nice list by yourself.

In order to protect the wildlife of the San Juan Islands Wilderness Area,

Whale-watching Etiquette

Seeing a group of whales is an exciting event; however, you are far more likely to be able to observe them for a length of time if your boat stays at a distance. Orcas might come quite close to boats if they do not perceive them as a threat; they seem fully aware of even small boats, and there has been no incident reported in the San Juans of even a canoe being overturned by a whale surfacing under it. The greatest problem is the danger boaters pose to the whales. There is a serious concern that heavy traffic by whale-watching tour boats, harassment by inconsiderate boaters and airplane pilots, and diminishing salmon supplies might lead the resident orca pods to abandon the San Juans for more hospitable surroundings. The following guidelines should be followed.

- Approach known or suspected whale-watching areas with extreme caution. Look in all directions before approaching or departing.
- Move parallel to the group of whales, at the speed of the slowest ones. A minimum distance of 100 yards is required by law. Failure to heed this can result in a severe fine. Aircraft should not fly lower than 1000 feet.
- If whales unexpectedly approach you, either slowly move out of their path or, if whales are within 100 yards, stop and wait until they move away.
- Do not deliberately move ahead of whales, positioning yourself in their path or between them and the shore.
- Do not throw anything at them, nor attempt to feed them.

SAN JUAN ISLANDS WILDERNESS AREA AND NATIONAL WILDLIFE REFUGE

1. Small Island
2. Rim and Rum Islands
3. Fortress Island
4. Skull Island
5. Crab Island
6. Boulder Island
7. Davidson Rock
8. Colville Island
9. Castle Island
10. Unnamed islands (3)
11. Unnamed rock
12. Swirl Island
13. Aleck Rocks
14. Unnamed islands (4)
15. Unnamed islands (3)
16. Hall Island
17. Unnamed island
18. Secar Rock
19. Unnamed rock
20. Unnamed islets (3)
21. Unnamed islets (13)
22. Mummy Rocks
23. Buck Island
24. Islets and rocks
25. Shark Reef
26. Harbor Rock
27. North Pacific Rock
28. Half Tide Rock
29. Unnamed rocks
30. Unnamed islands (7)
31. Low Island
32. Unnamed island
33. Barren Island
34. Battleship Island
35. Center Reef
36. Sentinel Island
37. Gull Reef
38. Ripple Island
39. Unnamed reef
40. Unnamed island
41. Gull Rock
42. Flattop Island
43. White Rocks
44. Mouatt Reef
45. Skipjack Island

46. Unnamed island
47. Bare Island
48. Clements Reef
49. Unnamed island
50. Matia Island
51. Puffin Island
52. Parker Reef
53. Little Sister Island
54. The Sisters
55. Eliza Rock ††
56. Viti Rocks ††
57. North Peapod Rocks
58. Peapod Rocks
59. South Peapod Rocks
60. Brown Rock
61. Unnamed rock
62. Shag Rock
63. Unnamed rocks (3)
64. Black Rock
65. Pointer Island
66. Lawson Rock
67. Dot Island ††
68. Bird Rocks (4)
69. Williamson Rocks (3)
70. Smith Island †/††
71. Minor Island †/††
72. Willow Island
73. Flower Island
74. Unnamed rock
75. Turn Island†
76. Turn Rock
77. Tift Rocks
78. Unnamed island
79. Unnamed island
80. Unnamed island
81. Low Island
82. Unnamed island
83. Nob Island
84. Bird Rock

†Nonwilderness status
††Not within area of map

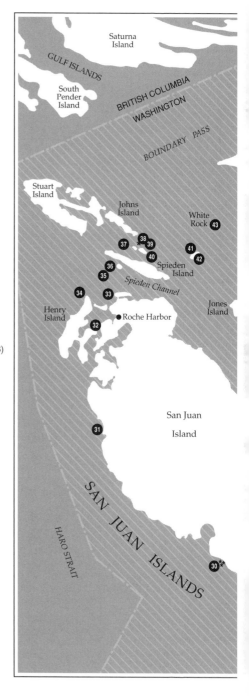

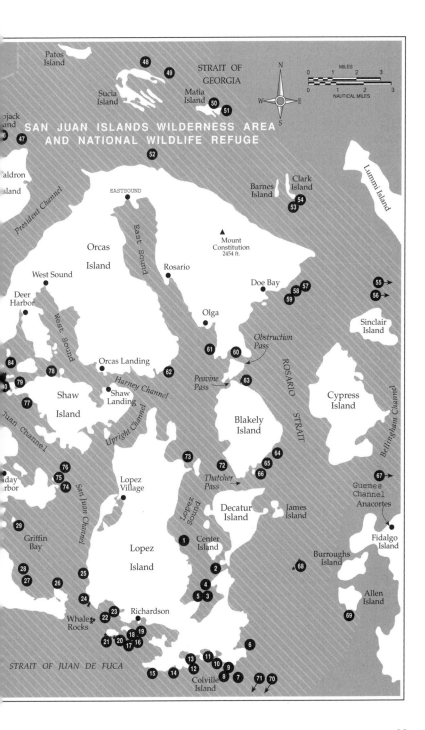

STRAIT OF
GEORGIA

Patos
Island

Sucia
Island

Matia
Island

SAN JUAN ISLANDS WILDERNESS AREA
AND NATIONAL WILDLIFE REFUGE

Barnes
Island

Clark
Island

Lummi Island

EASTSOUND

Orcas
Island

East Sound

Rosario

Mount
Constitution
2454 ft.

Doe Bay

West Sound

Deer
Harbor

Olga

Sinclair
Island

West Sound

Orcas Landing

Obstruction
Pass

Shaw

Shaw
Landing

Orcas Landing

Harney Channel

ROSARIO STRAIT

Peavine
Pass

Upright Channel

Island

Shaw
Island

Cypress
Island

Bellingham Channel

Blakely
Island

Lopez
Village

Thatcher
Pass

Guemes
Channel
Anacortes

San Juan Channel

Decatur
Island

James
Island

Griffin
Bay

Lopez

Center
Island

Fidalgo
Island

Lopez
Sound

Island

Burroughs
Island

Richardson

Whale
Rocks

Allen
Island

STRAIT OF JUAN DE FUCA

Colville
Island

President Channel

Waldron
Island

going ashore on any of the designated wilderness islands at any time is prohibited. Discharge of firearms is, of course, also prohibited and is subject to a stiff fine. Boaters, anglers, and scuba divers should stay at least 300 feet away from the islands to avoid disturbing the seals and nesting birds. Read the sidebar on pages 80 to 81 for more about the area.

Fishing, Scuba Diving, Seafood Harvesting, and Beach Foraging • To many, capturing fresh food for the dinner table is one of the greatest delights of oceans and lakes. Unfortunately, this resource is not limitless, and heavy use can seriously deplete areas. Because of this, fishing seasons vary by year and location.

LICENSES AND LIMITS. You must observe all state regulations on the taking of fish, shellfish, and any other food animal. A pamphlet of regulations, published by the state Department of Fish and Wildlife, available in most sporting goods stores, lists bag limits, seasons, and other restrictions. The following licenses are required:

Saltwater License is required to fish for halibut, herring, lingcod, rockfish, perch, cod, shad, tuna, shark, salmon, sturgeon, and related species. No license is required for smelt, carp, or albacore tuna.

Freshwater License is required for game fishing in all San Juan lakes, except for those entirely on private property.

Personal Use Shellfish/Seaweed License is required to harvest crab, clams, oysters, shrimp, sea cucumbers, sea urchins, squid, abalone, scallops, barnacles, cockles, mussels, octopus, crayfish, and seaweed. Dungeness crabs also require a Sports Catch Card, described later. The license tag must be displayed on the outside of clothing when harvesting shellfish or seaweed.

Combination License covers all three of the licensing areas.

Sports Catch Cards, in addition to the appropriate license, are required for sturgeon, salmon, steelhead, halibut, and Dungeness crabs. The catch location, date, species, and number caught must be recorded. The card must be turned in each year by April 30, even if nothing was caught.

If you dig for clams, state law requires that all holes be refilled. It might take several turns of the tide for displaced sand to be leveled, and in the meantime small marine animals brought to the surface by digging might die from exposure to the sun, and marine life covered by the pile of displaced sand might suffocate. In addition, such holes are hazardous to people walking the beach. Marine supply stores and bookstores have publications that give suggestions on digging clams and catching crabs and shrimp.

MARINE SANCTUARIES. All of the seashores and seabed of San Juan County and around Cypress Island in Skagit County are a marine biological preserve. The taking or destruction of any living specimen, such as starfish, sand dollars, or sea anemones, except those edible varieties defined and regulated by the state Department of Fish and Wildlife, is prohibited.

Although it is not illegal to take a small nonliving souvenir of a San Juan trip, such as an empty seashell or small rock, please use restraint in the quantity you take, or better yet, leave it to enhance the marine environment.

Many of these beach finds might harbor tiny marine life; check to see if a shell is inhabited before taking it home.

PARALYTIC SHELLFISH POISONING (RED TIDE). When the state Department of Health periodically issues a "red tide warning" and closes particular beaches, the public usually reacts with confusion or skepticism. A clearer understanding of the phenomenon of red tide will lead to a greater respect for its dangers.

The name "red tide" itself contributes to some of the public's confusion, for it is not always visibly red, it has nothing at all to do with the tide, and not all red algae are harmful. Paralytic shellfish poisoning (PSP) is a serious illness caused by *Gonyaulax catanella*, a toxic, single-celled, amber-colored alga that is always present in the sea in small numbers. During spring, summer, and fall, certain environmental conditions might combine to permit a rapid multiplication or accumulation of these microscopic organisms. Most shellfish toxicity occurs when the concentrations of *G. catanella* are too sparse to discolor the water; however, the free-floating plants sometimes become so numerous that the water appears to have a reddish cast—thus the name "red tide."

Bivalve shellfish such as clams, oysters, mussels, and scallops, which feed by filtering seawater, might ingest millions of the organisms and concentrate the toxin in their bodies. The poison is retained by most of these shellfish for several weeks after the occurrence of the red tide; butter clams can be poisonous for much longer. When the concentration of the toxin in mollusks reaches a certain level, it becomes hazardous to humans who eat them. The toxins cannot be destroyed by cooking and cannot be reliably detected by any means other than laboratory analysis. Symptoms of PSP, beginning with the tingling of the lips and tongue, might occur within a half-hour of ingestion. The illness attacks the nervous system, causing loss of control of arms and legs, difficulty in breathing, paralysis, and, in extreme cases, death.

Shellfish in all counties on Puget Sound are under regular surveillance by the state Department of Health. Red tide (or PSP) warnings are issued and some beaches are posted when high levels of the toxin are detected in tested mollusks. Warnings are usually publicized in the media; the state toll-free Marine Toxins/PSP Hotline at (800) 562-5632 has current information about beach closures. Crabs, shrimp, and fin fish are not included in closures because there have been no recorded cases of PSP in the Northwest caused by eating any of these animals.

Using the Public Parks: Fees, Regulations, and Courtesy

Regulations in the various parks are set up to preserve the natural environment and to maintain the safety and pleasure of all visitors, as well as park neighbors. The following comments apply specifically to the parks in the San Juans operated by the Washington State Parks and Recreation Commission. In general, these same rules, where relevant, also apply to county parks. Check for specific rules and regulations when using any area. They should be prominently posted on a bulletin board or are found in pamphlets available at park headquarters. While visiting, be courteous and considerate of other park users and treat the park itself with care.

FEES. Due to the state's budgetary problems, fees are charged for use of many state park facilities. In many parks, users are required to self-register and deposit fees in a locked metal box known as an "iron ranger." The fee schedule is published in newspapers and boating periodicals in the spring and is posted on information kiosks in camping areas. You can pay by personal check. Campsite reservations can be made online at the parks website, *www. parks.wa.gov*, or by calling (888) 226-7688 (CAMPOUT). Check the website or contact the specific park for information on group areas. For the Moran State Park ELC, call (800) 360-4240 or (360) 902-8600.

Following are the fees for 2007–2008. An asterisk (*) indicates added fees for premium sites and popular destination parks. Tax is added to all fees.

- Camping:

  Standard site: $17–22* for a maximum of four persons over age eighteen, maximum of eight persons per site

  Primitive site or Washington Water Trail campsite: $12–14* for a maximum of four persons over age eighteen, $2 for each additional person, maximum of eight persons per site

  Moran State Park ELC: $3.38 per person day-use, $9.30 per person overnight; full camp 70 people minimum, 144 maximum; main camp (October 1–April 30) 40 people minimum, 88 people maximum

- Vehicle overnight in parking area, or additional vehicle at campsite: $10

- Trailer dump station: $5 per use (fee waived if campsite or moorage fee paid)

- Advance reservation of facility through the central reservation system: $7 (nonrefundable); cancellation or change fee: $7. Advanced reservtion through non-central system: $25, non-refundable.

- Moorage (whether boats are tied directly to a float or buoy or rafted alongside another boat):

  Floats: $0.50 per foot, $10 minimum (annual permit: $0.50 per foot, $50 minimum)

  Buoys: $10 per any size boat, up to buoy capacity

  Anchoring: No charge

- Watercraft launch site permit: $5 (fee waived if campsite fee paid); annual permit: $50

CAMPING. Camp only in designated areas; camping is limited to 10 consecutive days at any one park. Do not ditch tents, cut green boughs for beds, hammer nails into trees, or in any other way mutilate nature. Clean up your campsite after using it.

FIRES. Build fires only in designated fireplaces and fire rings. Fire hazard can be extreme during the summer months, and fires on the remote islands are difficult to handle. Before leaving, be sure your campfire is completely extinguished and the embers are cold. Beach fires are prohibited. Report any out-of-control fire immediately. Emergency phone and radio contacts are listed in Appendix A at the back of this book.

Portable charcoal-burning barbecues or hibachis placed on the float beside a boat can badly char the float; when using any such stove, be sure the wood is properly shielded from the heat. Some places prohibit their use.

Gathering fallen trees, branches, and driftwood for campfires is prohibited in all state parks. Decaying wood provides nutrients to the forest ecology, and driftwood helps prevent beach erosion. Either bring firewood with you or, where it is available, purchase it at the park or at an island store.

GARBAGE. Trash receptacles are provided at the larger state parks; please use them. Many of the smaller, more remote marine state parks have neither garbage cans nor garbage collection. In areas where garbage cans are not provided, all trash must be removed. With the increasing waste disposal problem in the San Juans, a sensitive visitor will take garbage back home whenever possible. Recycling is encouraged.

When on boats, do not "deep-six" debris, whether it is cans, bottles, orange peels, or chicken bones. It usually does not come to permanent rest six fathoms down but will eventually wash up on some beach as ugly litter.

LIVING THINGS. As noted earlier, all of the seashores and seabed of San Juan County are a marine biological preserve. The taking or destruction of any living specimen, such as starfish, sand dollars, or sea anemones, except those edible varieties defined and regulated by the state Department of Fish and Wildlife, is prohibited. Feeding, hunting, or harassing of wildlife and discharge of firearms is prohibited within the state parks.

Green wood may not be gathered from the forests for fires or any other purpose. Plants may not be dug up, nor flowers picked.

VEHICLES AND BICYCLES. Motorized vehicles and bicycles are prohibited on service roads and trails, with certain exceptions for bicycles in Moran State Park, as noted in Chapter Eight. Observe posted speed limits on public roads within parks.

BOATS. In the moorage area of marine state parks, the boat speed limit is three mph (no-wake speed). In addition to being extremely annoying to other boaters, hot-rodding or racing, even in small outboard-powered dinghies, can create a wake that might swamp small craft, send hot food flying from a cruiser's galley range, or cause other damage. Boaters are legally responsible for any damage caused by their wakes.

Moorage on buoys, floats, and lineal mooring systems is on a first-come, first-served basis. The practice of individuals attempting to "reserve" space by tying a dinghy to a buoy or float space is not legal in the state parks. Continuous moorage is limited to 3 consecutive nights.

Mooring buoys provide secure places to tie up in most of the marine state parks.

It is courteous to use the minimum moorage space possible on a float. Beach small boats whenever you can, instead of tying up to a float. Berth small cruisers or runabouts as far inboard as possible, leaving the end of the float for larger boats that require deeper water and more maneuvering space.

During busy summer times, it is considerate (and often more fun) to raft together with a friend on a buoy, thus freeing a moorage for another boater. Because buoys can be displaced by having too heavy a load on them, observe the following restrictions:

- For boats less than 24 feet long, four boats may be rafted together on the buoy.
- For boats from 25 to 36 feet long, three boats may be rafted together.
- For boats from 37 to 45 feet long, two boats may be rafted together.
- Boats more than 45 feet long may not raft on buoys.

Lineal mooring systems have been installed at Echo Bay on Sucia Island and Reid and Prevost Harbors on Stuart Island. These consist of a 200-foot-long cable strung between a pair of pylons. Mooring eyes are provided along the cable, and boats can tie up to either side. This system allows more moorage in a small area, and in addition is easier on the environment, as it greatly reduces the damage done to the seabed by dragging buoy anchor blocks and boat anchor chains.

Reflecting concern about oil tanker traffic and the nearby mainland oil refineries, a series of buoys have been installed at Sucia Island (near the entrances to Echo and Fossil Bays and Fox Cove), Shaw Island (Blind Bay), and Lopez Island (Mud Bay). In the unlikely event of an oil spill, they are intended to serve as attachment points for containment booms to protect the bays. They may be used for recreational moorage unless needed for an oil spill emergency.

PETS AND HORSES. Pets must be on a leash no longer than 8 feet and be under control at all times. Pets are not permitted on designated swimming beaches.

Some boaters regard the land facilities of state parks merely as handy places for their dogs to relieve themselves. Even the most devout animal lovers find it hard to think kindly of these pets while trying to scrape doggy droppings from the grooves of their boat shoes. State park regulations state that pet owners must clean up after their pets; violators are subject to fines.

Horses are allowed only in designated state parks, in designated campsites, and on designated trails.

NOISE. Because sounds carry greater distances over water, use care that radios or overly boisterous noise do not penetrate to nearby boats or campsites. Report disturbances to park rangers.

VANDALISM. It probably does little good to talk about intentional vandalism here. The damaging or removal of park property is, of course, illegal, and if you see it, you should report it to the proper authorities.

Some acts of vandalism, however, are committed out of thoughtlessness or ignorance. Spray painting or scratching graffiti on rocks or other natural features might not be recognized by park visitors as vandalism until they are confronted with a lovely sandstone wall turned ugly with mindless scrawling. Such defacement is prohibited in all parks.

Safety Concerns

Safety is an important concern in all outdoor activities. No guidebook can alert you to every hazard or anticipate the limitations of every reader. Therefore, the descriptions of roads, trails, waters, and natural features in this book are not representations that a particular place or excursion will be safe for your party. When you follow any of the descriptions in this book, you assume responsibility for your own safety. The areas described herein vary greatly in the amount and kind of preparation needed to enjoy them safely. Some might have changed since this book was written, or conditions might have deteriorated. Weather can change daily or even hourly, and tide levels will also vary considerably. An area that is safe in good weather at low or slack tide might be completely unsafe during inclement weather or at times of high tide or maximum tidal current. You can meet these and other risks safely by exercising your own independent judgment and common sense. Be aware of your own limitations, those of your vessel, and of conditions when and where you are traveling. If conditions are dangerous, or if you are not prepared to deal with them safely, change your plans. Each year many people enjoy safe trips on the waters, beaches, and trails of the San Juan Islands. With proper preparation and good judgment, you can, too.

The Mountaineers Books

Emergency Assistance and Other Contacts • In parks where rangers are not on duty, the proper authority can be reached by marine or citizens band (CB) radio if immediate action is necessary. From cell phones, the quick-dial number, *CG, immediately connects the caller to the Coast Guard Vessel Traffic Center in Seattle. The center coordinates all marine safety and rescue activities in the region. Be ready to explain the nature of the emergency and your exact location.

The U.S. Coast Guard has primary responsibility for safety and law enforcement on the water. Marine VHF channel 16 is continuously monitored by the Coast Guard and should be the most reliable means of contact in case of emergencies on the water. The Coast Guard monitors CB channel 9 at some locations and times, but it has no commitment to full-time radio watch on this channel. Several volunteer groups do an excellent job of monitoring the CB emergency frequency and will assist as best they can with relaying emergency requests to the proper authorities

Overall legal authority in the San Juan Islands rests with the county sheriff. The emergency number is 911. Complaints or other business should be referred to the sheriff's office. A list of phone numbers and addresses for parks and legal agencies is included in Appendix A. In matters of less urgency, park rangers should be contacted by telephone or in writing.

A classic sailboat hangs on a buoy at James Island Marine State Park. In the distance a ferry heads for Thatcher Pass.

boating facility is a boat launch ramp on the north end of the island, at the end of the county road that crosses the island. A short dock located on the southwest end of the island on Reads Bay at the community of Decatur is for use by residents only. Nearby is the island airplane landing strip.

Several good spots to drop an anchor can be found around the island. Brigantine Bay, a bit to the north behind Trump Island, has good anchorages quite close to shore; however, when southerlies blow, the flat southern tip of Decatur offers no protection. Shrimp pots set here usually bring in enough to enhance a galley dinner.

Around a rocky headland is another fine anchorage at Sylvan Cove, known locally as Kan Kut Bay. The neat buildings and grasslands at the head of the bay are an idyllic scene from the water. The largest of the buildings was a boat-in restaurant many years ago, but today all property surrounding the cove, including the dock and buoys, is part of a private real estate development.

On the east shore of Decatur Island is a large curving bight with a gentle, sandy beach punctuated by the dramatic round knob of Decatur Head. The south end of the bight offers some anchorages to overflow crowds from James Island Marine State Park, but there is precious little wind protection from any quarter. Use care anchoring here, as it is quite shallow, especially on the west side. The county launch ramp faces on this bay.

The interesting formation of Decatur Head was once a separate little island, but the action of wind and waves over centuries of time built up the sand neck. This geological formation, known as a tombolo, now joins the head to the larger island. Spencer Spit, on Lopez Island just to the west, is an example of a tombolo in the process of forming as it stretches out toward Frost Island.

James Island Marine State Park Map 2

Boating • Paddling • Camping • Picnicking • Hiking • Scuba Diving • Fishing

Facilities: 13 primitive campsites, 3 Cascadia Marine Trail campsites, picnic tables, picnic shelter, fire grates, composting toilets, toilets, dock with a 40-foot float (removed in winter; a significantly longer float is planned for the near future), 5 mooring buoys, hiking trails; *no drinking water, no garbage collection*
Park area: 113 acres, 12,335 feet of shoreline
Trail hiking distance: $1/2$- to $1\frac{1}{2}$-mile loop, depending on route
Trail elevation gain: 200 feet, with numerous ups and downs
The island lies 4 nautical miles west of Sunset Beach and Flounder Bay, on Fidalgo Island, the nearest point where trailered boats can be launched. From Lopez Island, 4 nautical miles to the west, hand-carried boats can be launched at Spencer Spit.

Lacking the broad beaches and sheltered harbors of other San Juan marine parks, James Island is often ignored by boaters in favor of more spacious and glamorous spots. Its coves are frequently used only as an overnight stop for southbound boaters awaiting the turn of the tide at Deception Pass.

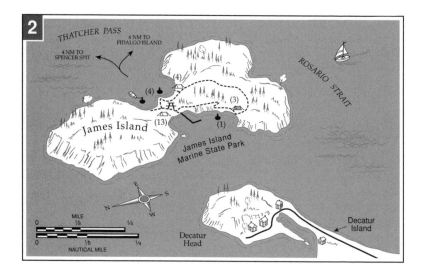

Nevertheless, the park offers pleasant camping and scenic hikes to those who linger awhile.

James Island is one of the most rugged of the San Juan Island marine state parks, with high, steep bluffs broken by coves. The eastern side of the island has two small adjacent coves, each holding two mooring buoys. These moorages are subject to weather and waves from Rosario Strait.

A cove on the west side, sheltered by Decatur Island, contains a mooring buoy and a dock, with a float large enough for three or four boats. Decatur Head lies immediately west across the ¼-mile-wide channel, tethered to its parent island by a narrow spit of land. Although this is the more protected side of James Island, the gravel bottom of the cove offers poor holding ground for anchors, and currents swirling through the small cove further complicate both anchoring and mooring.

Currents eddy in the cove from the northwest to the southeast, which can make docking on the south side of the floats a challenge at times, and winds from the southwest can make the moorage quite bouncy. Plans are to extend the float for added moorage and to place it in a better position. This should occur by 2005 or 2006. ❀ If heading from Lopez Island to James in a very small or paddle-powered boat, be aware that tidal currents can reach 2 knots in Thatcher Pass. Heavy boat traffic in the channel can add to the hazard.

Small boats can be easily beached in the coves on either side of the island. The western cove is a favorite scuba diving area; while fish are few, the invertebrate life is varied and colorful. Scattered in the trees on the narrow neck of land between the coves, and on the bluff above the northeast cove, a picnic shelter and a number of campsites provide picnic tables, fireplaces, and nearby composting toilets. Trails connect all the campsites.

From the dock area, a steep signed trail climbs over the headland between

Shallow-draft boats can draw up near shore at the cove on the west side of James Island Marine State Park.

the two sides of the cove, then switchbacks down steeply, arriving in ¹/₂ mile at a tiny beach on the far edge of the western cove. Three Cascadia Marine Trail campsites in the forest above the beach are reached via a staircase. Use care in following paths along the high grassy bluffs; overzealous exploration can leave a hiker hung up on the cliffs, or an unwary step can result in a bad fall.

If you are planning to camp, be forewarned of a horde of masked bandits that lie in wait onshore—raccoons. Although they might seem cute early in the evening as their bright eyes glimmer at the edge of your campfire, their charm palls when you wake at 2 A.M. to find them rattling cook pots and rifling groceries. To discourage these persistent pests, secure everything back on your boat or inside your tent.

chapter two

 Lopez Island

🚗 Lopez Landing is reached by ferry from Anacortes (about a 45-minute trip), or from Sidney, B.C., on Vancouver Island (slightly less than 2 hours from Anacortes).
🚤 Boating access is in several places around the island. The best access is at Spencer Spit State Park, 9½ nautical miles west of the city of Anacortes, and Fisherman Bay, 4 nautical miles from Friday Harbor.
✈ The island can also be reached via scheduled flights of San Juan Airlines, which stops at the local airfield, and by seaplane service from Seattle via Kenmore Air. Charter airlines also provide service to the island. A landing float is at the Islander Lopez Resort on Fisherman Bay.

HERE'S COW COUNTRY—AND SHEEP, and goats, and horses, too. A green patchwork quilt of fields and pastures, interrupted by sections of velvety forest rolling down to the edge of the sea; farmyards with chickens busily scratching around piles of fishing nets; arrow-straight roads edged by fences and hedgerows, disappearing into soupy San Juan mists. At the island's southern tip, the level land tilts upward to form steep, craggy cliffs and deeply notched, rocky bays. As if to compensate for its meek, pastoral nature, here Lopez Island presents some of the most rugged shoreline to be found in any of the San Juans.

Lopez, the most level of the three largest San Juan Islands, was once a

Lopez Island roads are a joy for bicyclists.

major agricultural supplier for western Washington. Its dry climate favored crops of grain and orchards of fruit. Dams built on the Columbia River during the 1930s later brought irrigation to the arid lands of eastern Washington, converting them to bountiful farmland with which the San Juans could not compete. Agriculture, and with it the islands' economy, declined. Only a few farms are still in operation today. A vineyard near the north end of the island now produces quality wines.

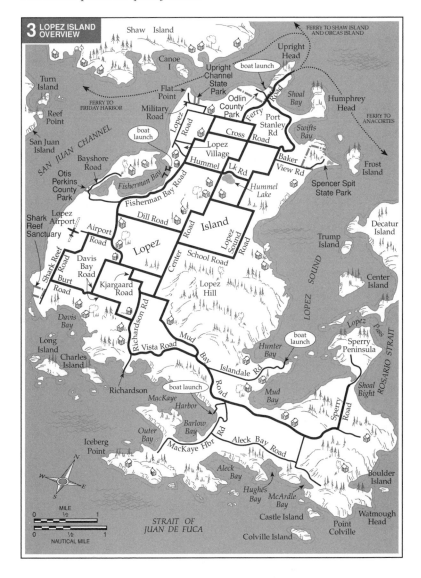

3 LOPEZ ISLAND OVERVIEW

Among an entire bevy of islands described as friendly and relaxed, Lopez is considered to be the friendliest and most laid back of all. The common phrase here is, "Wave, you're on Lopez." First-timers are surprised to find that drivers passing them on the road offer a salutatory wave and wonder if they have been mistaken for someone else. Usually it dawns on the visitor that this is simply a charming practice unique to an island where the population is so small that everyone is known, and even "outlanders" are welcome. As you travel around Lopez Island, take time to notice the lovely details of island life such as a lady scarecrow with a fancy bonnet, individualized mailboxes in imaginative shapes, or handcrafted fences and gates. Even a pasture gate might be a work of art.

Lopez Island does not display as much distinct marine flavor as Orcas and San Juan Islands. Its shoreline does not attract the usual San Juan hordes of yachtsmen, because it lacks good harbors. Bays on the north are quite shallow, while southern ones are farther from the boating mainstream, and those facing on the Strait of Juan de Fuca are subject to bad weather and uncomfortable swells. Nevertheless, a few choice spots along its shores make fine stopovers for boaters.

The island's gently rolling heartland is a joy to hikers and bicyclists, and it boasts an ever-growing reputation as the best of the San Juans for bicycling. A brief, steep uphill grade greets cyclists as they leave the ferry, but once this challenge is conquered, miles of quiet country roads stretch out. Several cycle shops offer rentals and repairs.

The ferry landing is in a small cove at the tip of Upright Head, where the only tourist facility is a small stand with a bit of seating that offers sandwiches and snacks. It usually is open only around the time of ferry arrival and departure. Public toilets are across the road, near the parking lanes.

City folk visiting the San Juans for the first time have been known to

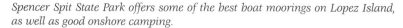

Spencer Spit State Park offers some of the best boat moorings on Lopez Island, as well as good onshore camping.

unload their cars at Lopez, drive down the timber-bordered road of Upright Head, make a quick loop around the island, and scurry back to the next departing ferry, shocked at the lack of such amenities of "civilization" as shopping malls, fast-food chains, or movie theaters.

Lopez Village, on the east shore of Fisherman Bay, is the island's "center of commerce." The few dozen businesses you'll find there offer food, lodging, groceries, and basic necessities, including some excellent restaurants. Marinas on the bay have fuel, moorage, and repairs. Auto fuel is available from stations at the intersection of Mud Bay and Mackaye Harbor Roads and at Lopez Village. On the south end of the island, the historic general store at Richardson, which was a popular tourist attraction, was destroyed by a fire in the fall of 1990. Now, the only commercial enterprise on that end of the island is a small gas station/convenience store/café.

Odlin County Park and Spencer Spit State Park, the only two car campgrounds on the island, provide a total of seventy-six sites. A privately operated campground on Fisherman Bay Road, 2½ miles south of the ferry landing, also has nice campsites as well as cottages. If these areas are all filled, it might be necessary to go elsewhere; check in early in the day to be sure you have a site.

Most island businesses and facilities are open daily, year-round, although at the end of the tourist season some drastically cut back their business hours and might be closed on Tuesdays.

THE NORTH END
Map 3

Odlin County Park   Map 4

Camping • Picnicking • Boating • Paddling • Swimming • Clam Digging • Fishing • Hiking • Scuba Diving • Snorkeling • Birdwatching • Beach Walking

Facilities: 28 standard campsites (reservations accepted), 2 CMT campsites, picnic tables, fireplaces, picnic shelter, group camps, drinking water, toilets, boat launch ramp, dock with float, 3 mooring buoys, children's play equipment, sports fields, hiking trails
Park area: 80 acres, 4000 feet of shoreline
The park is within minutes of the Lopez Island ferry terminal. To reach it, follow Ferry Road south for 1 mile; at the first two-way intersection turn right (west) and follow the road downhill for 300 yards to the campground.
The park lies 3½ nautical miles southeast of Orcas Landing, and 5½ nautical miles northeast of Friday Harbor.

Odlin is truly a family park, with a softball diamond for family ball games, a volleyball net, and an open field for Frisbee matches. All this and an outstanding beach, too!

The park, on a curving, sandy bay, makes a nice quick stop for lazing in the sun while waiting for the next ferry—you might even decide to linger awhile and catch a later one. Just offshore, the ferry on the runs to Friday

Harbor that bypass Wasp Passage sails by in Upright Channel.

As you enter the park, a launch for trailered boats is straight ahead, at the end of the park's main road. A narrow, unpaved road branching left, to the south, leads past the ball field to the camping area. The first of the park's campsites are just above the beach, with elbow-to-elbow picnic tables and fireplaces. This is the only park in the San Juans with campsites right along the beach. In summer, these sites frequently are more heavily used than those at Spencer Spit, which are some distance above the water.

The park road continues south into the trees to more private, sheltered sites and a small grassy clearing for group get-togethers. Bicycle and walk-in campsites are found beyond the road end, along the bank overlooking the bay. A dock with a float at the north end of the park is available for loading and unloading—no overnight moorage. The soft bottom of the shallow bay provides good anchorages, and residents claim the moorage here is one of the most protected from storms in the San Juans. Plans are to add a couple more buoys to the three existing ones. At the north side of the park, near the dock, the bottom begins to drop off quite steeply.

Scuba diving is excellent near the dock and along the sheer rock walls and submerged boulders on the west side of Upright Head. A rainbow-colored assortment of sea stars cling to the rock, and schools of curious fish swim by. Tidal currents outside the bay are quite strong. The sandy bottom of the bay is habitat for sea pens, sea cucumbers, and striped nudibranchs.

The fine sandy beach invites swimming, sand-castle building, and barefoot walks. At low tide, dig clams—if those ahead of you haven't found them already. Uprising cliffs halt beach walks on the north side of the park. South, at low tide, the gradual beach can be followed all the way to Flat Point, 1½ miles away. Do not attempt to walk the bank, as it is undercut and can be

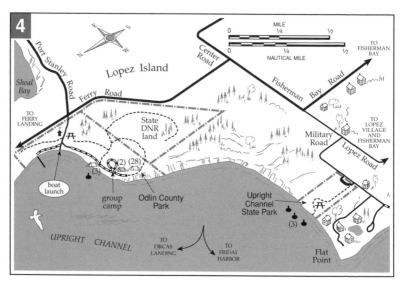

dangerous. In addition, walking the bank kills the vegetation needed to stabilize the embankment.

Trails out of the campground circle around in a flatland of second-growth timber and brush. Although they make nice walking, none have particular destinations; some dead-end, others loop back on themselves. Mushroom picking is good, in season. Additional trails are planned through the beautiful madrona forest on Upright Head, between the park and ferry landing.

Upright Channel State Park Map 4
Picnicking • Boating • Paddling • Clam Digging • Beach Walking

Facilities: Picnic tables, fireplaces, toilets, 3 mooring buoys; *no drinking water, closed October 1 to April 30*

🚗 From the ferry landing, go south on Ferry Road and in 2 miles, at a T intersection, turn west on Fisherman Bay Road. In ½ mile this road heads south; continue straight ahead on Military Road. In ¼ mile Military Road heads north, then shortly turns west again; ½ mile west of this last corner is a parking lot, gated except during daylight hours. Park here and walk the short distance down the service road to the park.

🚤 The park is immediately southwest of Odlin County Park and 2 nautical miles north of the entrance to Fisherman Bay, on Lopez Island.

This picnic area and beach access is a nice addition to the day-use recreational facilities on Lopez Island. The park, originally developed by the Department of Natural Resources but currently maintained by State Parks,

Trails at Odlin County Park offer a forest experience—and maybe some tasty mushrooms for those knowledgeable in identifying them.

has a couple of picnic sites nestled in dense brush upland from the beach and a few more with fire braziers and toilets sit in a grassy clearing on a low bluff. A path leads to the shore.

The gently sloping gravel beach, with tide-line driftwood and beach grass, looks out on Upright Channel. More than 1½ miles of shoreline can be enjoyed by walking east to Odlin Park or west around Flat Point to the end of the public beach 300 yards south from there. At the Flat Point residential area, only the beach below mean high tide level is public. Three offshore buoys give moorage to visiting boaters.

Lopez Village   Map 5

Historical Interest • Shopping • Bicycling • Nature Trail • Birdwatching

Facilities: Groceries, restaurants, stores, lodging, public restrooms with pay showers, museum, nature trail

Trail hiking distance: WEEKS WETLANDS TRAIL: ¼ mile round trip

Trail elevation gain: WEEKS WETLANDS TRAIL: None

From the ferry landing, follow Ferry Road south for 2 miles. At a T intersection turn right (west), and in ½ mile head south on Fisherman Bay Road. In 2 miles turn right on Weeks Road, which shortly reaches the town.

The town, at the entrance to Fisherman Bay, is 4 nautical miles from Friday Harbor. It is within walking distance of the marina on Fisherman Bay.

The hamlet of Lopez Village is the main commercial center of the island, with a cluster of businesses offering groceries, eateries, lodging, and some nice shopping. A public restroom is across the road, north of the grocery. Boater's facilities are ¾ mile to the south on Fisherman Bay.

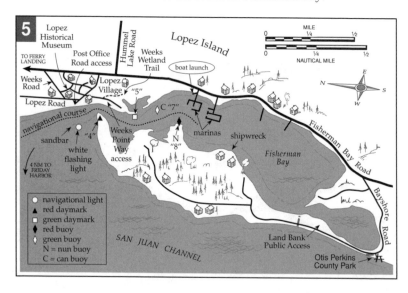

LOPEZ HISTORICAL MUSEUM. A block north of the shopping area, this nice museum, open on weekend afternoons, houses a collection of island photographs and memorabilia. Old farm equipment recalls the days when fruit, grains, and vegetables grown on the island flowed to dining tables in cities throughout Puget Sound.

WEEKS WETLAND TRAIL. Between the village and the north end of Fisherman Bay, this short nature trail wends past thickets of Nootka rose noisy with the songs and chattering of Savannah sparrows, song sparrows, violet-green swallows, and barn swallows, all protected by the thorny brush. Beyond, the trail crosses a field framing a saltwater marsh to reach a viewing platform overlooking the bay. The land was originally drained and farmed by the Weeks family in the 1850s. The berm that had been built to hold back the saltwater of the bay has been breached, creating today's brackish marsh. The Land Bank acquired this 22½-acre parcel in 1993 and later built the nature trail and supplied its interpretive signs. Only roadside parking is available at the trailhead.

WEEKS POINT WAY ACCESS. Although Lopez Village sits at water's edge, public beach access is limited. One access is on the west side of Weeks Point Way, two blocks south of the town, across the road from the Weeks Wetland Trail. Here, in a narrow strip between residences, is parking and a picnic table on the low bank above the Fisherman Bay channel, near daymark "4." On the tip of the peninsula across the channel, a couple of old hulls of reef netters are an interesting historical attraction. Reef netting was once the primary Indian method of salmon fishing. The hulls have moldered there for many years and someday might be gone.

Boaters leave Fisherman Bay. Lopez Village is on the left; the daymark at right warns of a shoal.

Reef Netting

The unique, colorful fishing method of reef netting was originated long ago by Indians in the San Juans, who fished from dugout canoes using nets fashioned from thin strips of willow or cedar bark. Pioneers adopted the method and added high, ladderlike lookout towers in the bows of the boats.

Reef netting, which is most commonly utilized for sockeye and humpback salmon, employs the use of two boats anchored about 50 feet apart in shallow water or around reefs, with a square net stretched between them and weighted at the bottom. In early times, the salmon chief, wearing a broad-brimmed hat that shaded his eyes, enabling him to see into the water, served as lookout. A cedar pole would be suspended horizontally a few feet under the water surface just ahead of the net, causing fish approaching the net to swim over the pole and break the surface of the water, making them easier to see. When a school of fish was spotted swimming into the net, the net was quickly pulled up and the catch dumped into holding nets. Very clear water and long, shallow reefs, such as are found in the San Juans, are necessary for this fishing method. This is the only place in the world it is used.

Reef netting has been modernized by the use of skiffs or barges with large outboard motors, modern nets of synthetic materials, and powered winches to haul in the catch. Lookouts today wear polarized sunglasses to aid their underwater view. Diminished salmon runs have made it less effective than other more high-tech methods; however, it is still practiced today by some fishermen.

Reef netters put lookouts on ladderlike towers to spot salmon.

POST OFFICE ROAD ACCESS. A second beach access is at the end of block-long Post Office Road, where stairs with a midway viewing platform descends to the shore. The rocky beach, which lies along the sinuous entrance to Fisherman Bay, features several interesting glacial erratics near the high tide level. The huge rocks were deposited here as the last Pleistocene ice sheet retreated. The public beach is a meager 100-foot strip at the foot of the stairs.

Fisherman Bay   Map 5

Boating • Paddling • Crabbing • Fishing • Bicycling • Birdwatching • Picnicking

Facilities: FISHERMAN BAY: picnic area, boat charters, dive shop, kayak rental, bicycle rental; **MARINAS:** guest moorage with power and drinking water, diesel, gas, marine supplies and repair, boat pump-out station, boat launch sling and ramp (fee), restaurant, snack bar, motel, restrooms, pay showers, coin-op laundry, swimming pool, hot tub for use of guests

🚗 From the ferry landing, travel to Lopez Village. Fisherman Bay is ¾ mile south on Fisherman Bay Road.

🛥 The bay's entrance lies on the west side of the island, facing on San Juan Channel. It is 4½ miles from the channel's southern entrance, and 4 nautical miles from Friday Harbor.

✈ Seaplanes can land on Fisherman Bay and use the float at Islander Lopez Marina (fee).

Fisherman Bay could more aptly be named Fisherman Lagoon; with its shallow bottom, brackish water, and mud-flat barrier built up by wave action, it is more closely related to a small lagoon than a clear, deep-water bay. But such a lagoon! Nearly a half-mile across and more than a mile in length, with shimmering, tranquil waters and evening sunsets that might bring tears of joy to the eyes.

Many boaters bypass Fisherman Bay, feigning disinterest: actually, they probably are apprehensive about the shallow entrance channel. Once this barrier is conquered, however, any skipper can lean back with the air of an experienced salt and play one-upsmanship with less accomplished pilots. It is claimed by businesses inside the bay that any boat that does not draw more than 4½ feet can enter the bay safely if the tide is not below zero. If that statement does not totally reassure you, enter on a rising tide to avoid the embarrassment of being stuck on a sand bar through a change of tide.

The accompanying map should be helpful when navigating. ❋ The channel runs quite close to the shoreline after rounding the tip of a long shoal extending north from the peninsula on the west side of the bay. The end of the shoal is marked with a navigation light—do not cut south of it! Once into the channel, keep red, even-numbered markers to starboard and green, odd-numbered to port when entering, the opposite when leaving.

If the anxious moments of the channel can be forgotten, the ½-mile journey is delightful, especially to large boats unaccustomed to such close quarters—cruising through the front yards of little waterfront homes, with the banks almost within arm's reach.

Moorage, fuel, boat servicing, supplies, and launch and haul-out facilities are available at both marinas on the east shore. Picnic tables and bicycle service and rentals are also in the vicinity. Perhaps treat yourself to dinner at the restaurant on the bay or in Lopez Village. Good anchorages can be had anywhere in the harbor.

The bay is superb for small-boat paddling. Put in hand-carried boats at the marina (fee) and explore the channel and bay. Drop off a crab pot near the western shore and return in the morning to find it filled with tasty Dungeness...perhaps.

Otis Perkins Park Map 5

Beach Walking • Birdwatching • Paddling • Picnicking

Facilities: Picnic tables; *no drinking water*

Park area: 1 acre, 60 feet of shoreline on San Juan Channel, 600 feet on Fisherman Bay

🚌 From the ferry landing, follow Ferry Road south for 2 miles. At a T intersection turn right (west), and in ½ mile head south on Fisherman Bay Road. In 4¾ miles, at the south end of the bay, turn west on Bayshore Road and follow it as it curves around the mud flat. The small park is clearly signed on the left. Park cars at the roadside pullout.

🛶 The park is 4 nautical miles from Friday Harbor. Kayaks can come up on the gravelly outer shore of the neck, on San Juan Channel; the inner shore, on Fisherman Bay, is too mucky for landing.

The south side of Fisherman Bay is enclosed by a sandspit so low that, from a distance, cars driving on it appear to be driving on water. At the south end of this spit, facing on San Juan Channel, is tiny Otis Perkins Park. The park is named for a longtime Lopez Island resident who donated the land. A pair of picnic tables and trash cans are the extent of the park's facilities—unless you count the sweeping views up and down the length of San Juan Channel, across to San Juan Island, and back to the lagoonlike stretch of Fisherman Bay. Prevailing westerlies whipping off the Strait of Juan de Fuca over the "toe" of San Juan Island can make the site quite breezy, so if you picnic here, you might have to hold down your bag of potato chips with a beach rock.

This narrow neck of land is interesting to drive or bike, but it is spectacular to walk, either on the beach or at road's edge. Within a few feet of one another are two entirely different saltwater environments. Inside the bay is grassy saltwater marsh, where crabs, clams, tiny fish, and myriad other small critters live, where pickleweed and marsh grass thrive, and where seabirds gather to feed and rest. Outside is smooth, clean beach with wave-swept sand and silvered driftwood, but little shore life. The constant movement of waves from San Juan Channel prevents the growth of marine life here.

The Land Bank acquired 3000 feet of the narrow peninsula running north from Otis Perkins Park, opening beaches on either side to public access. The road continuing on to a forested peninsula dead-ends at private property and offers no further public access or even views.

Hummel Lake Map 3

Paddling • Fishing • Birdwatching • Wildlife Watching • Hiking

Facilities: Boat launch ramp, dock, picnic tables, hiking trail, toilets
Trail hiking distance: ⅛ mile one way
Hiking elevation gain: None

Hummel Lake is on Hummel Lake Road, ¾ mile east of Lopez Village. To reach it from the ferry landing, follow Ferry Road south for 2 miles to a T intersection. Turn left (east), then in ¼ mile turn right onto Center Road, which can be followed to the lake, about 4½ miles total distance from the start.

Here's a modest little pond that packs a lot of interest into its 36-plus acres of surface. It is a favorite of fishermen, a pleasant spot for wildlife watchers, and large enough for boaters to take a brief paddle. Boats with gasoline motors are not permitted. The lake is stocked with trout, bass, and bluegill.

On Center Road, just south of the Hummel Lake Road intersection, an access with a launch ramp, a picnic table, racks of paddlecraft, and a stand holding several life jackets is maintained by local volunteers. There's ample parking; a toilet is adjacent. The life jackets are free for the borrowing, but the paddlecraft are all privately owned. Bring your own.

A second access, on 39 acres owned by the Land Bank, can be found on the south side of the lake. Look for a poorly marked road heading east from Center Road, ⅓ mile south of its intersection with Hummel Lake Road. This road leads to a day-use parking area with an adjoining toilet. A trail heads north through second-growth cedar, then breaks out into a woods-framed meadow. The path continues past picnic tables and benches to the lakeshore and a fishing dock. Boats may tie up but may not be launched from here.

The dock on Hummel Lake is reached via a short trail from the parking lot.

Cattails and blackberry brambles edging the lake rustle with bird life, including marsh wrens and colorful red-winged blackbirds. Virginia rails nest among the reeds; their narrow bodies and strong toes are adaptations for living in the muck and tightly packed vegetation of marshes. Because the lake is only 12 feet deep at its maximum, the water warms early in the spring, and it soon blossoms with algae. Although the green growth is unappealing, it is harmless to swimmers. The quiet water also fosters a prodigious growth of water lilies along the shore.

Spencer Spit State Park   Map 6

Camping • Picnicking • Boating • Paddling • Beach Walking • Birdwatching • Crabbing • Fishing • Clam Digging • Scuba Diving • Shrimping • Snorkeling • Swimming • Hiking • Wildlife Watching

Facilities: 30 standard campsites, 3 Cascadia Marine Trail campsites, 7 primitive campsites, 2 group camps, 2 Adirondack shelters, group day-use area, picnic tables, picnic shelters, fireplaces, beach fire rings, restrooms, showers, toilet, trailer dump, 16 mooring buoys, 2 miles of hiking trails; *closed November 1 to March 1*

Park area: 129³/₅ acres, 7840 feet of shoreline

Trail hiking distance: ¹/₂- to 4-mile loop, depending on destination

Trail elevation gain: 160 feet, depending on destination

🚐 From the ferry landing, go 1 mile to the first road junction and turn left on Port Stanley Road. At 3³/₄ miles turn left onto Baker View Road, continuing straight ahead to the park at 5 miles. The route is well signed.

⛴ The park lies 6¹/₂ nautical miles west of Sunset Beach on Fidalgo Island, the closest point on the mainland where boats can be launched, and 8¹/₂ nautical miles from Friday Harbor.

Although Spencer Spit State Park does not receive the gushing accolades that Moran State Park or the marine state parks do, its popularity grows each time it is newly "discovered" by campers, bicyclists, and boaters. Visitors delight in the marine view and the many activities the beaches and waters offer. To the north, tiny Flower Island nestles against the imposing backdrop of Orcas Island. At sunset, the channel is bathed in afterglow and the lights of ferries glimmer against Orcas's dark silhouette.

Spencer Spit is an excellent example of a sandspit enclosing a saltchuck lagoon. These lagoons, commonly found in the San Juans, are formed over a long period of time by the action of wind and tide on sandy beaches. In many cases, lagoons of this type eventually fill with sediment and progress from marsh to meadow. The perimeter of the lagoon displays a rainbow of colors from various algae and saltwater plants. A wide variety of birds pause at the lagoon during migration, including several kinds of gulls, a dozen species of ducks, great blue herons, kingfishers, black brant, and Canada geese. A billboard display near the parking lot explains the geology and ecology of this unique lagoon.

Inside the park entrance, a spur road leads to two loops of timbered campsites on the hillside above the beach. Nearly half the sites have enough

Ducks doze while a great blue heron oversees the action in the saltwater lagoon at Spencer Spit State Park.

space for RV trailers, although none have hookups. A walk-in group camp holds two large Adirondack shelters equipped with bunks. Walk-in campsites for cyclists and boaters are strung along the beach, and three Cascadia Marine Trail sites are located just above the beach, southwest of the lagoon.

Restrooms with outside showers are at the camping and parking areas, while the primitive sites make do with a toilet. Fire rings, stoves, and picnic tables along the shore invite daytime picnicking and evening bonfires. Build fires only in designated areas.

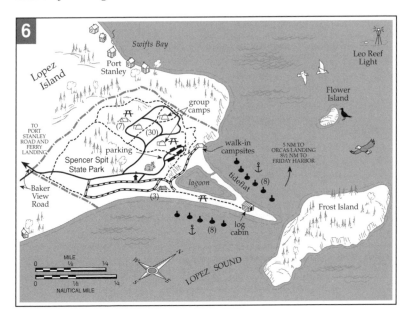

Silvered driftwood logs, tossed up by storms, edge the beach at Spencer Spit.
Photo: Heidi Mueller

Trails beginning at the lower campground road climb the hill to the other camp areas, continuing into the thick timber of the hillside. There are no views, due to the heavy growth, but it is still a lovely, cool hike on a warm summer day. These trails are primarily firebreaks that terminate at the park boundary.

Scattered on either side of the spit, sixteen mooring buoys accommodate boaters, with plenty of space for additional boats to drop anchor in the muddy bottom. Small boats can easily be hand carried the short distance to the beach from the loading area. Vehicles are permitted to drive on the service road from the park office to the beach for loading and unloading of boats or camping gear or to give disabled persons access to the beach.

Winter storms toss up driftwood and shells for beach walkers on the mile-long sandy beach. Butter, horse, and littleneck clams can be dug during summer low tides, and the waters yield crab, shrimp, and bottomfish. During warm summer days the broad beaches heat the usually frigid water to bearable swimming temperatures.

Rabbits tunnel in the soft soil of the hillside behind the beach and might appear in the daytime as well as in the evening. Raccoons roam the beaches at night, scavenging for tasty sea creatures or campers' tidbits left unattended. These animals, as well as the local black-tailed deer, can usually be seen during a quiet evening stroll along the beach or park roads.

A log cabin on the end of the spit has been reconstructed in the original style of a beach cabin that sat here more than 100 years ago. Some of the logs are from the original cabin; others were scavenged from the beach. The historic structure now serves as a picnic shelter, although heavy use by birds that roost in its rafters can make it unappealing. A second picnic shelter, built among remnants of the old Spencer family home, is at the base of the hill above the spit.

Frost Island lies just a stone's throw off the east end of the spit. Although all of its shores below the mean high-water-level are a public DNR beach, the rocky shoreline drops off so steeply that it is not walkable except at very low water. Property above the tideland is all privately owned. ☸When navigating small craft around Frost Island, use care, as the tidal current can be strong in the channel between the island and Spencer Spit.

Little Flower Island, less than 1/2 mile off Lopez Island, north of Spencer Spit State Park, is part of the San Juan Islands Wilderness Area. While the high, 4 1/2-acre island is interesting to explore by kayak or dinghy, do not go ashore, for such intrusion by humans disturbs nesting birds.

Harbor seals and sea lions are often seen sunning on rocks or peering curiously from the nearby water. Leo Reef, 1/2 nautical mile farther north, is also a favorite haul-out spot for these mammals. State ferry passengers with binoculars are almost assured of seeing them on the rocks or in the water as the boat passes by. The highest of the rocks has a lighted navigation mark. ☸Boats should give the reef a wide berth, as there are a number of submerged rocks in the vicinity.

LOPEZ SOUND

Map 3

This is one of the prettiest little cruising corners of the San Juans, with secluded bays, rockbound islets trimmed with ragged fringes of weather-torn evergreens, and a narrow pass with a bit of a navigational challenge, just to keep things interesting. The spacious channel, 5 nautical miles long and 2 nautical miles wide at its widest point, is squeezed between long Lopez Island and comma-shaped Decatur. It is just enough off the beaten path that it does not suit the boater hurriedly headed for somewhere else. Instead, it attracts cruisers willing to leisurely putt along, inspecting the shoreline, or sailboats looking for some wind.

Small Island, on the west side of Lopez Sound opposite the north end of Center Island, is a bird sanctuary of the San Juan Islands Wilderness Area. Other refuge islands in the sound are Fortress, Crab, and Skull Islands, between Hunter and Mud Bays. In addition to seabirds, seals can sometimes be seen basking on their sunny rocks.

Sperry Peninsula, a rounded bit of land south of Lopez Pass joined to the island by a slim tombolo, was long the site of a summer youth camp. The land was put up for sale and subsequently purchased for a private estate. The summer camp has been moved to Johns Island, near Stuart Island. At the south end of the sound, the Lopez Pass exit is guarded by the protruding reef of Rim, Rum, and Ram Islands. ❄Here, skippers heading out through the pass must continue south 200 feet beyond Ram Island to avoid kelp-flagged rocks tagged by red daymark "4," then make a hairpin turn to the left to run the tight little pass into Rosario Strait.

Some recent charts show Rum Island renamed as Cayou Island—evidently the State Board of Geographic Names gave it that title, not realizing it already had a dandy one. Rum it will always remain, however, to those who have a shred of whimsy in their heart.

The middle island, Rum (or Cayou, if you will), and Rim are part of the bird refuges of the San Juan Islands Wilderness Area. Ram, the larger wooded island on the south, is privately owned but has been designated as Open Space, and the public is permitted to go ashore. ❄Approach only with small boats, and even then use care, as the surrounding water is fouled with submerged rocks.

A buoy located halfway between Crab and Fortress Islands was installed as an anchor point for oil-spill protection booms. Recreational boaters may use the buoy when it is not needed for an emergency.

Hunter and Mud Bays Map 7

Boating • Paddling • Beach Walking • Birdwatching • Clam Digging • Crabbing • Fishing

Facilities: Dock, beach accesses

🚗 To reach the county dock on Hunter Bay, follow Ferry Road and then Center Road, south from the ferry landing. In about 8½ miles, where Center Road ends at a T intersection, turn left, and at the next intersection turn right (south) onto Mud Bay Road. Follow it for about 2 miles, and turn left (east) on Islandale Road. Follow this road for 1½ miles, avoiding private drives, as it winds downhill to the boat ramp and dock.

🚤 The bays lie 9½ nautical miles from Deception Pass and 10 nautical miles from the city of Anacortes, via Lopez Pass.

For boaters waiting to cross Rosario Strait and catch a favorable tidal current at Deception Pass, Hunter Bay offers peaceful anchorages in 20 feet of water. All mooring buoys in the area are private. A short county dock with a float and a launch ramp on the southeast side of the bay provide land-to-water access. The tideland on the tip of the peninsula separating Hunter and Mud Bays is a public DNR beach, although the shores drop off so steeply that there is little space for walking. Uplands are private.

There is parking for cars and boat trailers alongside the short spur road to the dock and ramp, with a 72-hour parking limit for boat trailers. The shorelands are forested or residential, with no stores or other facilities nearby.

Mud Bay, at the extreme south end of Lopez Sound, is too shallow for dropping an overnight anchor, but it has more extensive stretches of public tidelands. The obvious solution is to anchor in Hunter Bay and dinghy around to Mud Bay for beach walking, clam digging, and exploration.

Two upland accesses on Mud Bay provide a place for land-bound visitors

In Hunter Bay, a well-placed crab pot might yield a gourmet meal.

to reach the beaches. A public access near the head of the bay is reached by continuing past Islandale Road and taking the first road east of the end of Mud Bay, Mud Bay Dock Road, marked "Dead End." Head north on it along the shore; pass beach homes on a single-track dirt road that ends in ½ mile

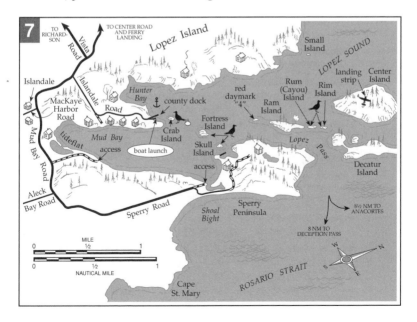

at a fence and parking space for a couple of cars. An easy scramble leads down to a beautiful flat beach. Most of the beach to mean high tide on Mud Bay is undeveloped state park land. Avoid any posted beaches and all upland property.

Another access is on the northeast edge of Mud Bay; to find it, continue on Mud Bay Road past the head of the bay and turn left on Sperry Road, heading north. When the main road curves right, a single-lane dirt road continues straight ahead for 300 feet to a turnaround at the road's end. Here boats can be hand-carried the short distance to the water. The nearby lagoon and pebbled beach provide interesting exploration by boat or foot; look for migratory waterfowl, in season.

THE SOUTHERN SHORE
Map 3

Two stretches of land on the far end of Lopez Island, Iceberg Point and Point Colville, are held by the Bureau of Land Management as lighthouse reservations. Iceberg Point houses a navigational beacon; Point Colville does not. The two areas can be reached only by boat; land access is closed.

The shores beneath the points are extremely rugged. The difficulty of landing boats varies with the tide level and the turbulence of the water. Between these rocky "toes" of the island are lodged a succession of intimate bays. The looming rock shorelines make these the most spectacular to be found in the San Juans.

Rocky walls along this end of Lopez Island plunge as dramatically underwater as they rise above. Undersea gardens that cloak these walls with a

Blind Island, right, and rocky bluffs at the south end of Lopez Island are seen from Hughes Bay.

colorful tapestry are a favorite of scuba divers who visit dive sites at Iceberg Point, Davidson Rock, and Colville Island. Marine life runs the gamut from red and green sea urchins, pecten scallops, bass, and rockfish, to wolfeels and octopuses. Strong winds, kelp, and the presence of commercial and sport fishing boats make this an area for alert, experienced divers.

The most easterly of the bays, Watmough Bay, faces east on Rosario Strait and is sometimes used as an overnight stop by boaters headed for Deception Pass. Although the narrow slot is well protected from weather, its rocky bottom might present some difficulty in getting anchors to hold.

Farther west, around Watmough Head and Point Colville, are McArdle and Hughes Bays. These two south-facing harbors offer reasonable anchorages along the eastern shore in northwest winds; however, they are exposed to southerlies and weather off the strait. Be wary of baring rocks near shore. Only the beaches below mean high tide at McArdle Bay are public.

Aleck Bay, which trends northwesterly for nearly ¾ mile, is the jewel among these inlets, with good protection and a muddy bottom for holding anchors. Clear days reveal a glorious sight—views all the way down Puget Sound to the white mass of Mount Rainier.

Shark Reef Wildlife Sanctuary   Map 8

Wildlife Watching • Birdwatching • Hiking • Picnicking

Facilities: Toilets, picnic tables; *no drinking water, no garbage collection*
Park area: 38 acres
Trail hiking distance: ½ mile round trip
Trail elevation gain: None

From the ferry landing, follow Ferry Road, which becomes Center Road, south from the landing. In about 8 miles, where Center Road ends at a T intersection, turn right on Kjargaard Road, then in ¼ mile, go left on Richardson Road. In ¾ mile turn right (west) on Davis Bay Road, and in 1½ miles, when Davis Bay Road turns north, continue west on Burt Road for ¾ mile to Shark Reef Road. Turn left (south) and in 200 yards reach the parking area at the trailhead to the beach.

The park lies 1 nautical mile from the southern entrance to San Juan Channel. Read the navigational warnings below.

Public land at Shark Reef, the legacy of a former military reservation intended to guard the entrance to San Juan Channel, now guards precious marine mammal and bird life and climax forest. The land, which had been held by the Department of Natural Resources, was scheduled to be logged in 1980 to provide money for funding state schools. At the behest of local groups, it was wisely decided that educational interests would be better served by preserving this unique forest as a wildlife sanctuary. San Juan County acquired it for use as a minimum-facility park. Toilets, picnic tables, and benches are near the beginning of the trail. No garbage cans are provided; please pack out all your trash.

A level, 10-minute hike through forest and shoulder-high salal leads to the rock and grass bluffs above the turbulent tidal currents of San Juan

Boats round Deadman Island near Shark Reef Wildlife Sanctuary as they head into San Juan Channel.

Channel. Shark Reef itself actually lies nearly a mile north of the park, and the view of it is blocked by Kings Point. The jumble of islets lying only 400 feet offshore from the park is a reef that is unnamed except for Deadman Island, the largest and highest of the rocks. With binoculars, seals and sea lions can be seen ponderously heaving themselves along the rocks to favored sunny

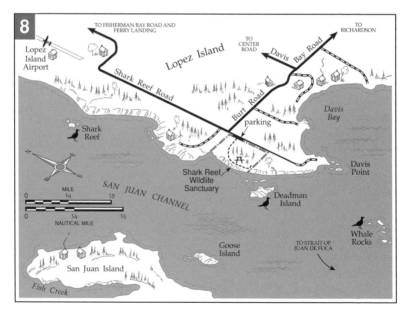

sites or slipping into the water with the grace of dancers. Harbor seals breed here, and glaucous-winged gulls and oystercatchers nest in rocky crevices. These islets are part of the San Juan Islands Wilderness Area.

The forest is one of the few remaining old-growth and late-successional second-growth forests on Lopez Island. Cavities in the trees provide nesting sites for screech owls and saw-whet owls; insects in rotting wood sustain a variety of woodpeckers. Four bald eagle nests are known to be in old trees in the vicinity.

Vague trails wind south along cliffs above the water for another ¼ mile, with views of nearby rocks and across the channel to the end of San Juan Island. The gull cacophony from across the channel at Goose Island offers atonal background music for the rugged scenery. Above, Cattle Point Light serves its lonely mission. A place to rest, observe, and meditate.

⚓ Boaters should stay well away from Shark Reef, Deadman Island, and all adjacent rocks; numerous rocks lie under the kelp-filled water, and currents are strong and tricky. Only experienced kayakers should attempt negotiating the narrow slot between the rocks and the island. Even the main channel entrance east of Goose Island can develop wicked tidal currents at extreme tide-level changes.

Richardson   Map 9

Bicycling • Boating • Paddling • Fishing • Scuba Diving

Facilities: Dock (no float), fuel for commercial vessels only

🚐 From the ferry landing, follow Ferry Road and then Center Road, south from the landing. In about 8 miles, where Center Road ends at a T intersection, turn right, then in ¼ mile, go left on Richardson Road and follow it to its end; total distance is about 10½ miles.

🛥 Richardson lies 12 nautical miles across Rosario Strait, west of Deception Pass, and 9 nautical miles southwest of Friday Harbor, via San Juan Channel.

Richardson, which looks directly into the Strait of Juan de Fuca from behind the limited protection of Iceberg Point and offshore islands, once was the southern outpost of the San Juans. At the turn of the century it was one of the major ports of the islands, shipping produce from the farms and orchards of Lopez Island via steamship to Puget Sound markets. A large fishing fleet, comprised of nearly fifty outfits, was based here, unloading their catches at the wharf or taking them directly to mainland canneries.

During this time, it is told, San Juan Channel ran thick with salmon, and at times nets were so full they could not be lifted into boats. Today, the great runs of fish are depleted, and fishermen are fewer and must go farther afield for their catches. Gillnetters and purse seiners still raft together in the harbor during fishing season, but the activity does not nearly approximate the days when the harbor burst with commerce.

The historic general store at Richardson, built on pilings over the water, was tragically burned in the fall of 1990, and there are no plans to rebuild it. The fuel tanks and dock were saved from the fire, so the dock still provides fuel for commercial boats. Aside from that, nothing remains of the bustling town except some private residences and a grand view into the strait.

The tour down-island to Richardson is a pleasure for bicyclists, with gently rolling blacktopped roads passing neat farms and cattle-filled pastures. Birds call from hedgerow and marsh, and San Juan rabbits dash across the road—perhaps just a breath ahead of a hawk. Watch for eagles soaring above the range of low hills to the south.

Mackaye Harbor and Agate Beach Picnic Area   Map 9

Paddling • Picnicking • Scuba Diving • Fishing • Wildlife Watching • Beach Walking

Facilities: MACKAYE HARBOR: launch ramp with boarding float; **PICNIC AREA:** picnic tables, toilets; *no drinking water*

Park area: 2 acres, 600 feet of shoreline

🚗 To reach Mackaye Harbor, follow Ferry Road and then Center Road, south from the ferry landing. In about 8 miles, where Center Road ends at a T intersection, turn right, then in ¼ mile, go left on Richardson Road. Just before reaching

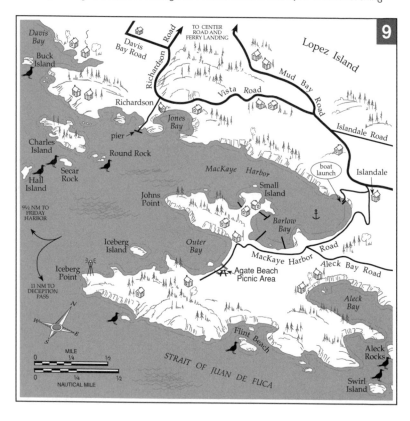

Richardson, turn left (east) onto Vista Road and follow it for 1½ miles to its intersection with Mud Bay Road. Turn right (southeast) onto Mud Bay Road, then in 1 mile, at Islandale, turn right again onto Mackaye Harbor Road. For the launch ramp, in a few hundred feet go right onto single-lane, dirt Norman Road, signed "Boat Ramp." The narrow road swings downhill to meet the corner of Mackaye Harbor at the launch ramp.

To find the picnic area, continue on Mackaye Harbor Road, which circles the shore, crosses a neck of land, then contours Outer Bay. In 1⅔ miles from Islandale, reach the small grassy picnic area on the east side of the road, near the middle of the beach.

The harbor is 12 nautical miles west of Deception Pass, 8 nautical miles south of Fisherman Bay, and 10½ miles south of Friday Harbor.

Mackaye Harbor, lying east of Richardson, offers some good anchorages at the east end of the harbor and in its southern extension, Barlow Bay. Two old fishing docks, previously used by commercial fishing fleets, occupy the south shore of Barlow Bay; the dock on the point to the northwest is privately owned.

A single-lane concrete launch ramp at the northeast corner of Mackaye Harbor offers access for trailered and hand-carried boats. The nearby parking lot can accommodate a dozen cars and trailers. The launch ramp is protected by a low rock breakwater and has a short boarding float.

Boats put in at the launch ramp can explore the multitude of bays and nooks along the south shore of Lopez Island. Remember to stay well away from the offshore islets and rocks of the San Juan Islands Wilderness Area, to avoid disturbing protected birds. Look, but give them clear berth.

The Agate Beach Picnic Area is farther along Mackaye Harbor Road, on Outer Bay. It is nothing pretentious, but it does offer a welcome rest spot

Kayakers prepare to launch at Mackaye Harbor.

and a lovely beach to walk. Across from the park, a stairway descends to the pebbled beach on Outer Bay, facing the "toe" of distant San Juan Island. Lying just offshore, a distinctive, smooth rock shaped like a shark's fin beckons to kayak explorers. Perhaps it can be reached by foot at extreme low tide. What else does low tide bring? Agates? Crabs? Stop and find out. Farther offshore is tiny Iceberg Island, an undeveloped state park property.

Outer Bay is a favorite with scuba divers, who explore the sand and cobblestone beach and offshore rocks. Sea urchins grow in particular abundance here. ❉Strong currents can present a problem in the outer portions of the bay, and in summer kelp growth is heavy in some areas.

Hughes Bay County Park   Map 10
Picnicking • Beach Walking

Facilities: Picnic table

🚗 To reach the park, turn south from Mud Bay Road onto Watmough Head Road, and in ¼ mile continue straight ahead on Huggins Road. Take the next dirt lane heading right, which goes to the parking area above the beach. The stairs are often closed, and the bank is much too steep and slippery to attempt.

🚣 Hughes Bay lies 8 nautical miles west of Deception Pass and 4½ nautical miles from the launch ramp on Mackaye Harbor.

This enchanting sand and gravel pocket beach on the east shore of Hughes Bay is a nice place to pause in your kayak explorations, and a pleasant spot for a picnic. A towering rock cliff bounds the southeast side of the beach. The narrow, 75-foot-wide strip of cobble beach grades to sand at minus tide. All of the remaining tidelands on Hughes Bay are private.

The steep, wooden staircase that drops down the high clay bank is often closed due to storm damage or hillside slippage. A plaque at the head of the stairs tells that this is Blacky Brady Memorial Beach.

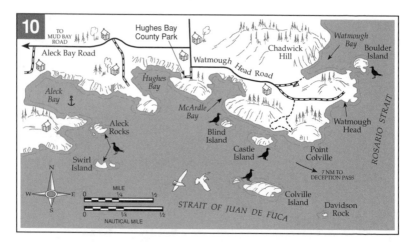

A high cliff edges the shore at Hughes Bay County Park.

Point Colville and Watmough Bay Map 10

Boating • Paddling • Hiking • Beach Walking • Birdwatching • Fishing • Scuba Diving • Views

Facilities: Hiking trail
Trail hiking distance: 1²/₃ mile round trip
Trail elevation gain: None

🚗 To reach the area, take Mud Bay Road east from Center Road for 4¹/₄ miles to Aleck Bay Road; head south on it for ¹/₂ mile to Watmough Head Road. Follow this road south, and then east, past McArdle Bay for 1 mile to the first unmarked spur to the northeast beyond Blue Darter Lane. A parking area and toilet are 500 feet downhill. A broad, flat, 300-yard trail leads along the marsh to the beach.

🛥 Point Colville lies 7 nautical miles west of Deception Pass, across Rosario Strait.

Chadwick Hill's steep rock cliffs frame the north side of Watmough Bay, but its west end has a tapering gravel beach below a long inland freshwater marsh. The surrounding land is protected by a Land Bank conservation easement and a BLM purchase, in recognition of its critical environmental features. Birdwatchers might see herons, teals, and various shorebirds.

Another BLM Area of Critical Environmental Concern offers access to Point Colville, with expansive views of the rugged coastline along the south side of Lopez Island and of offshore Colville, Castle, and Blind Islands and

79

Davidson Rock. To reach bluff-top viewpoints, continue a short distance past the spur road to Watmough Bay, to where the county road ends; the continuing track is passable only for four-wheel-drive vehicles. It is best to park at the Watmough Bay parking area and hike the road for ¹/₃ mile to the crest of a small rise, where the unmarked trailhead is found on the south side of the road.

The trail, vague but followable, heads south through open stands of second-growth fir, hemlock, and cedar to a Y junction in about ¹/₄ mile, the start of a ¹/₂-mile-long, bluff-top loop. The path to the southwest leads to the best viewpoints in a small wildflower meadow atop broad rock slabs. Offshore, the battlements of cliff-walled Castle Island rise more than 100 feet above the surf. The loop trail segment east from here is faint as it crosses more open slabs; it comes too close to the 80-foot-high cliffs for it to be safe for children.

What's a Wilderness Area Doing in the Middle of a Tourist Paradise?

It is well established that the numbers of sea birds have dramatically diminished throughout the world in the last century; civilization is almost totally responsible for this loss. Before the coming of humans, birds nested throughout the San Juans and raised their young here, and migratory birds used the islands as resting stops. Seals and sea lions sunned and rested on rocks and foraged the waters. Early Indians looted rookeries for eggs and killed birds for food and for their decorative value. The parrotlike beaks of tufted puffins were valued for ceremonial rattles and as adornment, and large numbers were killed just for that purpose. Despite this predation, the great flocks of birds survived.

Today civilization threatens their existence with subtler methods: It preempts their habitat, depletes their food sources, and poisons their environment. Aside from the moral and aesthetic issues raised by the loss of huge numbers of birds, this tinkering with one of the important links of the food chain must ultimately affect humans, too.

Anticipating people's insatiable demand for home and recreation sites, a number of these islands have been set aside as the San Juan Islands National Wildlife Refuge, providing sanctuaries for pelagic birds and animals. Most of these refuge islands have also been designated as wilderness areas, which offers them even greater protection.

On islands specifically designated as *wilderness areas*, going ashore at any time is prohibited, in order to protect the wildlife. Boaters and anglers are urged to stay at least 300 feet away from the islands to avoid disturbing the seals and nesting birds. Discharge of firearms is, of course, also prohibited and is subject to a stiff fine.

The three campsites at Blind Island Marine State Park have great views of ferry and boating activity.

☸Rocks around the island are a navigational hazard; a large one that has claimed a number of boat hulls lies southeast of the island, midway in the channel. A pole with a locally maintained caution sign displaying a white diamond marks it. Boaters approaching the mooring buoys should enter the bay on the east side of Blind Island, between the marker and the island, but favor the Blind Island side of the channel. Reefs west of Blind Island make entry via that route even more hazardous.

Low tide exposes rocky beaches all around the island; at that time, the best landing site for small boats is on the east side. Bring a sleeping bag and stay overnight to watch the evening show.

Parks Bay and Tift Rocks Map 11

Boating • Paddling • Birdwatching • Wildlife Watching

Facilities: None

Parks Bay lies 2 nautical miles northeast of Friday Harbor, on the southwest side of Shaw Island. Tift Rocks are 1 nautical mile northwest of Parks Bay.

On the southern end of Shaw Island, all the land of Point George and land surrounding Parks Bay is held by the University of Washington's Friday Harbor Laboratories as a biological preserve. Property here has been donated, purchased, or leased in order to maintain the shores and uplands in a nearly natural condition for research and educational purposes. Parks Bay is an excellent boat anchorage in 15 to 30 feet of water; however, going ashore is not permitted, due to its status as a nature preserve.

Grass-covered Tift Rocks, snuggled close to the shore of Shaw Island, usually go unnoticed by passing boaters. The northernmost and largest of the islands holds the deteriorating stone walls of a cabin that was built by a recluse who once lived here. Tift Rocks are part of the San Juan Islands Wilderness and host nesting seabirds and a number of seals that haul out to warm themselves in the sun. Going ashore is prohibited, but the animals and the rock walls of the cabin might be seen from the water.

South Beach County Park and Squaw Bay   Map 12

Camping • Picnicking • Paddling • Swimming • Beach Walking • Birdwatching • Clam Digging • Crabbing • Fishing • Hiking

Facilities: 10 campsites, 2 CMT campsites, toilets, picnic tables, fireplaces, picnic shelter, children's play equipment, drinking water, boat launch ramp
Park area: 65 acres, 3249 feet of shoreline

From the ferry landing, follow Blind Bay Road, which heads south and then curves west, to an intersection with Squaw Bay Road in 1¼ miles, signed to South Beach Park. Turn left (south); in ½ mile more, an inconspicuous sign points left to the South Beach Park camping area. There is another park entrance from Indian Cove Road ¼ mile east of its intersection with Squaw Bay Road.

Indian Cove lies just 3½ nautical miles east of Friday Harbor, where boats can be rented. Small boats are easily beached on the shore; deep-keeled vessels will have to anchor well out in the bay as it is extremely shallow.

Facing on Indian Cove, South Beach County Park encompasses 65 acres of prime Shaw Island real estate and one of the grandest sandy beaches on any of the San Juans. The land, once a military reservation, was purchased by Shaw Islanders for public use. Express your gratitude to these farsighted residents by observing posted regulations and respecting private property bounding the park.

The day-use picnic area is located on a slight embankment above the shore. A planked ramp at the end of the entrance road on the east side of

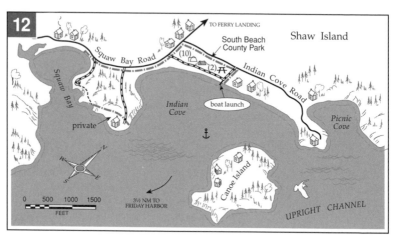

When Love Can Hurt

Jones Island, in a microcosm, reflects many of the problems besetting the San Juans as a whole. With its many attractions and convenient location, it might ultimately be "loved to death" by squadrons of boaters who arrive on its shores in greater numbers each year.

Today, ignorant visitors scar campgrounds by "ditching" their tents, injure trees with nails driven to support tent ropes, strip branches from anything green to fuel their campfires, pockmark the beach and shore with randomly built bonfires (and also risk setting the entire island ablaze), trample undergrowth by hiking carelessly, harass wildlife, and kill or cart away even inedible living beach creatures. Even well-intentioned campers who treat the land with care, simply by their presence have a negative impact on the environment. The space requirements and waste disposal logistics of tens of thousands of visitors create problems that must be dealt with.

As with all of the San Juans, Jones Island simply cannot tolerate the pressure of unlimited use and abuse by demanding recreationists. Without careful development and management, and sensitive, responsible use, the future might well see its beaches stripped naked, its meadows ground to dust, its forest destroyed, and its wildlife departed.

Black-tailed deer live on Jones Island. For their well-being they should not be fed or harassed.

A trail circles the low, wooded bluffs on the west lobe of the island, linking the southern and northern bays and the Cascadia MarineTrail campsite. Use care scrambling about the rocky embankment, as footing can be insecure; hikers have been injured here.

The west shore, at the edge of San Juan Channel, is a favorite spot for salmon fishing. Dungeness crab, which migrate around the island at some primitive whim, can sometimes be trapped in the south bay.

Until 1982, Jones Island was owned by the federal government, as a part of the San Juan Islands National Wildlife Refuge, and leased to the state as a marine park. Because the throngs of people using the island were not particularly compatible with its wildlife status, the U.S. Fish and Wildlife Service relinquished its claim and turned it over to the state in return for several smaller, more remote, state-owned islands.

chapter four

San Juan Island

🚐 Friday Harbor, on San Juan Island, can be reached via Washington State ferry from Anacortes or Sidney, B.C., about a 1½-hour trip either way. Foot-only private passenger ferries also provide service.

🛥 Private boats visiting the island will find guest moorage and supplies at Friday Harbor and at resorts on Roche Harbor and Mitchell Bay. Numerous fine anchorages are found around the island. Friday Harbor is 18 nautical miles from Anacortes, via the shortest route, and 19 nautical miles from Sidney, B.C. Several private ferries provide passenger-only service from Anacortes, Bellingham, and Seattle to Friday Harbor.

✈ For quicker access, San Juan Airlines has regularly scheduled flights from Anacortes and Seattle to the Friday Harbor airport. Kenmore Air also provides regularly scheduled floatplane service to Friday Harbor and Roche Harbor. Other air services offer charter flights.

Verdant, pastoral country punctuated by forested mountains. The most populated of the San Juan Islands, the center of commerce and industry and home port for the local fishing fleet. County seat and the largest (and only incorporated) town. Crossroads of these boundary waters, with a steady flow of international traffic through two customs offices. In short, the archipelago's busiest island.

Yet "busy" is a relative term in this slow-paced paradise. Even in summer, when tourists stream from crammed-full ferries, and harbors and bays swarm with boats, the customary tempo only slightly quickens. Many visitors, understanding the ambiance of the island, arrive with a bicycle or on foot with a backpack, prepared to enjoy it at a leisurely rate.

The early Spanish explorer Lopez Gonzales de Haro, who sailed through here in 1791, named this principal landfall of the archipelago San Juan. He noted its outstanding physical features and its important strategic location, facing on two major waterways. Arriving later, British settlers claimed it for the Crown and changed its name to Bellevue Island; eventually the original Spanish designation was restored.

Pioneers recognized San Juan Island as prime real estate, with its gently rolling farmland ideal for cattle and crops, its thick forests ripe to be turned into lumber, cabins, fences, and firewood, and its fine harbors providing sheltered access to the shores. Generation after generation they sank their family roots into the island soil.

Opposite: *Friday Harbor. The fuel dock is in the center; Spring Street Landing and the ferry dock are to the right, out of the photo.*

Many of today's full-time San Juan residents are retirees, artists, authors, and dropouts from the rat race who prefer their air without smog, their beaches without pollution slicks and beer cans, their highways without traffic jams, and their starry skies without obliterating city lights. Other property owners are the well-to-do or very wealthy who, probably for the same

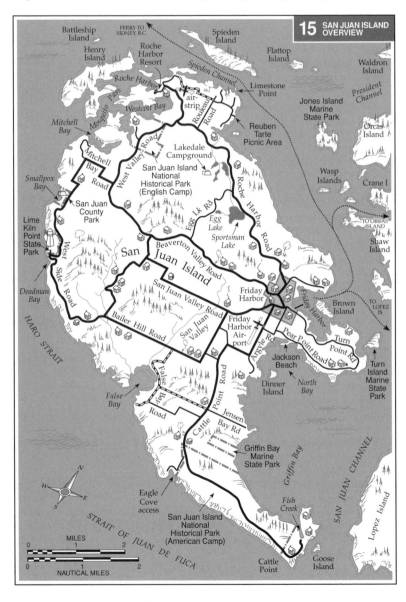

reasons, buy prime waterfront (or entire small islands) and build elaborate getaway estates. A few of these multimillion-dollar homes can be seen from the ferry.

Visitors will enjoy the gently rolling roads edged by pastures and forests, sometimes dropping down to round a salty bay, at other times skirting the edge of a bluff offering marine panoramas. Nearly all roads are two-lane blacktop with very little shoulder, but traffic moves at a relaxed pace, and, for hikers, cyclists, and moped riders, traveling the roads is quite safe if the simple precautions listed in the Introduction are observed.

Virtually all facilities and services found on San Juan Island are located at Friday Harbor. Small stores at Roche Harbor and Mitchell Bay pump fuel and carry supplies for campers, boaters, and anglers, but their selections are limited. A handful of resorts, hotels, and motels at Friday Harbor and a few other locations on the island provide overnight accommodations by

University of Washington Friday Harbor Laboratories

With shorelines ranging from quiet bays and saltwater lagoons to rocky shelves swept by swift-flowing tides, the San Juan archipelago provides an exceptional opportunity for marine research. Tidal fluctuations of nearly 12 feet expose vast tidelands harboring specimens of many diverse marine plant and invertebrate species.

Recognizing the unique character of the archipelago, the University of Washington established a marine biology research center on San Juan Island in 1904. When land from a former military reserve at Point Caution, just north of Friday Harbor, became available, the laboratories moved onto the 484-acre tract, there growing to become a fine educational and research facility, attracting visiting scientists from all over the world. The labs are open only to those involved in research. In the past, the laboratories offered guided tours to visitors. Unfortunately, funding constraints made it necessary to discontinue these popular tours.

Ferries arriving at Friday Harbor pass the attractive campus, on the north shore of the outer harbor. A modern-day aqueduct can be seen snaking along the bank; fashioned of polyethylene, the pipe delivers contaminant-free seawater to the laboratory aquaria.

The University of Washington also administers biological preserves at several areas in the San Juans. These lands have been donated, purchased, or leased to protect them in a nearly natural state for research and educational purposes. The largest of these holdings is on Shaw Island and includes most of the land and shoreline extending from Point George to Squaw Bay; others are at Argyle Lagoon and False Bay, on San Juan Island, and Iceberg Point and Point Colville, on the southern end of Lopez Island.

day or week, ranging from posh hotels to standard-fare motels and rustic beach cabins. Bed-and-breakfast inns offer lodging in a charming, comfy atmosphere. A local real estate agency carries listings of private homes that can be rented for a week or longer. Advance reservations are essential in summer for all lodging.

In addition to the county campground at Smallpox Bay, commercial camping facilities are available at a trailer park in Friday Harbor, at Lakedale near Sportsman Lake, and at the marina in Mitchell Bay. Some of the public campgrounds and all of the privately operated ones will accept reservations. Parking or tenting overnight along any road is not permitted.

The only public saltwater boat launch ramps on the island are at Jackson Beach and San Juan County Park. Commercial ramps, which may be used by the public for a fee, are located on the west side of the island at Roche Harbor Resort and Snug Harbor Resort. Numerous parks and road ends provide put-ins for kayaks and other hand-carried boats; all such put-ins are described in this book.

FRIDAY HARBOR
Map 16

Boating • Paddling • Bicycling • Historical Interest • Landmarks • Museums • Shopping • Nature Cruises • Festivals • Sightseeing

Facilities: FRIDAY HARBOR: Groceries, stores, gas, diesel, marine repair, boat rentals and charters, guest moorage, dock with water and electrical hookups, restrooms, pay showers, coin-op laundry, boat pump-out station, dump for portable toilets, portable pump for boat holding tanks, fishing tackle and bait, hotels, restaurants, movie theater, car rentals, bicycle and moped rentals, tour buses, U.S. Customs; **WHALE MUSEUM:** exhibits, gift shop, restroom; **HISTORICAL MUSEUM:** displays, gift shop, restroom

🚌 Friday Harbor can be reached via Washington State ferry from Anacortes and Sidney, B.C. Private, passenger-only ferries also make regular stops. The Whale Museum is three blocks from the ferry terminal, at 62 First Street North, the intersection of First and Court Streets. To find it, go south on Spring Street to First, and then head right two blocks to Court. From the Port of Friday Harbor dock, it is an easy walk via a staircase that leaves Front Street across from the road leading to the dock. The historical museum is about ½ mile from the Friday Harbor ferry dock, at 405 Price Street. Follow Spring Street to its intersection with Price; the museum is just north of the intersection. Park in the lot shared by the Saint Francis Catholic Church.

🚤 Friday Harbor is 18 nautical miles from Anacortes and 19 nautical miles from Sidney, B.C.

✈ The airport, about ¾ mile southwest of the town center, is reached by regular commercial flights, charter flights, and private plane.

Friday Harbor is an enchanting mix of old and new establishments, some shopping-center modern, some elderly but beautifully renovated, still others nostalgically decrepit—all with a dash of salt thrown in. Shopping facilities are within easy walking distance of the ferry landing and public boat moorages. A grocery store provides delivery service to boats moored at the Port of Friday Harbor dock, restaurants cater to tourists with offerings ranging from burgers to ethnic to gourmet, galleries offer quality work by local artists and craftspeople, while other shops have selections of souvenirs, books, and gifts for the folks back home.

Ferries from Anacortes, Sidney, and the other ferry-served islands arrive regularly during the day to disgorge their passengers. Sometimes two of the green-and-white behemoths are in the harbor, one patiently treading water in the outer bay, awaiting its turn at the slip. A host of smaller ferries arrive and depart regularly from Spring Street Landing, the long dock next to the state ferry landing. The Spring Street Landing dock complex also serves charter companies, and whale watch and nature cruises. The building at the end of the dock has waiting space, public restrooms, and a 400-gallon saltwater aquarium that displays an array of marine life from local waters.

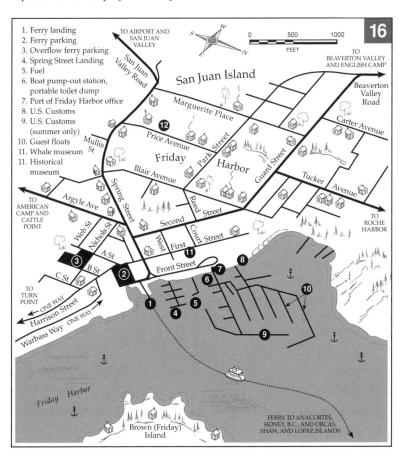

1. Ferry landing
2. Ferry parking
3. Overflow ferry parking
4. Spring Street Landing
5. Fuel
6. Boat pump-out station, portable toilet dump
7. Port of Friday Harbor office
8. U.S. Customs
9. U.S. Customs (summer only)
10. Guest floats
11. Whale museum
11. Historical museum

The Port of Friday Harbor docks host both recreational and commercial vessels.

Friday Harbor is virtually a nautical Times Square of the Northwest—stand here long enough and eventually every cruising boat you know will pass by. The public dock hosts more than 12,000 overnight transient boats in June, July, and August, and an equal number stop briefly to refuel, shop, or clear customs.

Even nonsailors will enjoy a stroll down the floats to admire, and perhaps envy, the many boats, some from exotic hailing ports. The commercial fishing fleet ties up on the larger docks—gillnetters and purse seiners with huge stern-mounted metal spools rolled fat with nets. A barge moored on the main dock sells Dungeness crab, shrimp, and clams fresh from a steaming pot, or other fish and shellfish from saltwater tanks and ice chests. It couldn't be fresher!

At low tide, dock pilings reveal underwater coatings of fluffy sea anemones, feather duster worms, opalescent nudibranchs, and spidery decorator crabs that glue bits of seaweed to their bodies as protective camouflage. Youngsters enjoy dipping nets for shrimp from along the edges of the floats.

If interest in the nautical scene of Friday Harbor palls, the rest of the island awaits. For persons arriving by boat or on foot via the ferry, various forms of transportation are available—some of them unique. Cars, bicycles, mopeds, and two-person scooter cars similar to golf carts are available for rent, tour buses make regular guided circuits of the island in summer, and planes can be chartered at the airport for aerial sightseeing.

Port of Friday Harbor Marina • The building at the head of the Port of Friday Harbor dock complex houses the harbormaster's office and has restrooms with showers for visitors. The float on the southeast side of the main dock has a station for pumping out marine heads and a place to empty portable toilets. In addition, the port has available two pumps with holding tanks that can be wheeled to your boat for emptying your holding tank.

U.S. Customs is located at the head of the Port of Friday Harbor dock, near the harbormaster's office. During summer daytime hours, customs official can also be found at a shed on the outer breakwater. Booths at the end of A

On Turn Island, an erratic nearly 10 feet high on its lower side was deposited by a glacier some 14,000 years ago.

of the island, the trail passes an enormous rock erratic, silent testimony to the geological forces that shaped this region. It was dropped here some 14,000 years ago, as the last Pleistocene ice sheet retreated.

Rabbits and other small mammals inhabit the forest; resident raccoons can be a major headache for campers who do not thoroughly secure food containers. Black-tailed deer have also been seen here. These deer, which can be found throughout the San Juans, swim from island to island, sometimes across extremely broad and swift-flowing channels.

Turn Island at one time held a huge bald eagle nest; however, the tree supporting it broke during a storm, destroying it. Reported to have been in continuous use by several generations of eagles for more than seventy years, the nest had been abandoned at the time of its destruction. Frequent disturbances by humans can cause the birds to abandon a nesting site, or they might be driven out by infestations of vermin brought to the nest on captured rodents. There are other eagle nesting sites in the vicinity; as you hike, you might be startled by a huge bird taking flight from a nearby tree.

Turn Point Road Access Map 17

Paddling • Birdwatching • Clam Digging • Tidepools • Snorkeling

Facilities: None

To reach the access, follow Harrison, a one-way street heading east along the shore of Friday Harbor. In a few blocks Harrison joins Warbass Way and then becomes Turn Point Road. The road winds around Turn Point and, about 2 miles from Friday Harbor, arrives at a gravel parking lot.

Put in hand-carried boats at a public access area on San Juan Island just spitting distance from Turn Island. From the parking lot, a path leads to a bike rack and benches in a nice grassy patch above the beach. Turn Island can be seen ¼ mile or less across the channel, depending on the tide level.

Intertidal Life

Intertidal lands in the San Juan Islands are vast displays of marine life, where the competition and predation of these animals and their peculiar adaptations for survival can be seen. Delicate interrelationships are easily disrupted by public misuse, and overcollecting of any particular species, even natural predators such as starfish, can have far-reaching effects on the overall marine balance.

Sea anemone and sea urchins line a San Juan tidepool

Especially sensitive are very slow-growing species, which must not be harvested in quantity due to their long replacement cycle. While the edible mussel is fast-growing and readily replaces itself, the California mussel (larger, with a rougher, ribbed shell) is much slower to replace itself in chilly Northwest waters. Goose barnacles, which sometimes are gathered for food, are also slow growing in the San Juans. Overharvesting of abalone has depleted their numbers, and harvesting is now closed until the population recovers.

A rockfish two feet long needs thirty years to grow that large, compared to a salmon, which will grow to an equal size in three to four years. It makes a lot of sense to protect large rockfish, because they contribute relatively enormous numbers of young fish to the population annually, in addition to taking a long time to achieve their large size. Taking smaller individuals, for example, one to three pounds, has a lesser impact on future generations.

With an increasing scarcity of choice butter clams, oysters, and Dungeness crabs, human beach-foragers are displaying a greater interest in adding to their gastronomic fare the more bizarre marine forms: leathery chitons, limpets, and moon snails, grotesque sea cucumbers and goose barnacles, and a variety of edible seaweed. In Washington, the taking for food use of nearly every form of marine life and the gathering of seaweed is controlled by state law.

Even the removal from the beaches of nonliving things, such as driftwood or empty shells, can have negative effects on marine life. For example, at Lime Kiln Light, hermit crabs have severe competition for shells. People removing shells that could serve as shelters can cause these invertebrates to become exposed to predators or the environment.

In order to protect marine lands, all of the seashores and seabed of San Juan County and around Cypress Island in Skagit County are designated a marine biological preserve. They are open for public recreation, but state law prohibits the taking or destruction of anything living, except for food use.

At low tide, the area between Turn Point and Turn Island becomes a big tideflat, although even then there is 10 feet of water in the channel. Clams and mussels await harvesting. Tidepools are exposed at mean lower low water, or they can be observed by floating just offshore in a dinghy and gazing down into the water at the dazzling undersea world of marine life: brilliant purples, oranges, and reds; pastel pinks, greens, and lavenders—the color range is limitless. Polarized sunglasses reduce glare on the water and make viewing easier. The shallow water is excellent for snorkeling.

Jackson Beach Park and Boat Launch   Map 17

Boating • Paddling • Picnicking • Swimming • Beach Walking • Birdwatching

Facilities: Boat launch ramp, toilets, kayak rentals and tours
Park area: 10 acres

🚗 Head south out of Friday Harbor on Argyle Avenue, and in ¾ mile turn east on Pear Point Road. Just after a large, former sand and gravel operation is reached, Jackson Beach Road branches left (south) and heads downhill to the launch ramp.
🛥️ Jackson Beach is 4 nautical miles west of Fisherman Bay on Lopez Island and 5 nautical miles from Friday Harbor.

A public launch ramp for trailered boats in the vicinity of Friday Harbor is found at Jackson Beach. More than just a boat launch, this narrow strand also includes a day-use park with one of the nicest beaches on this end of the island, sloping, and with a jumble of driftwood logs at the high-tide level. Three pullouts above the beach, with adjacent picnic tables and fire braziers, provide parking. The north end of the beach is wide, flat sand,

Jackson Beach occupies a long sandspit, with North Bay on the left and a saltchuck lagoon on the right.

with a volleyball court and ample space for kite flying, Frisbee games, or other beach pastimes.

The road along the spit enclosing Argyle Lagoon ends at a two-lane concrete ramp with adjacent float dropping into a small, protected cove. The nearby defunct fish cannery is home base for a kayak tour company, although a local group is trying to purchase it and convert into a wooden boat and sailing center. With the exception of the commercial property and the lagoon, the spit is public.

Argyle Lagoon, on the inside of the spit, is a research area for the Friday Harbor Laboratories; one condition for public use of the beach is that the lagoon will be protected and restricted from any public access. The lagoon is used primarily for short-term research projects, as it functions as a "mini-ocean." In such a controlled environment, distinct populations can be followed and small plots can be manipulated in order to observe the effects.

THE NORTH END
Map 15

Sportsman and Egg Lakes   Map 15
Birdwatching • Fishing • Paddling

Facilities: SPORTSMAN LAKE: boat launch ramp; **EGG LAKE:** float
Area: SPORTSMAN LAKE:87 acres; **EGG LAKE:**6½ acres

🚐 Sportsman Lake lies to the left of Roche Harbor Road, 4 miles northwest of Friday Harbor. To reach Egg Lake, continue west on Roche Harbor Road for another short ½ mile, to the intersection with Egg Lake Road. Turn left and follow this road for ¾ mile; through the trees on the left, the lake and a small float can be seen. Parking for a couple of cars is adjacent the road.

Bird heaven! Cattails and bogs edge the open water of two lakes only a few minutes' drive from Friday Harbor. Red-winged blackbirds perch sidesaddle on cattails; an array of wild migratory waterfowl coexist with plump domestic ducks and geese from neighboring farms. During mating season, marsh birds loudly advertise their territorial boundaries. All this and fish, too!

At Sportsman Lake, a short spur road from Roche Harbor Road, on the northeast side of the lake, leads to a gravel boat ramp. Turn around room at the ramp is tight; it is probably best to back down or park alongside the road and hand-carry your boat to the water.

Open to fishing year-round, the shallow, 87-acre lake contains largemouth bass and spiny ray. All surrounding lands are private, but no matter—for the beauty lies in the bogs, birds, and tranquil water. Drop in a boat for fishing, birdwatching, or just paddling around the lake.

Sportsman's tiny counterpart, Egg Lake, lies just 300 yards to the west. The small float is the only public access. Egg Lake is regularly stocked with rainbow trout. Fishing is permitted from April 16 through October 31; gasoline motors are not legal. Aside from the public dock, all bordering lands are private.

Sportsman Lake is a delight for birdwatchers and anglers.

Lakedale Campground Map 15

Camping • Paddling • Swimming • Fishing • Birdwatching

Facilities: 88 standard campsites, 10 bicycle campsites, 19 RV sites, 6 group campsites, 3 tent cabins, 6 cabins with a shared gazebo and hot tub, lodge with 10 guest rooms and a dining/meeting room, restrooms, pay showers, drinking water, picnic tables, fireplaces, boat and fishing-gear rental, fishing docks, groceries, camping equipment rental and sales

Area: 82 acres

🚗 From Friday Harbor, follow Roche Harbor Road and in 4 miles pass the Egg Lake Road intersection. The entrance to the campground is ¼ mile beyond the intersection.

The overburdened little county campground at Smallpox Bay is the only public facility for campers on San Juan Island; however, a 200-acre commercial campground and recreation area located just north of Egg and Sportsman Lakes offers everything a camper might wish—and then some. Here, former marshes have been dammed to form a network of three private lakes for fishing, swimming, rowing, and canoeing. Shorelands are available for camping, picnics, or comfortable stays in cabins or a lodge.

Nearly a hundred campsites are scattered along the shores of the lakes, some in timber, others in open grassy areas. Because the lakes are private, fishing licenses are not required, but a fee is charged.

Reuben Tarte Picnic Area   Map 15

Scuba Diving • Birdwatching • Picnicking • Wildflowers • Paddling

Facilities: Toilet (summer only)

Park area: 6 acres, 600 feet of shoreline on Spieden Channel

🚐 Follow Roche Harbor Road for 8 miles from Friday Harbor and turn right (north) onto Rouleau Road. In 1 mile, at the intersection with Limestone Point Road, turn right again (east). At a T-intersection in 1 mile, turn right (south) on San Juan Drive. In about ¼ mile a steep paved road goes left down to the beach.

🚤 The beach is 7 nautical miles from Friday Harbor, at the confluence of Spieden and San Juan Channels.

Reuben Tarte Picnic Area is located on a rocky prominence southwest of Limestone Point, on the north side of San Juan Island. This out-of-the-way corner is an interesting little nook that has a certain appeal. The shores drop off rapidly, so anchoring is not feasible, but small boats can be landed on the rocky beach.

The park is open for day use only; a gate limits access from sunset to sunrise. Parking at the road end is restricted to 15 minutes for unloading and loading only; longer-term parking is at the top of the hill. Trailers, motorcycles, and ORVs are not permitted on the last section of road.

The picnic area is on a grassy knoll that pokes into San Juan Channel between two tiny coves, offering expansive views to the east across San Juan Channel. Sedums and other wildflowers are sprinkled across the rock. Look for the bright blue springtime blossoms of camas. In early days, camas bulbs were a dietary mainstay of local Indians. The underwater rock formations of the point and offshore reefs are home for copious amounts of marine life, making the area a favorite with scuba divers, who explore along the channel and northwest to Limestone Point.

San Juan Limestone

Colonies of coral, clams, and other sedentary marine animals, growing in the warm waters of a Triassic sea, created the beds of white limestone that distinctively mark the 80-foot-high knob of Limestone Point. These beds, laid down some 200 to 250 million years ago, are thought to have originated near the equator and migrated north nearly 1000 miles as part of tectonic plate movement. Fossils of a unique clam found here date the rock to that time.

Other limestone deposits found in the island, such as those at Roche Harbor, appear to have been formed earlier, during the Paleozoic era. Fossils found there are different from those found at Limestone Point. The Roche Harbor deposits once supported fifteen quarries and, until they were depleted, provided most of the lime for concrete manufacture in western Washington.

Blue-purple blossoms of great camases, left, and brown and yellowish green blooms of exotic chocolate lilies, right, can be found at Reuben Tarte Picnic Area.

Westcott Bay Nature Reserve and Sculpture Park   Map 18

Outdoor Sculpture Park • Birdwatching

Facilities: None
Reserve area: 19 acres

🚐 From Friday Harbor, head southwest on Spring Street and turn right on Second Street. In three blocks turn left on Guard, and after 1 more block, go right on Tucker. At a Y in the road, bear left on Roche Harbor Road. In 10 miles, just inside the entrance to Roche Harbor Resort, a large parking lot enclosed by a white wooden fence is on the left.

A number of well-known, talented artists make the San Juan Islands their home. Many do commissioned work for off-island clients, and most also sell their art locally. An outdoor sculpture park, established by a volunteer group of artists, business people, and art patrons, showcases the works of both local and other Northwest sculptors. The long-range goals are to build a Westcott Bay Center for Interpretive Education and Art at the site, and to grow a fund for long-term support of the Westcott Bay Institute.

The park, on a broad grass field donated by Roche Harbor Resort, centers on a willow-edged pond. Mowed paths lead across the field and around the pond from one piece of sculpture to another. About forty pieces are displayed at any one time, all of which are for sale. However, as with any gallery, you needn't buy in order to enjoy a fine art experience—and unlike most galleries, touching is okay. Donations are accepted for admission.

The pond on which the park centers hosts great blue herons, Canada geese, and a variety of ducks. Some nest along the shore; in spring watch for babies, but give them a wide berth, as Mom can be very protective. A bird list, available at the parking lot, names more than 100 species of birds that might be seen here.

Roche Harbor Resort   Map 18

Sightseeing • Historical Interest • Landmarks • Boating • Paddling • Fishing • Hiking • Scuba Diving • Bicycling • Views • Nature Cruises

Facilities: Guest moorage, dock with water and electrical hookups, mooring buoys (fee), boat launch ramp (fee), airstrip (fee), seaplane float, boat rental, holding tank pump out, gas, diesel, restrooms, pay showers, coin-op laundry, groceries, hotel, cabins, restaurants, swimming pool, tennis courts, moped rental, gift shop, U.S. Customs

Trail hiking distance: MAUSOLEUM: 1-mile loop; **QUARRIES:** 1³/₄-mile loop
Trail elevation gain: MAUSOLEUM: 150 feet; **QUARRIES:** 150 feet

To reach Roche Harbor from Friday Harbor, head southwest on Spring Street, turning right on Second Street. In three blocks turn left on Guard and after one more block, go right on Tucker. At a Y in the road, bear left on Roche Harbor Road, which continues to the resort 10¹/₄ miles from the ferry landing.

The harbor is 11 nautical miles northwest of Friday Harbor and 22 nautical miles northeast of Victoria Harbor, on Vancouver Island.

A small landing strip at the entrance to the resort is suitable for landing small private or chartered airplanes. It is owned by the resort. Seaplanes can land at a float in the harbor.

Reminders of an earlier, much different era mingle easily with the trappings of a modern-day vacation resort. A few feet from where a log cabin stood 100 years ago are now busy tennis courts and an Olympic-size swimming pool. Most vestiges of the industrial heyday of the town are gone, and instead posh fiberglass cruisers bob at their moorings. Visitors register at the hotel, which in the 1850s saw duty as a Hudson's Bay trading post and later hosted Presidents Teddy Roosevelt and William Howard Taft.

In summer the bustling docks are a happy mingling of Canadian and Yankee boaters. Old friends are met, new ones are made, and sea stories are swapped. Rows of buoys in the harbor are filled by early evening, and courtesy boats from the resort, like large water bugs, transport boaters from their buoys to the shore and back. A special barge, the *Phecal Phreak*, tootles around, offering to pump out holding tanks.

On the week of Dominion Day (July 1) and Independence Day (July 4), the harbor is jammed with upwards of 500 boats and is even more festive, with fireworks and special events. The evening flag-lowering ceremony, which takes place throughout the summer months, holds special meaning at this time when Canadians and Americans join together in friendship to honor their countries.

Trailered boats can be launched for a fee at a surfaced ramp just south of the resort parking area. Boat trailer parking is on the hill south of the quarries. The resort can also be reached by private plane at the resort airfield nearby.

The historic old Hotel de Haro and restaurant in the former McMillin mansion, graced with a prize-winning formal flower garden, are the center of harbor activity. A display in the lobby of the hotel tells of Roche Harbor's history. A young Indiana lawyer, John S. McMillin, built the largest lime-producing company west of the Mississippi and for fifty years "ruled" the town. He became one of the richest and most influential men in the state, ran (unsuccessfully) for the U.S. Senate, and even entertained hopes of becoming governor of Washington.

After McMillin's death in 1936, his son operated the business until the lime deposits began to play out. In 1956 the town was sold; the lime kilns were shut down shortly thereafter. Subsequent owners have restored the deteriorated buildings and developed the property into a modern resort that offers fine vacation and boating facilities to visitors. Plans are to expand the resort with a row of two-story buildings just above the shore, with retail shops and condominium apartments, creating a small village at the site.

1. McMillin Mausoleum
2. Cemetery
3. Roche Harbor Resort Airstrip
4. Westcott Bay Nature Preserve and Sculpture Garden
5. Resort parking
6. Lime quarry hiking trails
7. Boat trailer parking
8. Resort suites
9. Company Town Cottages
10. Tennis courts and swimming pool
11. Our Lady of Good Voyage Chapel
12. Restaurant
13. Historic Hotel de Haro and gardens
14. Abandoned lime kilns
15. Boat launch (fee)
16. General store
17. Café, restrooms, showers
18. Fuel and holding tank pump-out
19. Main guest dock
20. Resort mooring buoys (fee)
21. Harbormaster and U.S. Customs
22. Seaplane float
23. Resort condominiums

From the hillside above Roche Harbor a portion of the resort's guest moorages can be seen. More docks are to the right. Henry Island lies beyond the mouth of the bay.

Afterglow Vista Mausoleum • Forsake the activity of Roche Harbor for a stroll through quiet woods to rub elbows with the McMillin family ghosts. From the Hotel de Haro, follow the path northwest past the church, toward the swimming pool; in ¼ mile it joins Roche Harbor Road. Turn left (north) and follow the blacktopped road past a small cemetery that sits just above the road, and in ¼ mile find a dirt side road on the right. This side road is barred to vehicles, although it is often used by horseback riders and bicyclists. In 200 yards the path reaches the gateway arch of the mausoleum.

Several tiers of stairs lead to a platform encircled with Doric columns. In the center is a round stone table surrounded by six stone chairs. The encroaching forest adds to the eerie calm of the spot. It is a privilege to be permitted to visit this unique shrine; please treat it with respect.

John McMillin chose this spot for his final resting place because he enjoyed the splendid sunset afterglow on Spieden Channel; however, today second-growth timber obscures the view he prized. The significance of the construction of the tomb is based on the family history and on the Masonic

Order, of which McMillin was a member. The intentionally broken column represents life broken by death, while the ring supporting the remaining columns represents eternal life after death.

The table and chairs are placed just as they were in the family dining room, with McMillin at the head of the table and an open space at the foot facing westward, so that all could enjoy the sunset. The chair bases are said to hold ashes of the deceased family members, who rest here for eternity, their spirits watching the sun set just as they did in life.

Beyond the side road to the mausoleum, the main road drops downhill to end at private drives. The one to the left can be walked southward; near the swimming pool/tennis court complex watch for trails dropping through timber to the beach. From here walk the beach back to Roche Harbor.

The intentionally broken column of the McMillin family mausoleum symbolizes life broken by death.

Lime Quarry • A row of abandoned lime kilns overlooks the waters of Roche Harbor. For a closer inspection of the kilns and the quarries that once were the lifeblood of the town, take a loop hike along the road, pausing to inspect the rusted railroad tracks and machinery, visualizing the quarries at the height of their productivity, when 15,000 barrels of lime per day were turned out from thirteen quarries.

To begin the hike, walk southwest from the grocery store along the road at the water's edge. Immediately to the left are the lime kilns, with their gracefully arching brickwork still intact. Continue uphill, following the road left when it turns sharply at the first intersection. Pass gaping quarries where undergrowth is creeping back to gentle the harsh outlines. A short, marked trail wanders through the forest that now grows in the quarries, reaches a hilltop viewing platform, and then drops back down to the road.

From the road near the top of the hill, stop to enjoy a sweeping view of Roche Harbor, Spieden Channel, Mosquito Pass, and Henry Island before the road climbs back into the timber, losing sight of the harbor. Turn left at the intersection with a road, then left again at a driveway that drops steeply downhill past some private homes, headed back to the bay. The driveway dead-ends at a path that brings the hiker back to the plaza between the hotel and the restaurant, a short distance from the grocery store.

Posey Island Marine State Park   Map 19

Camping • Picnicking • Boating • Paddling • Views • Fishing • Scuba Diving • Snorkeling • Tidepools • Beach Walking

Facilities: 2 campsites (16 persons maximum), Cascadia Marine Trail campsite, picnic tables, composting toilet
Park area: 1 acre, 1000 feet of shoreline on Spieden Channel
🛥 The island lies less than 1 nautical mile northeast of Roche Harbor, the nearest place where boats can be launched.

This dot of an island just outside Roche Harbor provides a lovely afternoon picnic spot or, in fair weather, a campsite with a superb sunset. The accommodations at Posey Island are meager, with a couple of scruffy picnic tables and space for a couple of tents, but its proximity to Roche Harbor, and the protected, shallow water, makes this a popular destination. Unfortunately, its single toilet gets heavily used as a potty stop for commercial kayak tours, increasing the wear and tear on the island.

❄Boaters in small craft headed for the island from Roche Harbor can

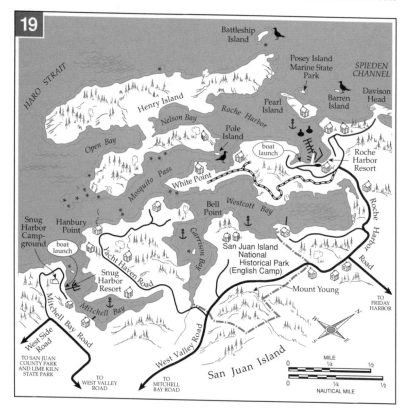

take a shorter route through the channel at the east end of Pearl Island, while deeper draft vessels are advised to stay in the main channel at the west end of Pearl and anchor well out, as the water surrounding Posey Island is quite shallow and reefs extend out on the north and east.

Because the sun goes down in the rainy district of Vancouver Island, the San Juans have exceptionally vivid sunsets. The crimson and gold colors, intensified by the black masses of the islands, linger in the sky and sea long after the sun has disappeared. The open views of Haro Strait and Canadian islands make Posey Island a prime spot for savoring the afterglow.

Battleship Island lies ³/₄ nautical mile northwest of Posey Island. With its chunky shape and "smokestacks" of trees, it surely does resemble a battleship in both size and shape. Underwater rocks host abundant sea life. Sea urchins, encrusting sponges, and anemones create a colorful fantasyland that attracts scuba divers. Battleship Island, Barren Island (east of the entrance to Roche Harbor near Davison Head), and Pole Island (in the north entrance of Mosquito Pass) are all part of the San Juan Islands Wilderness Area.

Henry Island and Mosquito Pass Map 19

Boating • Paddling • Fishing • Scuba Diving

Facilities: None

Henry Island encloses the west side of Roche Harbor and Mosquito Pass, on the nortwest corner of San Juan Island.

Resembling a letter H crudely scrawled in the water to the west of Mosquito Pass, Henry Island shelters San Juan bays from waves off Haro Strait. The island rests on the protruding edge of an underwater shelf, and bluffs on the west side plunge steeply downward to a depth of 120 fathoms. The edges of this shelf, especially areas off Kellett Bluff on the south and McCracken Point on the north, provide fine fishing and scuba diving. At Kellett Bluff, deep caves that harbor enormous lingcod are a major attraction for divers.

Open Bay, indenting the bottom of the H, and a small bight north of Nelson Bay, at its top, give anchorage to boaters escaping the summertime bustle of Roche Harbor. Most of the island is privately owned, except for a number of acres that were purchased by the Land Bank and Preservation Trust in order to preserve them in their natural state. Approximately 80 acres at Kellett Bluff on the tip of the southwest lobe of the island are a lighthouse reservation; however, the steepness of the shore makes landing there impractical.

Mosquito Pass, a skinny, 1¹/₂-mile-long waterway separating Henry and San Juan Islands, connects Roche Harbor and Westcott, Garrison, and Mitchell Bays. The pass and the three shallow bays are ideal for small-boat exploration, with some care. ❈Tidal currents can be strong and unpredictable in Mosquito Pass itself, where paddle-powered boats should be wary. Deep-keeled vessels should not attempt the channel without the aid of charts, as there are many rocks and shoals where the unwary can find themselves embarrassingly aground. A phalanx of reefs and shoals marks the south end of the channel. Pay close attention to navigational markers and observe the 7-mph no-wake zone in the pass.

Westcott Bay   Map 19

Boating • Paddling • Shellfish

Facilities: None

🛥 From Roche Harbor, the entrance to Westcott Bay is 1½ nautical miles via Mosquito Pass.

Although most boaters visiting the English Camp portion of San Juan Island National Historical Park drop anchor in Garrison Bay, some choose to stop in Westcott Bay and dinghy ashore to walk the short trail along Bell Point. For descriptions of adjacent Garrison Bay and English Camp, see Chapter Five, San Juan Island National Historical Park.

Two protruding points on either shore divide Westcott Bay into two areas. The best anchorage is in the southwest portion of the bay; the northeast end becomes quite shallow. An extensive aquaculture operation on the southeast shore raises oysters, mussels, and clams for sale to restaurants. Give the underwater pens a wide berth. The sea farm has oysters for sale to visitors.

HARO STRAIT
Map 20

Mitchell Bay   Maps 19 and 20

Camping • Boating • Paddling • Fishing • Whale Watching • Scuba Diving • Crabbing • Nature Cruises

Facilities: SNUG HARBOR RESORT: Guest moorage, gas, outboard mix, boat launch ramp (fee), 5 cabins, campground with 8 sites, restrooms, boat rental and charter, limited transient moorage, whale watch tours, marine repair and supplies, groceries, fishing tackle, scuba air

🚐 To reach Mitchell Bay by land, head south from Roche Harbor Road on West Valley Road, and in 3¾ miles turn west on Mitchell Bay Road. The road winds downhill to the resort in 2 miles.

🛥 The bay is 2¾ nautical miles from Roche Harbor, at the south end of Mosquito Pass, facing on Haro Strait.

Snug Harbor, the small marina/resort on the south shore of Mitchell Bay, is well named, as the entrance to the harbor is, indeed, very snug. However, once inside this cozy haven, the water is adequately deep for most small craft in all but extremely low tides. ❄ At the entrance, a shoal marked by a small island extends from the south side of the bay; stay well to the north of this rock. Anchorage space is limited, and the bay is shallow at low tides.

All beaches and docks are private, except for the resort. On the hillside

Snug Harbor Resort has some nice moorages on Mitchell Bay.

behind the resort eight campsites are laid out on a series of graded platforms in the woods; a row of cabins stretches along the beach from the resort entrance.

San Juan County Park Map 20

Camping • Picnicking • Scuba Diving • Snorkeling • Boating • Paddling • Tidepools

Facilities: 20 campsites, CMT capsite, picnic tables, picnic shelter, fireplaces, restrooms, groceries, group camp, boat launch ramp, mooring buoys
Park area: 12 acres

🚙 Follow Second Street northwest out of Friday Harbor. Turn left on Guard Street, and in about two blocks head right on Beaverton Valley Road, which becomes West Valley Road. In about 6 miles turn left on Mitchell Bay Road, and in just under 1 mile turn south on West Side Road. The park is on the left in 3³/₄ more miles.

🛥 Smallpox Bay lies 4³/₄ nautical miles south of Roche Harbor, via Mosquito Pass.

The story is told that long ago, a number of Indians stricken with smallpox plunged into the icy San Juan waters to rid themselves of their burning fever; as a result, they died of pneumonia. The tiny bay on the west side of San Juan Island where the tragedy occurred has since that time been called Smallpox Bay.

Despite its unfortunate history, today the bay is of more pleasant significance, for it is the site of popular San Juan County Park. The park occupies land at the head of the bay and in an old orchard on a bluff. Although the park officially has only twenty campsites and a group camp near the office/store, more than a hundred people might be crammed into its 12 acres on summer weekends. To be assured of a site during busy times, make reservations well ahead.

123

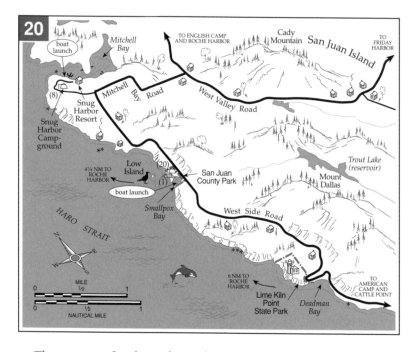

The pressure of such numbers is beginning to show in the irascibility of local residents, who are unable to find a place to camp in their own park. To better enjoy the area and be appreciated by San Juan Islanders, visit off-season. In winter, when it is uncrowded, the park is a relaxing spot with exquisite nighttime views across Haro Strait to the lights of Vancouver Island. Explore the shores of the bay or saunter through twisted madronas to the top of the bluff—but even the healthy risk pneumonia by attempting to swim in the bay.

The tiny log cabin in the campground was built around 1890 as a home for a widowed homesteader and his daughter. While the building was under construction, the pair lived in a cave that he dug in the side of a nearby hill. The cabin once had an outside stairway to provide access to the daughter's bedroom on the second floor. As of 2004 the cabin was badly deteriorated. Hopefully, it can be restored

With dive spots within walking distance of campsites, the park is a favorite among scuba divers. Easy snorkeling is found in the bay, while the rocky bottom that plunges steeply to 80 feet just offshore is a challenge to more experienced divers. In addition to the usual bright palette of anemone, urchins, and starfish, look for abalone clinging to rocks and octopuses hiding in crevices.

Gulls, and sometimes seals, congregate on Low Island, 100 yards offshore—another of the bird refuges of the San Juan Islands Wilderness Area. From shore, use binoculars to spot them.

Bicyclists enjoy the view of Haro Strait from West Side Road.

against the rugged flank of San Juan Island. In spring, masses of California poppies flame between rocky outcrops. The paved road makes the route appealing for bicyclists.

False Bay Map 21

Beach Walking • Tidepools • Birdwatching

Facilities: None

To reach False Bay by land from Friday Harbor, go west out of town on Spring Street. At an intersection 1½ miles from town, turn left (south) onto False Bay Road, which can be followed 3½ more miles to the bay. Small pullouts for parking are adjacent to the road at both the south and north ends.

Shallow, nearly circular False Bay is located on the southern end of San Juan Island, with its narrow mouth opening onto Haro Strait. Quite a number of unfortunate boaters, seeking shelter from weather, have discovered the significance of its name when they've become hung up on a tideflat, for the entire bay holds less than a fathom of water at mean low water.

The shores provide a pleasant beach walk at moderate-to-high tides, but the real fun comes at low water, when the entire bay nearly drains. Don rubber boots and wander through the muck to observe seashore life. Investigate more than 200 acres of strange creatures: skittery purple shore crabs; two-foot, flame-colored ribbon worms; prehistoric-looking clingfish; shoe-shaped chitons; barnacles and rock oysters (jingle shells) fated to spend life fastened to one rock, with never a change of scenery.

The bay is owned and carefully monitored as a biological study area for the University of Washington. Several scientific theses have been written on the ecological systems found here. The contained environment, sheltered

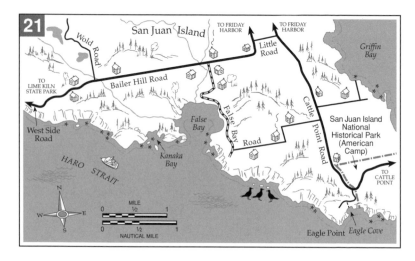

from the disturbing action of large waves, allows the study of discrete marine populations. Do not disturb rods, sticks, tubes, or anything that looks peculiar; these usually mark a research project in progress. Avoid any such staked-out areas, and do not dig in the vicinity. Look all you wish, but do not kill or collect any specimens anywhere in the bay. Walk carefully to avoid damaging any of the marine life. Camping and beach fires are not permitted.

Eagle Cove Public Access Map 21

Beach Walking • Picnicking • Paddling • Swimming • Scuba Diving

Facilities: None
Park area: ¼ acre, 100 feet of shoreline

🚗 In Friday Harbor, head southwest on Spring Street, and at the Y intersection on the south side of town, bear left (south) on Argyle Avenue. Follow it south and then west to its intersection with Cattle Point Road. Follow signs to American Camp. In 5 miles, just before the American Camp boundary, turn south on Eagle Cove Road. In ½ mile reach a blacktopped parking area for a few cars, signed "Public Access. No Overnight Camping."

🚤 Eagle Cove lies 1 nautical mile north of South Beach in American Camp, the closest point where hand-carried boats can be put in. The nearest launch ramp is at Smallpox Bay, 8½ nautical miles to the north, or Roche Harbor, 5 nautical miles beyond.

Just outside San Juan Island National Historical Park's American Camp is a small public cove fronting on the Strait of Juan de Fuca. This rock-rimmed inlet is surrounded by a high bank that protects its beautiful sandy beach from much of the wind that whips the shoreline to the east.

From the parking area, a 100-yard-long path descends through a tall, cool

Cattle Point Light faces on the Strait of Juan de Fuca and is backed by sand dunes.

south into the Strait of Juan de Fuca for nearly a mile to capture salmon runs headed into San Juan Channel. The area is still a popular fishing ground.

Fish Creek • Why the enchanting little corner called Fish Creek has this name is a puzzle, for it is not a creek at all but a slotlike saltwater cove at the extreme end of San Juan Island. The "fish" part of the name is more understandable: During the 1850s the Hudson's Bay Company had a fish-packing station here.

All the shoreland, docks, and floats around Fish Creek are private, so there is no way to reach the water by land. For boaters, however, it offers a handy protected anchorage for waiting out fog or bad weather in the Straits of Juan de Fuca.

South Beach at American Camp has small coves and huge driftwood logs.

guardhouse. Next to it, a tidy white picket fence encloses a traditional formal garden that is typical of those planted during the time. Near the barracks grows a spreading big-leaf maple tree; once it was the largest of its kind in the world, but parts have broken off, and it is now slightly outranked by one in Oregon.

The 1½-mile boat excursion from Roche Harbor to English Camp winds through lovely Mosquito Pass and the narrow entrance to Westcott Bay. ❋Consult a good chart for the location of numerous shoals along the way; Garrison Bay is shallow throughout and deep-keeled vessels should enter with care. The two protected bays are ideal for kayak or dinghy exploration.

Tiny, wooded Guss Island, lying only 300 yards offshore in Garrison Bay, was named during British occupation for a San Juan storekeeper. Although it is also part of the park, it has been designated as an archaeological preserve and is closed to the public.

HISTORICAL INTERPRETIVE TRAIL. An interpretive trail leads a short distance uphill from the formal garden to a grassy flat overlooking the bay where the officers' quarters were located. On a second, higher flat, quarters were built for the commanding officer of the Royal Marines and his family. The small stone obelisk seen here was erected on October 12, 1904, to commemorate the thirty-second anniversary of the resolution of the boundary dispute.

Vague remnants of one of the old docks built by the British are still visible near the blockhouse. A small dock with space for a few dinghies is now located farther north along the beach. In summer the bay is often filled with boats anchored and rafted together. Skippers can also anchor at Westcott Bay, then dinghy to Bell Point and walk the trail to English Camp.

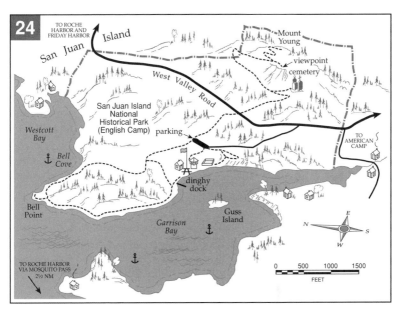

BELL POINT. A level hike through madrona and fir leads to pretty Bell Cove on Westcott Bay. The signed trail starts on the north side of the English Camp clearing, near the shore. Tides permitting, Bell Cove can also be reached by walking the beach.

The beaches of Bell Point might be closed to clam digging during certain seasons, although Bell Cove is normally open year-round. Observe posted signs. Dig clams only if you intend to use them, and observe limits; heavy public use of the clam beds could exhaust them, causing the beaches to be closed in order to let them reestablish.

For an alternative return to English Camp, follow the old wagon track heading east from Bell Point, skirting Westcott Bay. In about ¼ mile the route reaches a clearing. Turn right (south), following the grassy track between the old-growth timber of Bell Point and a thick stand of recent-growth firs. Listen here for the distinctive trilling song of the chipping sparrow, which nests in the area. The track eventually emerges at the north corner of the English Camp clearing.

A larger, more distinctive bird that sometimes startles visitors by its presence at English Camp is the wild turkey. These nearly domestic fowl were introduced on San Juan Island almost a decade ago and have become well established. Even occasional poaching by Thanksgiving-minded hunters has failed to make a dent in the population.

British Military Cemetery and Mount Young　Map 24

Historical Interest • Hiking • Birdwatching • Views

Facilities: None

Trail hiking distance: less than ½ mile one way from parking lot to cemetery; 1½ miles one way from parking lot to Mount Young summit

Trail elevation gain: 250 feet from parking lot to cemetery; 650 feet from parking lot to Mount Young summit

🚐 From Friday Harbor, head northwest on Roche Harbor Road. At a major intersection 8½ miles from Friday Harbor, turn left (south) onto West Valley Road. The entrance to English Camp is on the right in 1½ miles. Locate the trailhead at the picnic area in the northeast corner of the parking lot. Although the route crosses West Valley Road in ¼ mile, there is no parking space along the road.

A small plot on the slopes of Mount Young holds the graves of five marines and one civilian who died during the British occupation of San Juan Island. From the English Camp parking lot, the signed trail wends steadily uphill along an old overgrown wagon track. Sun filters through second-growth alder, fir, and madrona. Walk quietly and perhaps you will be rewarded with glimpses of black-tailed deer or occasionally great horned owls blinking sleepily in the trees. An owl's favorite perching spot can sometimes be located by watching for piles of droppings beneath the tree. The owls take large numbers of rodents and are responsible, even more than eagles and hawks, for controlling the island's rabbit population. The winter wren nests here; listen for its lovely, sustained warbling song as you hike.

CEMETERY. About ¼ mile after crossing the road, the Mount Young trail branches left, and a short spur trail leads to the cemetery in a grassy clearing. A neat white picket fence encloses tombstones for men who died in accidents while serving at English Camp. The stones tell the story of each mishap; note that one commemorates two marines who drowned at sea. Two other graves are unmarked. Gravestone inscriptions have been duplicated on interpretive signs along the fence to prevent people from going inside the fence to read them.

Several of the trees in the clearing were killed or badly scarred by a 1972 fire. Even more than thirty years later the damage can be seen. Take heed of the havoc a cigarette ash accidentally dropped in dry grass can cause.

Five men who died during the Pig War impasse were buried on Young Hill.

MOUNT YOUNG. To reach the top of Mount Young, return to the trail intersection and continue uphill. The route climbs steadily to round a north-facing rib of Mount Young, then heads south on a path cut through high arching brush. At a flat area 100 feet below the summit, the trail forks. Switchbacks to the left lead to the top of the 650-foot mountain; at the end of the path to the right is an interpretive display on an open, grassy rock platform. The British Marines maintained an observation post on the summit during the Pig War.

Views, views, views: This is probably the most spectacular outlook on San Juan Island. Henry Island, White Point, Bazelgette Point, Mosquito Pass, Westcott Bay, and Garrison Bay all merge in a mosaic of land and water. Mitchell Bay, its entrance obscured by land, looks like a small lake—but with a fleet of large pleasure boats bobbing on it! Southward can be seen the snowy peaks of the Olympic Mountains, while to the north are the Canadian Gulf Islands, marked by the imposing profile of Saltspring Island. Across Haro Strait lies Vancouver Island, where, more than 100 years ago, British frigates sailed forth to uphold the sovereignty of the Crown. The display at the lower viewpoint identifies major landmarks. Note the north-to-south grooves in the bare summit rock. These scratches were made by rocks carried by continental glaciers that spread across this area about 14,000 years ago.

Stroll to the east side of the hill for views through timber of Mount Baker. Looking southeast from the summit, immediately above the silhouette of Mount Erie on Fidalgo Island, on a very clear day Sloan Peak can be seen. Ranging southward are the misty outlines of Mount Baring, Mount Index, and other Stevens Pass peaks more than 90 miles distant.

AMERICAN CAMP
Map 25

Historical Interest • Hiking • Beach Walking • Fishing • Boating • Paddling • Birdwatching • Nature Trail • Views

Facilities: Picnic tables, restrooms, drinking water, fire pits; *no open beach fires, no overnight camping*
Park area: 529 acres, 7920 feet of shoreline
Trail hiking distance: INTERPRETIVE TRAIL: ³/₄-mile loop; **SOUTH SHORE WALK:** 3 miles one way
Trail elevation loss: INTERPRETIVE TRAIL: minimal; **SOUTH SHORE WALK:** 180 feet

To reach American Camp from English Camp, continue south on West Beach Road and in 3³/₄ miles turn right (south) onto Boyce Road. In 1 mile turn left (east) on San Juan Road and in 2³/₄ miles go right (south) on Douglass Road. In 1¹/₂ miles turn left (east) on Little Road, which ends shortly at a T intersection with Cattle Point Road. Here head right (south) and in 2³/₄ miles reach the American Camp entrance. Total distance from English Camp is 12 miles.

To travel directly to American Camp from Friday Harbor, at the Y intersection on the south side of town, bear left (south) on Argyle Avenue. Follow the arterial south and then west to its intersection with Cattle Point Road. The route is well signed. Total distance to the park is 5 miles.

For visitors traveling by boat, there are no docking facilities or buoys at American Camp; however, in calm weather paddlecraft can be beached on the gentle shores on either side of the park. Griffin Bay provides the only semiprotected anchorage. ❋ When entering the bay, carefully check nautical charts and depth finders for the location of numerous submerged rocks. The north beach of the park is about 6¹/₂ nautical miles from either Friday Harbor or Fisherman Bay.

American Camp is a marked contrast to English Camp. Instead of the protected harbor and wooded enclave, here are vast marine panoramas and miles of surf-swept beach. First-time visitors might be struck by the austerity of the park, but it holds amazing diversity, ranging from rippling summer grass on Mount Finlayson to winter storms pounding on South Beach.

The small building that houses the park headquarters and some historical displays is just inside the park entrance. Bicyclists making the long, dry trek from Friday Harbor should note that the only drinking water in the park is here. Restrooms are here as well; other locations have toilets.

Kayaking the waters around the park is interesting, especially along the exposed south shore; however, it is recommended only for experienced paddlers. ❋ Great care must be used in small boats as the wind and current can be extremely strong; attempting to maneuver an underpowered boat under such conditions can be a frightening experience. Shark Reef, lying to the east immediately across San Juan Channel, along the shore of Lopez Island, is an inviting destination for those skilled enough to attempt it.

PARK HISTORY PROGRAMS AND TOURS. On summer weekends, programs are presented at American Camp by park rangers and volunteers, sometimes wearing dashing replicas of British and American military uniforms or other costumes appropriate to the time. Programs have presented old-time folk music, prehistory of the San Juans, birds, pioneer folkways, and stargazing. Check the park website, *www.nps.gov/sajh*, for a schedule of programs.

Volunteer-guided tours are held daily throughout the summer at American Camp. These walks, which begin at 11:00 A.M., leave from the park headquarters and information center and cover the areas of Pickett's Redoubt and the Hudson's Bay farm. Large groups planning to visit the park can request a tour with a guide in costume.

INTERPRETIVE TRAIL. For those who miss the excellent guided tour or who would rather walk at their own pace, a ¾-mile-long self-guided interpretive trail covers the historical section of the park. Its start is at the picnic area east of the park information center. Signs at numerous stops along the way relate Pig War history and point out interesting features of the park.

At the top of the ridge, Pickett's Redoubt commands views of American Camp and waters stretching to Victoria. Still in evidence is the earthworks (redoubt) thrown up by the troops, who dubbed it "Robert's gopher hole," after its construction officer, Second Lieutenant Henry M. Robert. Five earthen platforms around the perimeter were to be the sites for thirty-two-pound naval guns borrowed from the war steamer USS *Massachusetts*. Although eight

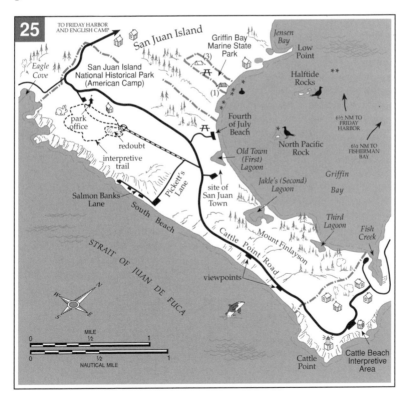

Volunteers, such as these garbed as a laundress and an officer, dress in costumes from the Pig War era and conduct tours and lectures at the park.

guns were hauled up the hill from South Beach, only one was ever mounted, and it was fired only once, as a salute to the U.S. commander Lieutenant General Winfield Scott when his ship was anchored offshore. Lieutenant Robert went on to historical fame as the author of *Robert's Rules of Order.*

SOUTH SHORE WALK. Leave the interpretive trail and wander open slopes above the ocean to enjoy the austere beauty of the park. There are no formal trails. In late summer the inland section of the slope is covered with patches of stinging nettles and Canadian thistles, so long pants are advised. Warrens burrowed by rabbits in the soft till of the hillside can cause a twisted ankle or other injury if stepped in.

Near the edge of the cliff, the harsh environment causes the vegetation to be miniaturized. Many of the species of plants are so tiny that novice botanists can identify them only when they bloom. *Collinsia* grow less than an inch tall, showing quarter-inch blue-purple blossoms in late May. Lupine, whose distinctive leaf whorls grow more than four inches across on the alpine slopes of Mount Rainier, here have ground-hugging leaves smaller than a thumbnail.

Bays along this section of the island are unlike those found anywhere else in the San Juans. The soft glacial till, scooped out by winds from the Strait of Juan de Fuca, form perfect, grassy amphitheaters dropping steeply to beaches jammed with huge driftwood logs. Explore the small coves if you wish, but bear in mind the difficult, 50-foot scramble back to the top. Grandma's Cove, the largest rounded bay to the west, was the site of the original Hudson's Bay Company settlement.

Rabbits

The long arm of San Juan Island is largely covered with soft glacial till deposited centuries ago by retreating ice. The loose mixture of sand, stone, and boulders, ideal for tunneling, made American Camp a nirvana for San Juan rabbits. The rabbits are believed to be descendants of domestic animals brought here during the 1880s by settlers. They either escaped from captivity or were turned loose and, finding local conditions to their liking, multiplied—and multiplied—and multiplied!

By the late 1970s, an estimated 250,000 bunnies (give or take a few) populated San Juan Island. Their evidence was everywhere at American Camp at this time: droppings covered the ground to the extent that in places more dung than dirt was visible, and park rangers swept the walks daily to enable visitors to walk. Tunnel entrances made the ground look like a bombed battlefield. At one point, the Cattle Point Light was so undermined by rabbit warrens that it was in danger of collapsing.

In the mid-1980s, for reasons not entirely understood, the rabbit population decreased dramatically. One plausible theory is that plants such as vetches, when subjected to overgrazing by large numbers of rabbits, produce a chemical that acts as a birth-control agent. When grazing returns to normal, this chemical is no longer produced. Another theory credits an increase in the population of animals that prey on young rabbits. Whatever the reason, the rabbits seem to be making a slight comeback. Hunting or trapping has not been permitted since 1966, when the park was established. This allows useful data to be gathered on population cycles.

The rabbits are a major food source for eagles, hawks, great horned owls, and other predatory birds living on the island. Fluctuations in the rabbit population can also be reflected in the natural balance established between the predators and their food supply. European ferrets and red foxes were brought in some time ago to control the rabbit population. It is believed the ferrets have died out, but the foxes are doing nicely, and seem to fit in with the overall balance of life here—although farm chickens sometimes augment their diet.

San Juan rabbits, a result of crossbreeding between wild and domestic bunnies, are a distinct species.

If hiking legs need further exercise, traverse the bank eastward, staying well above the shore. Do not walk near the edge, as the earth is soft on the high bank, and footing might be insecure. When the slope gentles, drop down to South Beach near the parking lot and return to the information center via the road.

South Beach Map 25

Beach Walking • Views • Tidepools • Historical Interest

Facilities: Toilets, picnic tables, fire pits; *fires permitted only in fire pits*

🚐 From the park entrance, turn right off American Camp Road onto Pickett's Lane. In ½ mile is the first parking lot; Salmon Banks Lane leads west to three more parking areas.

🛥 Lightweight boats can be carried the short distance from the parking areas for launching, surf permitting.

South Beach offers access to 2 miles of unbroken sand and gravel shore edging on the Strait of Juan de Fuca. When storms kick up in the straits, heavy wave action along the beach is exciting to watch. Drift logs are dangerous at these times; stay well away from moving logs. Such storms toss flotsam and jetsam onto the beach, making this the prime area on the island for finding beach treasures.

With calm weather and favorable tides, the beach can be walked all the way east to Cattle Point, 2 miles from the parking lot. Very little marine life is found on the gravel beach; constant movement of the surf-tumbled sand and gravel lets nothing survive for long. Low tide exposes rocky shelves to the west where tidepools hold fascinating critters. During the summer and fall salmon runs, numbers of commercial fishing trawlers are frequently seen spreading their nets just offshore.

San Juan Town Site and Griffin Bay Map 25

Historical Interest • Boating • Paddling

Facilities: FOURTH OF JULY BEACH: Picnic tables, toilets

🚐 To reach Fourth of July Beach, turn north (left) off Cattle Point Road at a signed intersection 1 mile east of the park entrance. For the trail to the area of San Juan Town, continue east on Cattle Point Road. Just past the Pickett's Lane intersection a side road branches north (left), ending in a short distance at a gate and small parking lot; use care not to block the gate in case of emergency.

🛥 Broad Griffin Bay is 4½ nautical miles southwest of Fisherman Bay on Lopez Island and 5 miles south of Friday Harbor. Paddled boats are easily drawn up on the beach at American Camp.

When American troops built their stronghold on San Juan Island, a shanty town sprang up on the shore of Griffin Bay, just outside the military camp boundary. Shopkeepers in San Juan Town sold a few supplies to the soldiers, settlers, and Indians, but it was soon apparent that liquor was the commodity in greatest demand. Other enterprising merchants brought in Native American women for "nefarious purposes." Robberies, assaults, and sometimes murders took place, with open defiance of civil and military officers. Authorities were able to tame the town a bit, but it always remained a center for booze, brothels, and brawls.

In 1873, when San Juan County was established, the new commissioners felt that San Juan Town, with its rowdy reputation, was unsuitable for a county seat. Instead, they selected a few acres at Friday Harbor to the north. In time businesses drifted away from Old San Juan Town (especially after Friday Harbor also acquired a saloon), and by the late 1800s the once thriving village was a ghost town. The deserted buildings were accidentally burned to the ground in 1890, bringing to a close the career of the colorful, if somewhat tarnished, village.

SAN JUAN TOWN. The saltwater lagoon visible on the north side of American Camp Road is just west of the old town site. From the parking area, a trail wanders down an open grass slope. A few footings of the original buildings have been excavated and can be found by searching the grassy fields. Halfway down the hill, the track of an old road is faintly visible.

GRIFFIN BAY. Early sailing ships hove to in Griffin Bay waiting out westerlies whipping the Strait of Juan de Fuca. Today, fast-moving powerboats

Harbors of Refuge

During the late 1800s, the U.S. naval strategy was to develop "Harbors of Refuge" that were safely out of range of the capabilities of naval bombardment at the time and that could be protected by land-based weaponry. Griffin Bay was designated as such a Harbor of Refuge, and land was set aside for military reservations on Lopez Island (at Shark Reef and Upright Head), Shaw Island, and San Juan Island (at Cattle Point and Point Caution near Friday Harbor). Other such harbors of refuge were planned on the Olympic Peninsula at sites such as Neah Bay, Sequim Bay, Discovery Bay, and Port Townsend Bay.

It was intended that Griffin Bay would serve as a safe haven for both commercial and military vessels if adjoining waterways were blockaded by an enemy's superior naval forces. Ships coming in or going out of the Strait of Juan de Fuca could hide here until it was possible for them to make a run for their destination or the next harbor of refuge.

About this time the strategy of naval combat changed, with the U.S. Navy no longer taking a passive defensive role of protecting home shores but assuming an aggressive stance and taking the battle to the enemy. The military reservation land in the San Juans was no longer needed; over the years some of it was transferred to the DNR or other government agencies, and some was sold off to private interests. The parks at Shark Reef, on Lopez Island, and the DNR picnic area at Cattle Point are a result of these land holdings.

whiz by in San Juan Channel, rarely stopping to enjoy the languid pleasures of the bay. ❀ Even though the water of the bay is inviting when seas are calm, boaters should be aware that a number of rocks are scattered at or near the water's surface. Consult a good, large-scale chart and approach with care. Barren Halftide Rocks lie northeast of the park boundary, near a row of rotting pilings. About ½ nautical mile south of these rocks is North Pacific Rock; it is unnamed on most charts but is shown as a rock baring at tides of minus 2 feet or less. Harbor Rock lies farther east, just off the tip of Cape San Juan. These three groups of rocks, nesting grounds for marine birds, are part of the San Juan Wilderness.

❀ Between North Pacific Rock and Harbor Rock the approach to the beach is clear, except for rocks lying quite close to shore. Some good anchorages can be found in this section of the bay, although those to the west are exposed when winds are stiff—which is most of the time. The best spot to drop an anchor is to the east, in or near Fish Creek.

FOURTH OF JULY BEACH. The gentle shore of Fourth of July Beach, which extends west for ½ mile from San Juan Town Lagoon (First Lagoon) to the park boundary, holds driftwood and some interesting marine life. Here is a parking lot with a picnic area, picnic tables, and a large grassy field for kite flying or tossing Frisbees. A path leads past toilets to the beach. Carry a small boat or kayak the short distance to the beach to be rewarded with a leisurely paddle the length of the park.

Jakle's Lagoon, Third Lagoon, and Mount Finlayson Map 26

Hiking • Birdwatching • Wildflowers • Wildlife Watching • Paddling • Views

Facilities: None

Trail hiking distance: JAKLE'S LAGOON: 1½ miles round trip; **NATURE LOOP TRAIL:** 1½ miles round trip; **THIRD LAGOON:** 4-mile loop trip or round trip; **MOUNT FINLAYSON:** 2-mile loop

Trail elevation gain: JAKLE'S LAGOON: negligible; **NATURE LOOP TRAIL:** 120 feet; **THIRD LAGOON:** 130 feet; **MOUNT FINLAYSON:** 200 feet

🚗 From the park entrance, continue east on Cattle Point Road. Just past the Pickett's Lane intersection, a side road branches north (left), ending in a short distance at a gate and small parking lot; use care not to block the gate.

🛶 Paddlers can explore the lagoons by following the shoreline south along Griffin Bay. They are quite shallow and often are choked with driftwood.

While American Camp is impressive, it can at times seem bleak. Jakle's and Third Lagoons, in a secluded nook of the park, offer a delightful contrast, with ferns, a rich moss carpet, and tall firs. At the urging of The Nature Conservancy, the road to the lagoons is closed to vehicles to protect eagle nesting areas as well as the delicate lagoon habitat. Jakle's Lagoon itself has been set aside as a natural environmental study area; it is used by the University of Washington as a collecting site for marine specimens and has been the subject of several studies and Ph.D. theses. Smoking is prohibited while on the trail, and campfires are forbidden in the forest and on the

Trees hang low over driftwood-filled Jakle's Lagoon.

beaches. In the dry summer the fire hazard here is extreme and a spark could start a blaze that would destroy the entire wooded area, bringing death to the birds and animals living here.

This land was originally farmed by Frank Bryant, an American soldier stationed at Garrison Bay. After Bryant died in a drowning mishap, his widow married another U.S. soldier, George Jakle. The site is know to have been actively farmed by them at least as late at 1927.

JAKLE'S LAGOON. From the parking area, walk the abandoned road downhill, dipping into the forest. Hikers will find a network of old roads crisscrossing the hillside. If side roads are confusing, keep bearing downhill and eastward to reach the lagoon. As the road levels off, look for two trails taking off from the left side of the road. The first path heads out to a medium-high bank above the west side of the lagoon, then swings west and heads toward First Lagoon. The second spur, a few hundred yards farther, leads along the east side of the lagoon to a grassy point protruding into the southeast side of the lagoon. Here is a fit spot for a Hobbit home—in winter, when the forest drips with San Juan mist and fog lies heavily over the lagoon, one can easily imagine magical creatures scurrying in the undergrowth.

With moderate to low tides, the Griffin Bay beach can be walked between Jakle's Lagoon and the site of San Juan Town for a loop trip with the added interest of a beach walk.

NATURE LOOP TRAIL. The Jakle's Lagoon Trail is also the first leg of a loop nature trail. This trail focuses on the two contrasting natural communities on Mount Finlayson. A marked route follows the road to Jakle's Lagoon (with side paths to the lagoon itself) and then climbs to the crest of Mount Finlayson, where the forest ecosystem transforms into grasslands on the south side of the mountain. The return path follows the Mount Finlayson Trail back to the trailhead. A brochure available at the park office describes differing ecosystems and identifies the plant families found along the trail.

THIRD LAGOON. Another, smaller, lagoon lies ½ mile east of Jakle's Lagoon. San Juan Town Lagoon is first, Jakle's is second, and this, appropriately, is known simply as Third Lagoon. It can be reached one of several ways: The easiest route, tide permitting, is to walk the gravel beach east from Jakle's Lagoon. For an inland route, return to the abandoned road from Jakle's Lagoon and continue east. The beauty of the forest makes this route worthwhile. In spring, find calypso orchids, twinflowers, and bleeding hearts popping through the carpet of rich moss.

The road climbs to the top of a ridge, where it joins a road from higher up the hill, then descends again. Where it levels off at the bottom, watch for an old road on the left leading to the east side of Third Lagoon. A faint but followable path crosses the spit outside of the lagoon, then climbs along the edge of the high bluff between Third and Jakle's Lagoons to rejoin the road near the junction mentioned earlier.

Just east of the road to Third Lagoon, a trail heads right (south) next to a marsh. This path climbs uphill through thick timber, emerges at a meadow, and joins the Mount Finlayson Trail. Just beyond the lagoon, the road is gated at the eastern park boundary; from here follow Marina Lane east about 25 feet to the Fish Creek marina (private). Return the way you came, or follow the Mount Finlayson Trail back.

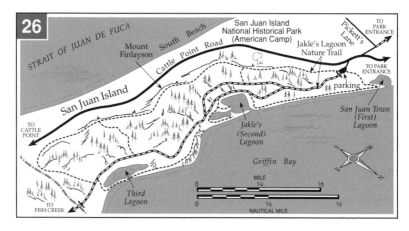

Calypso Orchid

The lovely calypso orchid *(calypso bulbosa)*, found in moist, shady spots in the San Juan Islands, holds a delicate single blossom on an arched, 6-inch-high stem. The pinkish-lavender blossom, brushed with white and deep red, is commonly known as fairy slipper or Venus's slipper—you can certainly imagine them being put to that use. The name calypso comes from the Greek word meaning "hidden" and refers to the goddess Calypso, who was often hidden beneath the waves. After the blossom withers, the single leaf dies back and the plant lies hidden beneath the soil throughout summer. A new leaf grows in fall, and a new blossom appears in May.

If you are fortunate enough to see one of these exotic flowers, do not pick or remove it. The plant grows in association with certain fungal and plant hosts, and the corm, a bulblike swelling at the base, will die if removed from this habitat.

A calypso orchid curves around a tuft of grass.

MOUNT FINLAYSON. The 200-foot high, rolling hill of Mount Finlayson is the highest point on this end of San Juan Island. A trail that follows a mowed firebreak leaves the Jakle's Lagoon parking area and wends through the meadow near the edge of the forest. Magnificent examples of wind-shredded Douglas-fir tower beside the track. Along the way, two faint trails head north into the forest; the westernmost one is the return loop of the Jakle's Lagoon Nature Trail, the farthest east leads down to Third Lagoon.

From the round summit, look north to Griffin Bay, east to Lopez Island and the Cascades, and south across the Strait of Juan de Fuca to white Olympic peaks. Ocean freighters ply the strait, bearing cargoes from exotic lands headed for Puget Sound ports. Once they carried silk, tea, and spices; today they are laden with plywood and Hondas.

From the top of Mount Finlayson, the trail continues east out of the park and onto state- and Land Bank-owned land, then drops steeply down the eastern ridge line to an abandoned gravel pit near Cattle Point Road. A faint trail leads northeast across a boulder-strewn meadow to an old overgrown road heading northwest into the trees and back into the park. Watch in the

Mount Finlayson rises above South Beach.

open old-growth timber for woodpeckers and brightly colored western tanagers. The road fades to a trail and ultimately joins an old road from Fish Creek near the east end of Third Lagoon.

ROAD VIEWS. Returning to Cattle Point Road and following it east toward the end of the island, the road traverses the open lower slopes of Mount Finlayson. Here are astounding roadside views south across the Strait of Juan de Fuca, east to Cattle Point Light, and beyond that to the rocky southern end of Lopez Island.

Within the sweep of your eyes are more public lands than can be seen from any other viewpoint in the United States. From the North Cascades to Mount Rainier, from the national forests spanning the Cascades to the onetime forts, now parks, of Admiralty Inlet, and then to the heights of the Olympics are national wilderness treasures set aside for recreation and preservation. Two pullouts along the road have interpretive plaques identifying these areas and paying credit to the legislative accomplishments of Senator Henry "Scoop" Jackson, who helped make these reserves possible.

chapter six

North from Spieden Channel and President Channel

Traveling north from the busy thoroughfares of Spieden Channel and President Channel, boaters encounter Spieden, Waldron, and Stuart Islands and their associated smaller islands. These landfalls, which are similar geologically to the Sucia Islands group to the north, are composed of folded, eroded sedimentary beds with long ridges extending underwater as a network of reefs and shoals that make boat pilots wary but offer habitat for marine life and thus beckon to anglers and scuba divers.

Lying deep within the rain shadow of Vancouver Island, the islands' climate is dry enough that the Cactus Islands do, indeed, support cactus. The brittle prickly pear cactus, *Opuntia fragilis,* the most northerly occurring species of cactus, blooms here with a delicate, yellow, tissuelike flower in early summer. Although more common in the prairies of the Great Plains, this cactus species is becoming rare in the San Juans; it is found in small colonies on only nine of the islands. The stress of invasions by other plants, climate change, wildfires, and loss of habitat due to spreading civilization might, sadly, drive it to extinction here.

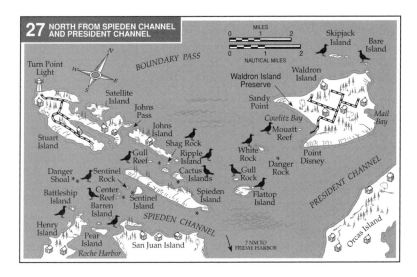

White Rock is one of the protected islets of the San Juan Islands Wilderness Area. Its distinctive white "patina" is a result of bird guano.

These are islands to enjoy from the deck of your boat, for aside from the state parks on Stuart Island and The Nature Conservancy reserves, all shoreland is privately owned or held as a wildlife refuge, and there are no commercial developments.

SPIEDEN CHANNEL
Map 27

Spieden and Sentinel Islands   Map 27
Boating • Paddling • Birdwatching

Facilities: None

The islands lie along the north side of Spieden Channel, 7 nautical miles from Friday Harbor.

The most striking in appearance of this northwestern group, 480-acre Spieden Island, with its long northern slope neatly forested and its southern side barren except for tawny grass, appears as if a prankish barber had been at work. Lying alongside to the south, 15-acre Sentinel Island is a miniature duplicate of its neighbor.

Spieden, which is the only large San Juan island without a bay or harbor of any sort, has not been commercially developed, and for many years its life was pleasantly bucolic. In 1969 an abortive attempt was made to capitalize on its dry climate and open rangeland by transforming it into an African game farm and renaming it "Safari Island." The island was stocked with ungulates such as Japanese sika deer, European fallow deer, Indian blackbuck antelope, and wild goats. No predators were brought, assuming that hunters who paid to come to the island would keep the herds under control.

Immediately there was a loud outcry from conservationists protesting this "sitting duck" type of sportsmanship. Whether it was because of the voice of the conservationists or because the project was ill conceived, the business went broke and the land was sold to other interests, but some of the wildlife remained. A couple of attempts to round them up and relocate them were unsuccessful, and thus far, some of these strange imports from

It's a Hard Life on a Rock

You would think that bird nesting grounds are a comfy nursery, but such is not the case. Life can be tough, and egg destruction or death of chicks is a constant concern. The harshness of Mother Nature makes it difficult enough for birds; don't make it worse. Even the most minor disturbance by humans, such as the close approach of a boat, can pose a threat to eggs or young birds. Thus, it is crucial that humans stay away from nesting grounds.

When birds are frightened from their nests, even for a short period of time, the unattended eggs might be broken by either predatory birds or competing birds of the same species. If the parents remain gone for any length of time, eggs might chill and fail to hatch. Nesting gulls are extremely territorial and will viciously defend their foot-square domain against intrusion by other birds; if a mother is chased from her nest, the frightened small chicks often scatter into foreign territory and are killed by rival birds.

If eggs or young are destroyed for any reason, the female might lay a new clutch. However, studies show that second- and third-clutch chicks are not as healthy as those that hatch from first clutches, and mortality is higher. Also, if it is too late in the season, weather or food conditions could be unsuitable for young chicks, or, in the case of migratory birds, the flock might leave before these second-clutch chicks are mature enough to make a journey.

As tempting as it might be to see wildlife, stay at least 300 feet away from offshore rocks and islets that hold nesting areas.

This herring gull mom chose pilings to nest and raise her chick. However, most San Juan seabirds require the privacy of offshore rocks and islets.

The unique pattern of vegetation makes Spieden Island, left, and Sentinel Island, right, easy to identify.

foreign lands remain. Passing boaters with binoculars might spot gazelle or antelope. The island is privately owned.

Sentinel Island, Spieden's small companion, was acquired by The Nature Conservancy in 1979 as a nature preserve. It is an active eagle-nesting area, it holds a nesting community of pigeon guillemots, and its rocky shores are used by harbor seals for resting and sunning. Unlike nearby Yellow Island, which is also owned by The Nature Conservancy, Sentinel Island is not open to public visitation.

Flattop Island and Other Bird Refuges Map 27

Boating • Paddling • Birdwatching

Facilities: None

⛴️ The islands lie in the vicinity of Spieden and Waldron Islands.

Sentinel Rock and Center Reef (southwest of Spieden Island); Shag Rock, Gull Reef, and Ripple, Little Cactus, and Flattop Islands (northeast of Spieden Island); and Gull and White Rocks, and Mouatt Reef (between Flattop and Waldron Islands) are all part of the San Juan Islands Wilderness Area. These islets, rocks, and submerging reefs are nesting sites for glaucous-winged gulls, pelagic cormorants, black oystercatchers, and pigeon guillemots. Large flocks of harlequin ducks and occasionally some loons can be seen here in the summer.

Although in the past boaters have stopped at Flattop Island, the largest of these bird refuges, public recreational use of Flattop, as well as the less-hospitable rocks, is now prohibited in order to protect bird nesting areas.

STUART ISLAND
Map 28

Boating • Paddling • Hiking • Historical Interest • Fishing

Facilities: None

Stuart Island lies 3½ nautical miles north-northwest of Roche Harbor on San Juan Island, and 11½ nautical miles from Friday Harbor.

Stuart Island thrusts far toward the Canadian border, only 3 miles from several of the Gulf Islands, making its protected harbors popular stops for B.C.-bound vacationers and for Canadians headed south for U.S. destinations. Indeed, the outline of the island itself, ignoring its deep harbors, suggests a boat headed for Canadian waters, and Johns Island is its dinghy in tow. At 1786 acres, the island is the eighth largest of the San Juan Islands, and it has 5130 feet of shoreline on Haro Strait and Boundary Pass.

Stuart Island has a population of some forty permanent residents living in homes scattered about the island. A small private airfield on the northwest tip of the island serves these residents. Fishing and farming have provided a livelihood for islanders since the days of early homesteading; the reef-netting site off the entrance to Reid Harbor has been fished by Indians for six generations. Other residents are retirees or people who can manage their jobs from here, with an occasional boat or airplane commute.

Reid and Prevost Harbors, the location of Stuart Island Marine State Park, provide fine overnight facilities for boaters. Those who stay a while longer

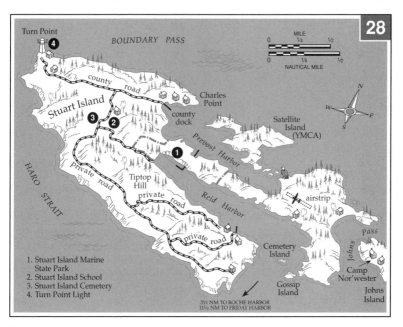

1. Stuart Island Marine State Park
2. Stuart Island School
3. Stuart Island Cemetery
4. Turn Point Light

enjoy the fishing, the beaches, and the shellfish, while the more energetic might even sample the forest hikes and pastoral road walks revealing the serene inner beauty of the island.

Stuart Island is a fine destination for kayakers, with enough nooks and crannies to fill several days' worth of exploration; however, the distance and strength of tidal currents encountered en route to the island make this a trip only for experienced paddlers.

❀ When planning a trip from Roche Harbor to Stuart Island in a small boat, consider strong tidal currents and shoal areas in Spieden Channel. The entrance to Reid Harbor is constricted by submerged rocks and shoals. Stay west of Gossip and Cemetery Islands, in the middle of the channel or slightly to its west side, to avoid running aground. Boats cruising the north side of the island via Johns Pass should use care at the south entrance to the channel. Kelp marks several rocks and a ¹/₂-fathom shoal extending well out from the eastern tip of Stuart Island. Give all obstructions a wide berth. Check a good navigation chart for exact position of hazards. On the north side of Prevost Harbor, tucked behind the protective wing of Charles Point, is a county dock and a few homes. No facilities or provisions are available here, so visitors should limit their stops to the state park docks.

The shores do not exhibit the sculptured sandstone cliffs so characteristic of the northern Sucia Islands group; instead, the steep banks are heavily covered with vegetation almost down to the waterline. The rounded, forested dome of Tiptop Hill, the highest point on the island, rises 640 feet above Reid Harbor.

Johns Island lies so near Stuart Island that it would be a part of it except for the narrow channel of Johns Pass. The slender island is home to Camp Nor'wester, a youth camp formerly located on the Sperry Peninsula of Lopez Island. It relocated here when that property was sold. The camp's canoes, bearing a colorful Indian design, can often be seen in nearby waters.

Stuart Island Hikes Maps 28 and 29

Trail hiking distance: SCHOOL: 1¹/₃ miles round trip; **CEMETERY:** 1¹/₂ miles round trip; **LIGHTHOUSE:** 5 miles round trip

Trail elevation gain: SCHOOL: 250 feet; **CEMETERY:** 250 feet; **LIGHTHOUSE:** 250 feet

⬤ The trails begin at the head of Reid Harbor, in Stuart Island State Park. ❀ At Turn Point, offshore water is so turbulent and shores so steep and rocky that a boat approach is not wise. Experienced kayakers could land in a small cove on the south side of the point.

An easy stretch of the legs gives visitors an opportunity to gain insight into the history and lives of the people who make this island their home. For all hikes, at the head of Reid Harbor, follow the trail through the woods to its junction with the county road. Continue west on the road, which grinds uphill through pleasant forest. The old ridge-top trail that once led between the park property and the school is closed to public use because it crosses private property.

STUART ISLAND SCHOOL. The schoolyard is reached ²/₃ mile from the Reid Harbor dock. On the edge of the clearing is the classic, one-room, white clapboard schoolhouse that served generations of children living on Stuart, Johns, and Spieden Islands. The building is currently used as a library for the modern school nearby. Next to it, in a small companion building, is The Teacherage Museum, with displays lining the interior walls and a pair of kiosks describing life on the island and telling the history of the Turn Point lighthouse.

This, perhaps the most interesting school in the state, has been featured on television. In early days the children from nearby islands would row to Stuart daily, in all weather, and then hike overland to school. Later, outboard motors made the trip easier, although still somewhat hazardous at times. One December day in 1961, while all of the school's youngsters were on a boat outing, the boat sank in bad weather and all aboard were drowned. The school remained closed for sixteen years following the tragedy, and local children commuted to San Juan Island. In the fall of 1977 it reopened with an enrollment of eight.

Modern times dictated the need for a newer facility, and in 1980 the new school standing nearby was opened. Although it is more spacious and its modern design provides a flood of cheery light, the building is still one room and is heated with a wood stove. At one time enrollment numbered up to twenty-three; in recent years it has been around a dozen, and in 2003 enrollment had dwindled to only four, fostering the concern that the school might close.

STUART ISLAND CEMETERY. To find the historic little Stuart Island Cemetery, continue west on the path past the school to its junction with a dirt road. Turn right, down the county road, and in 30 yards watch on the left for an unmarked, seldom-used road leading to the cemetery.

Spanning almost a century of island time, the gravestones tell the story of the many settlers who lived here for long years and others who enjoyed this lovely, though sometimes harsh, land for only a brief time. The land for the cemetery was originally donated by Chris Cook, in memory of his mother, Maria Cook, who, in 1910, was the first person buried at the site. The area was chosen because of its central location, beauty, and solitude. It is still used today.

Several generations attended historic Stuart Island School. The building has been replaced by a newer facility.

When the deed was recorded in 1910, no one realized that the legal description was in error and it actually described a spot beneath 200 feet of water in Haro Strait. In the early 1980s, because of the description error, the islanders found out they did not own the cemetery when the actual property owners wanted it closed. The residents of Stuart Island then formed a cemetery district, with the power to tax, purchase property, and/or take the property through the power of eminent domain. Finally, in 1989, a young woman who had purchased the land several years before sold the 480-square-foot site to the Cemetery District for the modest sum of $500.

In the past the cemetery had been protected only by a rusty fence. To provide better security, the Cemetery Board has now surrounded the area with a low chain-link fence. Wide gates swinging from brick columns are surmounted by concrete lions. A nearby kiosk tells the story of the cemetery and offers brief obituaries of those buried here. Examine the gravestones and speculate about the lives of these people, but treat the cemetery with respect.

TURN POINT LIGHT. Far on the western tip of Stuart Island, a lighthouse blinks warning to freighters, fishermen, and pleasure boaters traveling through Haro Strait. Turn Point Light, so named because it marks the point where boats must turn in the channel, was established in 1893 on a tract of land high atop a rocky cape, with a sweeping 300-degree view of the surrounding sea.

Freighters pass offshore from Turn Point Light.

The current concrete tower, housing the light and a foghorn, was built in 1936.

In 1974 the lighthouse was automated; it seems unfortunate at times that fine old traditions must give way to modern technology. The residence fell into disrepair, but has recently been restored, and there are attempts to find someone to use the property and care for it. Treat this historic site with respect.

Turn Point is best reached by an overland hike from Reid or Prevost Harbors. The steep cliffs below the point and the treacherous water offshore make landing a boat impractical. Catch the trail to the school, described above, then continue a short distance past the school to the junction with a dirt county road. Follow the road north past a farmhouse and a barn. Walking the quiet, tree-shaded road is like stepping into time suspended. The nautical bustle of the state park harbors seems a planet away, and rarely is anyone seen along the deserted track. Even if some of the buildings appear unoccupied, all the land is private property; do not trespass.

About 1¼ miles from Reid Harbor, the route intersects the Prevost road. Several homes can be seen down the road on the right; beyond is Satellite Island, and on a clear day Mount Baker hovers above. Turn left at the intersection and continue past rolling fields, where cattle share pasturage with deer. To the left of the road are reminders of modern-day technology: several parked cars and tie-downs for aircraft that use the private strip to the southwest. At 2½ miles from Reid Harbor, reach Turn Point Light.

A Lighthouse Drama

Originally, Stuart Island's dramatically scenic Turn Point was the home of Indians who fished nearby waters. After construction of the lighthouse, a succession of lighthouse keepers lived here, raised their families, and often left their names imprinted on the history of the area. The fine, spacious home and idyllic island were an ideal place to raise a family.

Edward Durgan was one such lighthouse keeper. In his book, *Lighthouses of the Pacific*, Jim Gibbs describes an incident that earned Durgan a certificate of merit. On a February night in 1897, the tug *Enterprise* ran aground near Turn Point and the barge under tow was cast adrift with men still on its deck. As Durgan and his assistant, Peter Christiansen, were attempting to rescue the men on the tug and on the barge, one drunken member of the crew went berserk, attacking the lighthouse keeper with a knife. Durgan and Christiansen subdued the man and the rescue was successfully carried out. By morning's light, all were safe in the lighthouse, except for the drunken assailant, who was chained in the chicken house.

This same assistant lighthouse keeper, Peter Christensen, began the first Stuart Island school in 1897 so his children could have an education.

Views spread in all directions across Haro Strait to Canadian islands and down the 50-foot cliff to the sea churning against the flanks of the point. Walk with care; the footing at the edge of the cliff can be insecure.

Take the hike in the late afternoon to enjoy the fiery sunset behind Vancouver Island and the crimson afterglow, but pack along a flashlight for the return trip through the forest. Fires and overnight camping are not permitted anywhere except the state park.

Stuart Island Marine State Park   Map 29

Camping • Picnicking • Boating • Paddling • Scuba Diving • Clam Digging • Crabbing • Fishing • Hiking

Facilities: Docks and floats, 22 mooring buoys (2 lineal mooring systems planned), 15 primitive campsites, 4 Cascadia Marine Trail campsites, picnic tables, fire rings, drinking water, toilet and composting toilets, marine pump-out station, hiking trails

Park area: 88 acres, 4130 feet of shoreline on Reid and Prevost Harbors

The park dock on Reid Harbor is 5 nautical miles from Roche Harbor on San Juan Island and 12½ nautical miles from Friday Harbor. The Prevost Harbor dock is 6 nautical miles from Roche Harbor on San Juan Island and 13½ nautical miles from Friday Harbor.

The ½-mile recess of Reid Harbor is one of the best anchorages in the San Juans. The enclosing arms of the island drop off sharply to 5 fathoms, giving good anchorages almost up to the shoreline, while the gravel beach at the head of the bay is gradual enough for small craft to land easily.

A dock and float on the north shore, two floats anchored near the head of the bay, and fourteen mooring buoys spaced about the harbor provide easy tie-ups for about thirty boats. The large blue-striped buoy in the center of the harbor is for use of Coast Guard vessels when stationed in the vicinity. State Parks plans to install a lineal mooring system between the Coast Guard buoy and the existing park buoys, which will increase the number of moorages. It is expected to be in place by the summer of 2004. The float anchored to pilings about 100 yards south of the dock is a marine holding tank pump-out station.

On the north side of the island, Prevost Harbor and its broader beaches offer a different perspective. The only safe entrance to the harbor is by Charles Point, west of Satellite Island. ✵ Do not attempt the channel on the east with boats of any draft, as it is dangerously rocky and shallow. The harbor contains a dock with float, seven buoys, and good anchorages, although there might be some difficulty getting hooks to dig through the thick eelgrass at the bottom of the harbor. A lineal mooring system is also planned for here.

✵ Boats opting to anchor in the superb little bay on the north side of the harbor at Satellite Island should be aware of a large rock, submerged at tides above 8 feet, that lies near the center of the entrance. Satellite Island is owned by the YMCA, which maintains a summer camp here and does not encourage visitors. The tideland below mean high water is a Department of Natural Resources beach, however, and is open for clam digging during favorable tides.

In the state park, nineteen campsites with fire grates are situated on a pleasant knob north of the Prevost Harbor dock, on the high rib between Prevost and Reid Harbors, and on either side of the marsh at the head of Reid Harbor. All are pleasantly shaded by light timber. Four spots at the head of Reid Harbor are designated Cascadia Marine Trail campsites for kayakers.

The beaches of Prevost Harbor offer interesting low-tide exploration. Walk carefully to avoid crushing Dungeness and red rock crabs that burrow in the eelgrass. Gentle (and cautious) probing of the grass

A clam is an uncertain trophy for this young lady.

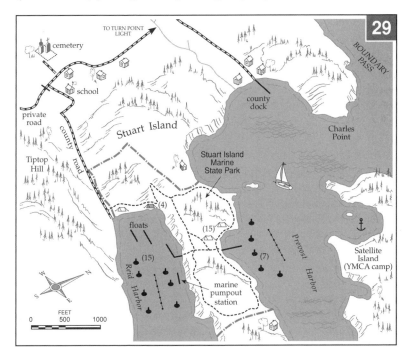

Prevost Harbor, sheltered by Satellite Island, has buoys, a dock with float, and plenty of anchoring room.

might yield some of meal size. Undersize and female Dungeness crabs, or any others you don't plan to eat, should be returned to a protected, damp spot or put into the water. Any crabs left stranded in the sun might dry out and die.

The park's gravel beaches, especially the one at the head of Reid Harbor, provide good clamming for littlenecks and butter clams. Those with the stamina to dig deep enough might claim some geoducks. Tidelands on Reid and Prevost Harbors lying outside the park are privately owned and are posted.

A ½-mile trail connects the Prevost dock with the head of Reid Harbor. Catch the cross-island trail northwest of the dock and follow it past the side trail to the toilets. In about 300 yards this trail joins another along the top of the high rocky bank above Reid Harbor, where twisted, red-barked madronas frame views of sleek boats bobbing at their moorings. Here, head south along the bank to return to the Reid Harbor dock, or drop down a switchbacking staircase (127 steps!) to the beach at the head of Reid Harbor. At the bottom, in a marshy flat, continue south on a clearly marked trail for 300 yards, emerging at the county road leading to the south corner of the beach.

Cemetery and Gossip Islands, lying on the east side of the Reid Harbor entrance, are two undeveloped marine state park islands. The larger of the two, Gossip Island (also known as George Island), is about an acre of rock and grass and a few scruffy trees; at low tide it nearly joins Stuart Island.

Smaller Cemetery Island, lying slightly farther into the harbor, is nearly barren. It gains its somber name from reported historical use of the island by natives as a burial site.

Because of several rare and endangered plant species found on the islands, they are closed to public access. The water surrounding the two islands is designated as an Underwater Marine Recreational Area for use by scuba divers.

WALDRON ISLAND
Map 27
Boating • Paddling • Birdwatching • Wildflowers • Scuba Diving • Fishing

Facilities: None

The dock on Cowlitz Bay is 10 nautical miles from Friday Harbor and 9 nautical miles from Orcas Landing. The nearest launch ramp is at West Beach on Orcas Island, 4½ nautical miles away.

Waldron is a staunchly individualistic island, defying categorization, either physically or socially, with any other in the San Juans. Although it is quite close to Orcas Island, lying only 2 nautical miles west of Orcas's West Beach, geologically it is related only to that island's extreme north shore.

The people of Waldron display this same individualism, along with a strong sense of self-sufficiency, for the island has no electricity, water district, telephones, stores, or regular ferry service, and most residents prefer it that way. This is not a primitive island, however, for many homes are modern, with either private gasoline generators or tanks of propane to power lights, radiotelephones, appliances, and furnaces.

The island is one of the more unusual pieces of topography to be found hereabouts. More than half the island is a marsh and meadow flatland covered by glacial drift, rarely more than 100 feet in elevation; however, at the southern tip, the cliffs of Point Disney suddenly rush up to a height of more than 600 feet. The imposing fortresslike walls of the point display beautiful banding of exposed fossil-bearing sandstone and conglomerate.

The walls of Point Disney drop off just as steeply underwater, providing an excellent dive site for scuba divers. This is a spot for the experienced, due to the strong current. Undersea walls and niches hold a colorful world of anemones, basket stars, and scallops.

Point Disney was the site of the island's only commercial enterprise—a sandstone quarry that operated here during the early 1900s. When concrete paving became favored over sandstone cobbles, the quarry closed. Some of the workmen departed while others remained to farm.

Waldron has less than a hundred year-round residents, with most homes located along the two broad bays of the northwest shore. The "village" of Waldron consists of a few abandoned buildings clustered around the county dock on Cowlitz Bay. There is a small float attached to the dock, but passing boaters rarely stop here as there are no onshore facilities and visitors are regarded with suspicion. The open bay is a marginal anchorage, even in

A 600-foot-high cliff marks Point Disney, at the south end of Waldron Island.

good weather. ✳Mouatt Reef, which is exposed at low tide, lies at the entrance to the bay, 300 yards off the end of the dock.

The island's only other harbor is rock-bound Mail Bay, on the east side, which in early days was the local mail stop when seas were too rough at Cowlitz Bay; apparently "neither rain nor snow nor sleet nor hail (nor towering seas) could stay these couriers...." Mail Bay offers a few anchorages in 10 to 40 feet of water. ✳Skippers should be wary of submerged pilings, the remnants of earlier docks, along the north side of the bay.

Waldron Island Preserve Map 27

Birdwatching • Wildflowers

Facilities: None
Preserve area: 273 acres, 4000 feet of shoreline
🚤 The area is east of Sandy Point, 11 nautical miles from Friday Harbor and 10 nautical miles from Orcas Landing.

The Nature Conservancy has purchased 273 acres of beach, meadow, and marshland on the west side of Waldron Island, facing Cowlitz Bay, between Sandy Point and Point Disney. This purchase was fostered by Waldron residents who wanted to preserve it in its natural state. Especially important from an ecological standpoint are 52 acres of wetland that provide a haven for migratory waterfowl and resident muskrats and river otters. Another 205 acres on Disney Mountain, adjoining The Nature Conservancy property, was purchased by the San Juan Preservation Trust in order to establish a sanctuary for native flora and fauna.

The area should be visited only by those seriously interested in viewing and studying the birds and flora. Going ashore is permitted, subject to restrictions necessary to maintain this as a nature preserve: Remain on designated trails; no pets, picnicking, camping, or fires; no collection of plants or animals; prior permission must be obtained for groups of more than six. To arrange for group access, call (206) 360-4344.

Douglas-fir, oak, and madrona forests attract colorful goldfinches, red crossbills, western tanagers, and nuthatches, while red-winged blackbirds, long-billed marsh wrens, and myriad other marsh birds inhabit the wetlands. Ponds are resting grounds for migratory freshwater ducks such as cinnamon, blue-winged, and green-winged teals, and occasional groups of whistling swans. Eagles nest in the forested heights above the island, as well as across President Channel on Orcas Island. The nesting sites are carefully protected by island residents and conservation organizations.

Skipjack and Bare Islands   Map 27

Birdwatching • Wildlife Watching • Fishing • Scuba Diving

Facilities: None

The islands are 4½ miles from North Beach Resort, where boats can be launched.

Lying near the northwest shore of Orcas Island, in the past Skipjack Island has been a popular destination for small-boat adventurers. However, the island, along with a nearby unnamed rock and Bare Island, ¾ nautical mile to the east, is part of the San Juan Islands Wilderness Area and is now closed to any public use. Landing on the islands is prohibited.

The islands, which lie due north of Waldron Island, support large rookeries of pigeon guillemots, black oystercatchers, auklets, glaucous-winged gulls, and other pelagic birds. As human use of the other San Juan Islands increases, it is vitally important that some of these islands be reserved exclusively as refuges. Any intrusion, no matter how cautiously done or well intentioned, can frighten birds from their nests, leaving their eggs and young open to predation by rival birds. Even after the nesting season, it is important that the birds have rocks on which to rest undisturbed.

The waters south and east of the islands are popular salmon fishing grounds, and the long underwater reefs nearby are frequented by scuba divers. Boaters engaged in these activities should stay well away from the bird refuges.

Eagles

A black silhouette with a 6-foot wingspan, soaring, wheeling in the summer sky, its white head glinting in the sun, then swooping downward to alight in a skeletal tree snag—a bald eagle is one of the most spectacular sights in the San Juans. At times they seem so common that tourists become blasé about them, but those who understand the significance of their presence can never fail to be thrilled by sightings of these elegant raptors.

The San Juan Islands have the largest and healthiest concentration of nesting bald eagles in the continental United States, with about fifty pairs that are known to breed here. The local population thins briefly in the fall when spawning salmon lure them up inland rivers, although a few prefer their local diet and remain year-round. Other migratory bald eagles summer in the islands after nesting in Alaska and coastal British Columbia.

About 10 percent of the eagles found in the San Juans are golden eagles. Some of these also nest here, although they prefer more protected sites inland, in trees and cliffs away from the water, to the seaside snags that the bald eagles choose. The two birds are not closely related; golden eagles are considered true eagles, while bald eagles are sea eagles, as are ospreys.

Immature bald eagles are often mistaken for golden eagles, because they do not display their dark body and snowy white head until their third or fourth year. Young bald eagles are evenly brown-colored with white mottling as they mature, while golden eagles display patches or bands of light-colored feathers at the base of the tail and in the wing linings at the base of the primary feathers.

Bald eagles frequent the many tree snags in the San Juan Islands.
Photo: Bob and Ira Spring

It is remarkable to find such a concentration of these strongly territorial birds in one area, along with large numbers of hawks, vultures, owls, and other predators with competitive feeding requirements. With the bountiful supply of fish, rabbits, and other favorite tidbits, coupled with the isolation of the islands and the current protective attitude of human residents, the eagles have modified their behavior to a more social existence. While golden eagles take large numbers of live rabbits and rodents and thus are valuable to the islands in the control of these prolific animals, bald eagles prefer fish, waterfowl, and carrion. They frequently will steal captured prey from other birds.

Eagles, which can be seen almost anyplace in the San Juans in spring and summer, are often spotted in snags of forested areas, surveying the sea from beach-front rocks, gliding low over quiet bays, or rising in concentric circles in the thermals above the mountains. Sometimes they are seen even near such bustling places as Roche Harbor or Sucia Island.

A number of San Juan residents, assisted by The Nature Conservancy, have attempted to locate all bald eagle nesting sites in the islands and have taken steps to protect them by obtaining conservation easements of 20 to 40 acres as a "buffer zone" around each nest tree, to prevent logging or public disturbance of the site. The trees are surveyed by air and boat each year to determine activity. About fifty chicks are believed to be successfully raised in San Juan nests each year.

In addition to the serious threat of loss of nesting sites by human encroachment, the birds also succumb to such natural hazards as storms, disease, and predatory raccoons, crows, and hawks. Although they are placed on the list of threatened species and are protected from being killed (except in Alaska), they are occasionally shot by irresponsible hunters. Severe penalties can result from killing or disturbing eagles. In the 1980s, some persons who deliberately cut down a tree containing a nest subsequently paid $10,000 in fines.

Still another threat to these majestic birds are poisons in the environment. Eagles have exceptional longevity, living up to thirty years in the wild. During this time, their bodies become storehouses of agricultural and industrial toxins absorbed or ingested from air, plants, and water. In addition, they eat large quantities of carrion, some of which died as a result of poisoning. These poisons, if they do not kill the bird outright, can cause sterility, thinning of eggshells, failure of eggs to hatch, and weakened chicks, ending the reproductive capabilities of the adult. It is imperative that bald eagles be given every possible protection if the species is to survive in the lower U.S. Visitors to the San Juans should stay well away from nesting sites, enjoying these birds from a distance with field glasses.

Bald eagle nesting sites are selected with a goal of overseeing territory. The birds choose the tallest tree and construct a platform of sticks, moss, shredded bark, and mud. Nests are reused from year to year and eventually are used by the eagles' offspring. Each year the nest is redecorated and expanded with additions of sticks and mud until, over a period of decades, it can become many feet across and weigh more than a ton. Such huge nests have been known to come crashing down during storms or to fall from their own weight. One to three eggs are laid in the nest, although usually only one chick will survive. Nesting eagles in the San Juans have been known to be accustomed to residents but become agitated by the presence of strangers. The best means of viewing them is from inside a car or boat, with binoculars.

chapter seven

Orcas Island

🚗 Orcas Island is served by the Washington State ferry from Anacortes (about a 1-hour trip) and from Sidney, B.C., on Vancouver Island (about 2 hours away).
⛴️ Orcas Landing is 15 nautical miles from Anacortes and 8 nautical miles from Friday Harbor on San Juan Island. Several private ferries provide passenger-only service from Anacortes, Bellingham, and Seattle to Rosario Resort and Obstruction Pass.
✈️ The Orcas Island Airport, which is 1 mile north of Eastsound Village, is a daily stop on the schedule of San Juan Airlines. Charter air services also provide flights to the islands.

ORCAS ISLAND IS UNIQUE AMONG THE SAN JUANS. Its three long inlets thrust deep into the interior of the land, giving it more shoreline and more protected waters than any of its neighboring islands. In addition, it has taller mountains and more surface area than any of the others. However, it exceeds San Juan Island in area by a mere 1½ square miles.

Proud residents can certainly boast that it has more of everything, including the largest park, Moran State Park. But with all this bounty, Orcas Island has only limited saltwater lands open to public use. With the exception of the hike-in park at Obstruction Pass, public waterfront is limited to a few meager road ends at Cormorant Bay, Buck Bay, West Beach, and near Smugglers Villa on the north shore.

Although initially one might think that Orcas Island was named for the orca whales that are seen in the surrounding waters, it was in fact named by Francisco Eliza in 1792 for the viceroy of Mexico. It is doubtful this early Spanish explorer deliberately chose the name for its double meaning, for the major landfalls such as this were always named after important political figures, not for any mere wildlife.

Islanders today, however, care little for Don Juan Vincente de Guemes Pacheco y Padilla Orcasitees y Aguayo Conde de Revilla Gigedo (yes, all that was his title) and generally prefer to relate the island to the magnificent mammal. Eliza further honored his patron by giving the name Isla y Archipelago de San Juan (Islands and Archipelago of Saint John) to the entire group of rocks. Guemes Island and Padilla Bay to the east also honor him.

While San Juan and Lopez Islands have had a history of bustling industry and agriculture since the time of early settlement, Orcas holds a long tradition as a vacationland. Ever since the 1890s, when ferries first made

Opposite: *Eastsound Village sits at the head of East Sound.*

runs to the San Juans, mainlanders have flocked here to summer at gracious inns or to rough it in canvas tents set up at beaches around the island. Several of the original inns have been modernized and are still in operation.

Today, hamlets at Orcas Landing, Eastsound Village, and Deer Harbor have groceries, general stores, and interesting shops, while outstanding meals can be had at a number of restaurants. A few other businesses are scattered around the island. Daily or weekly lodging is available at resorts, inns, and bed-and-breakfast inns ranging from rustic to posh. In summer, reservations are strongly recommended.

The only public camping areas are at Moran State Park and at a small hike-in campground at Obstruction Pass. A commercial resort at West Beach

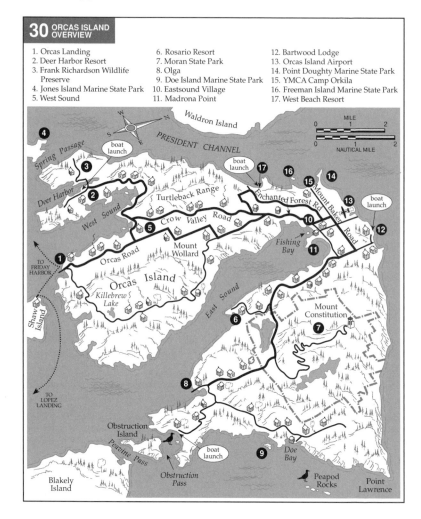

30 ORCAS ISLAND OVERVIEW

1. Orcas Landing
2. Deer Harbor Resort
3. Frank Richardson Wildlife Preserve
4. Jones Island Marine State Park
5. West Sound
6. Rosario Resort
7. Moran State Park
8. Olga
9. Doe Island Marine State Park
10. Eastsound Village
11. Madrona Point
12. Bartwood Lodge
13. Orcas Island Airport
14. Point Doughty Marine State Park
15. YMCA Camp Orkila
16. Freeman Island Marine State Park
17. West Beach Resort

The Orcas Hotel, which has operated since 1904, is on the National Register of Historic Places.

also has some camping space. In summer, campsites fill rapidly; be sure of overnight accommodations before planning to camp on the island. Most campgrounds accept reservations.

The major marinas are at Deer Harbor and West Sound. Orcas Landing, West Beach Resort, and Bartwood Lodge also have some boating facilities, although of a more limited nature.

Bicycling is a favorite mode of travel on Orcas Island, as anyone can testify who has witnessed the droves of bicycles exiting from the ferry in summer. Orcas roads, however, are two-lane affairs with limited shoulders and plenty of ups and downs and curves. Although auto traffic often is light, cyclists should use both care and courtesy when traveling here. Several of the steeper and slower sections of the main roads have marked bicycle pullouts; use them to allow backed-up traffic to pass and for rest stops. Public restrooms are available at Orcas Landing, in Eastsound Village, and in Moran State Park.

Nearly all island roads are blacktopped, and they wind through forest and farmland, at times edging some of the many miles of shoreline. Until recently, few of the roads carried names, and those that did changed their names seemingly at random. Most roads are now named and signed, a concession to the growing population and the need for emergency crews to quickly and correctly locate places. However, locals giving directions still refer to landmarks and names that do not appear on either maps or signs, such as "OPALCO Road" (which, incidentally, means the road where Orcas Power and Light Company is located—it's signed as Mount Baker Road).

Many of the old directional signs remain at intersections, pointing to one destination or another. The one reassuring thing is that you cannot get seriously lost. If you do end up wandering a bit, you will probably discover a pretty corner of the island you otherwise might not have found.

You are sure to see waterfowl at any time of year, although their numbers are far greater during the winter migratory season. A startled deer might dash across the road, then pause to stare back curiously at passersby. The greatest scenic viewpoint of all, whether by bicycle, foot, or car, is the top of Mount Constitution, in Moran State Park, with its panorama out to a sea of islands. This park is so stupendous that in this book it is covered in a chapter by itself.

ORCAS LANDING
Map 31
Shopping • Historical Interest • Nature Cruises • Picnicking

Facilities: Float (for fuel and charter boat use only), gas, diesel, groceries, fishing tackle, bait, marine supplies, whale-watching charters, 2-person scooter car and moped rentals, bicycle rentals, kayak rentals, restrooms, shops, restaurants, hotel; *no drinking water available at the float*

🚗 Orcas Landing can be reached via Washington State ferry from Anacortes and Sidney, B.C.

🛥 Orcas Landing is 15 nautical miles from Anacortes and 8 nautical miles from Friday Harbor, on San Juan Island.

A small cluster of stores next to the ferry landing caters to tourists waiting for the ferry and visiting boaters stopping to fuel up and resupply ship's stores. The marina adjacent to the west side of the ferry landing is equipped

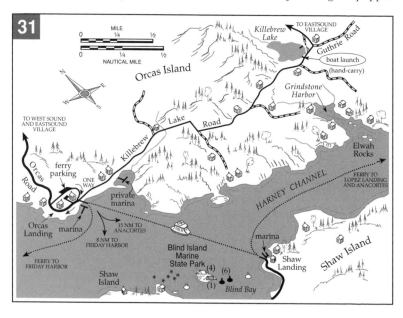

to meet boating fuel needs, and the grocery store has provisions for wheeled or keeled visitors. A number of gift shops and snack bars line the road on the slope above the ferry ramp, offering tourists pleasant places to browse, pass time, and purchase a few remembrances of the island while their cars sit in line.

Most interesting of the buildings overlooking the bay is the three-story, Victorian-era Orcas Hotel, which attests to the longtime role of the island as a resort center. Constructed in 1900, it began accommodating vacationers in 1904 and did a flourishing business for many years. Extensively restored and remodeled, the hotel has modern guest rooms furnished in the style of the original hotel, as well as a restaurant and bar. It is on the National Register of Historical Places.

Ferry line parking is in a large lot uphill from the Orcas Hotel, where there is ample space for cars awaiting the ferry; restrooms are adjacent. Purchase tickets for westbound destinations at the booth, then park in the appropriate lane for your destination. Ferry arrivals and departures are announced on a public address system, and lighted signs at the head of each lane indicate when boarding has begun. An open grassy area adjacent to the stairs that lead from the lot to the terminal has a few picnic tables for open-air relaxation and a nice view of the goings-on. In summer the wait for the ferry might be long, but at least it is fairly enjoyable.

The shops and businesses of Orcas Landing sit on the hillside above the ferry terminal. Photo: Heidi Mueller

Killebrew Lake   Map 31

Fishing • Paddling • Birdwatching

Facilities: Public float, hand-carried boat put-in; *gasoline motors are not permitted*
Area: 13 acres

🚐 Turn right immediately after leaving the ferry and follow Killebrew Lake Road east. It first parallels the shore, then winds through thick forest, arriving in 2³/₄ miles at a Y intersection, where White Beach Road continues to the east and Dolphin Bay Road heads north. To the left are the lake and a small pullout with parking for a car or two.

Here's a lily-pad lake, its quiet waters reflecting the cattails, skunk cabbage, pussy willows, and fir trees along its margins. Land bordering Killebrew Lake is owned by the state Department of Fish and Wildlife, but there are no developed public facilities. A short float on the northeast shore, patched and somewhat the worse for wear, provides the only foot access.

From the parking area, a path, once road, follows along the brushy lakeshore to the float. This spot can also be reached by continuing on Dolphin Bay Road to the first dirt road on the left and then following it to the lake; the end of this road is quite brushy, and you might prefer to walk it.

A steep dirt ramp on the south shore alongside Killebrew Lake Road permits launch of hand-carried boats, but it is not suited for trailered launching. Spend some time paddling about the lake, floating and watching the array of birds that visit the marsh and the dragonflies darting among the lily pads, or fish for the cutthroat trout with which the lake is stocked. The marshy nature of the shoreline limits any approach from any place other than the float and launch ramp.

Grindstone Harbor   Map 31

Boating • Paddling

Facilities: None

⛵ Lying on the north side of Harney Channel, 2 nautical miles east of the Orcas ferry landing, the small, deeply indented cove has space for just a few boats to drop a hook.

Grindstone Harbor has no public facilities from either land or sea, but it is a secure anchorage worth trying. ✸A wicked reef, just below the surface in all but minus tides, lies in the center of the entrance 300 yards offshore. Its slightly more obvious companion reef lies on the east, just inside the entrance. A slow and cautious approach, somewhat favoring the west side of the harbor, leads past a channel-pinching point to the pleasant inner harbor and anchorages in 10 to 15 feet of water. The upper end of the bay is quite shallow. Respect the privacy of the shoreline.

The harbor received its name because Paul Hubbs, an early settler who lived here, owned a grindstone. He was often called upon to sharpen the axes, knives, and other tools of neighboring pioneers.

In 1983, Grindstone Harbor achieved notoriety when the (then) captain of the ferry *Elwha* attempted to steer the 382-foot vessel close to the entrance to the harbor while showing a lady friend the sights, and hung the ferry up on a reef. The event has since been immortalized in story, song, and a bar drink called "Elwha on the Rocks." The reef has now been officially named Elwha Rock.

DEER HARBOR
Map 32

Boating • Paddling • Fishing • Crabbing • Wildlife Tours

Facilities: RESORT: inn, cabins, swimming pool, restaurant, deli; **MARINA:** guest moorage, power, drinking water, diesel, gas, marine supplies, marine pump-out station, restrooms, pay showers, coin-op laundry, groceries, deli, gift shop, bicycle rentals, kayak rentals, boat rentals, charters, wildlife tours; **DEER HARBOR BOAT WORKS:** paved launch ramp with boarding float (fee)

🚗 Go 2½ miles north from the ferry landing on Orcas Road to the Deer Harbor Road intersection. Turn left here and follow the road as it curves around West Sound and then heads south to Deer Harbor, 4 miles from the community of West Sound.

🛥 The village of Deer Harbor lies 6 nautical miles north of Friday Harbor, along a route threading through the Wasp Islands.

Smallest of the Orcas Island inlets, Deer Harbor indents the western lobe of the island for a mere mile. The small village at the head of the bay, primarily made up of a marina and vacation resort, is a handy stop for boaters seeking to replenish fuel and ship's stores. Several of the buildings are neat, clapboard structures dating from the 1890s, when the historic resort was first established. Adding to the atmosphere, all types of interesting boats tie up at the docks, ranging from sleek plastic runabouts to beautiful old classic sailing vessels.

Good anchorages can be had in the bay, although its extreme head is quite shallow. A little wooded islet, appropriately named Fawn Island,

The docks at Deer Harbor Marina have everything visiting boaters need, including picnic tables and a handy place to clean their catch.

lies near the entrance; ✿passage can safely be made on either side of it, although a shoal extends from its southern end.

Landlubbers and seafarers mingle in the shops and eateries of the charming little village. All the lodging interiors have been updated to plush resort standards, and several modern one- and two-story cabins provide vacation accommodations for families or small groups.

The resort and marina are separate businesses; the only shared facility is the resort swimming pool, which is also open to both resort and marina guests. The shared water system, along with the marina facilities, has recently been modernized, making chronic water shortages a thing of the past. At the outside edge of the floats, A and B docks have a number of permanent moorages, and the outside of the floats on B, C, and D docks are reserved for various area yacht clubs. The remainder of the floats are available for guest moorage.

There is a small charge to nonguests for kayak put-ins and long-term parking. Kayakers with experience in handling tidal currents can paddle 2 nautical miles west from Deer Harbor to Jones Island Marine State Park, investigating Fawn Island en route, or can head southeast for 1¼ nautical miles to Pole Pass, then on around Caldwell Point into the expanse of West Sound. ✿The current can be strong in Pole Pass; refer to a tidal current chart for the best time to attempt the channel.

Although it is more difficult to locate, a second launch facility with a single-lane concrete ramp and adjoining boarding float is found at the head

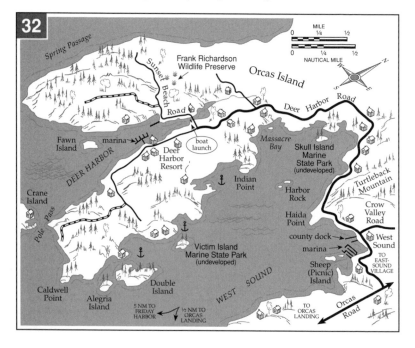

The Deer Harbor post office dates from the 1890s.

of Deer Harbor at the Deer Harbor Boat Works. A launch fee is charged, and the boat yard doesn't provide any parking. ❄The water off the end of the ramp can be quite shallow at low tide.

Frank Richardson Wildlife Preserve Map 32

Birdwatching

Facilities: None
Area: 20 acres
🚗 To reach the preserve, take Sunset Beach Road west at the head of Deer Harbor. The road curves around the head of bay, then goes steeply uphill. In 1¼ miles from the Deer Harbor Road intersection the marshland lies on the right.

The Frank Richardson Wildlife Preserve encompasses portions of a marsh on top of the hill west of Deer Harbor. The marshland teems with bird life year-round. In spring look for hooded mergansers, cinnamon teals, mallards, and American coots with their broods. Marsh wrens and red-winged blackbirds call from the rushes.

The narrow road has no shoulders and no parking alongside the preserve; find pullouts at either end of the marsh and walk the road to observe the birds. A few breaks in the dense roadside brush offer views, and viewing is better in winter and early spring before brush has leafed out.

The Land Bank has purchased a conservation easement on two nearby pieces of property. One surrounds Cayou Lagoon, at the head of Deer Harbor, and a second is a 109-acre wildlife corridor between the tidal lagoon and the Frank Richardson Wildlife Preserve.

Frank Richardson was a professor of zoology at the University of Washington. He lived on Orcas Island from shortly after the time of his retirement until his death in 1985. The preserve was established to honor him and his important contributions to the study of wildlife.

WEST SOUND
Map 32

Boating • Paddling • Birdwatching • Shrimping

Facilities: WEST SOUND: county dock with float, café/deli; **WEST SOUND MARINA:** guest moorage with power, drinking water (limited), diesel, gas, restrooms, pay showers, marine supplies and repair, boat launch sling (fee)

🚗 From the ferry landing, follow Orcas Road north for 2½ miles to Deer Harbor Road and turn left. The village is a mile farther.

⛴ The entrance to West Sound is ½ nautical mile from Orcas Landing and 5 nautical miles from Friday Harbor.

✈ The West Sound Marina has a float for seaplanes.

The "middle" of Orcas Island's three main inlets, West Sound is middle both in size and in location, lying between East Sound and Deer Harbor, and running north for 3 miles to the base of the Turtleback Range. Prevailing northerly or southerly winds make the waterway a favorite with sailors who happily leave the busy traffic of Harney Channel for brisk sails up the sound. ❄A long rock at the entrance to Massacre Bay, midway between Haida Point and Indian Point, is marked by a daybeacon. At high tide considerable portions of the rock are submerged—give it a wide berth.

The remarkable outline of the Turtleback Range, with the "shell" formed by 1500-foot Turtleback Mountain and the "head" created by Orcas Knob, is easily recognized from the waters of West Sound. Another good view of the turtle can be had from the north end of President Channel, northwest of Orcas Island.

On the eastern "thumb" of the roughly mitten-shaped sound is the village of West Sound, where there is a marina, yacht club, café, and county dock. The southernmost dock at West Sound is the property of the yacht club. Immediately north of this private dock is the county dock, with a 50-foot float that is accessible to the public for day use only. A staircase at the head of the dock provides access to the beach. A café/deli is across the road. The marina, tucked behind Sheep Island, is the largest and best on Orcas Island, with both permanent and guest moorages, fuel, repair and maintenance services, haul-out, and chandlery.

Boats planning to drop a hook for the night will find Massacre Bay quite shallow and open to southerly winds; the most protected anchorage is on the northwest side of Double Island, near the entrance to the sound. Two other indentations into the west side of the sound offer limited anchorage in all but southeasterly winds. One is a small cove just northwest of Victim Island; the second is the bight south of Indian Point.

The inlet offers little to the land-bound visitor aside from the very scenic

Sailing is great in West Sound. In the distance is Turtleback Mountain, with the head of the turtle on the left.

route around Haida Point. Pretty little Skull Island is visible from the road near the head of Massacre Bay, but once the road rounds the head of West Sound, it ducks into timber and all marine views are lost. In winter, Massacre Bay fills with great rafts of all kinds of migratory waterfowl—buffleheads, scaups, goldeneyes, grebes, and scoters—squawking and skittering about uneasily at every imagined menace from shore. When startled by the sight of a human or a stopping car, they depart in huge flocks of whirring wings, to alight farther down the sound.

Skull Island and Victim Island Marine State Parks   Map 32

Paddling • Picnicking • Crabbing

Facilities: None
Park area: SKULL ISLAND: 2 1/2 acres; **VICTIM ISLAND:** 3 acres
Located only 400 feet off the shore of West Sound, Victim Island lies a third of the way up the sound, just north of Double Island, while Skull Island is near the head of Massacre Bay.

Skull and Victim Islands bear grisly names for such innocuous bits of land; but—rather than any recent problem—they, along with Massacre Bay, recall the area's early history of bloody Indian raids.

Although the islands lie nearly within arm's length of the nearby shore, there is no access to the parks from land. They are small ("intimate" if you prefer) and rocky, with a few picturesquely scrubby trees. Skull is most accessible from low banks on the north and south ends of the island, while Victim has steep banks on all but the north end. After a day of paddle exploration of the shore of West Sound, either is a fine spot to pause for a snack or a snooze. These are undeveloped parks, thus there are no amenities such as water or toilets. Fires or overnight camping are not permitted; please take all garbage home with you.

The shoreline of West Sound wanders in and out, forming coves and bays ideal for small-boat perusal and peaceful anchorages. The only public tidelands in West Sound are those surrounding Sheep (Picnic), Skull, Victim, Double, and Oak Islands. Uplands are private except for Skull, Victim, and Oak Islands and a small rock north of Sheep Island.

Indian History

A number of tribes of Indians who lived along the Northwest coast, and whose languages shared a common root, are as a group known as the Coast Salish. They include the Clallam, Samish, Skagit, Nooksack, and Lummi tribes, who lived in the vicinity of the San Juan Islands, as well as many others who lived farther south. These tribes traded, intermarried, and, at times, warred.

The bounty of the Northwest provided the Coast Salish tribes with all they required. Fish, shellfish, deer, birds, and small animals provided meat. Bird eggs, as well as berries, camas bulbs, seaweed, and a variety of other plants, enhanced their meals. Some nutritionists believe they had a diet superior in vitamins to that of modern man. Cedar trees, which grew in abundance, were utilized for nearly every purpose: Wood was used for building homes and creating dugout canoes; shredded cedar bark was made into clothing and was even used for baby diapers (early Pampers!). Animal skins were also utilized for clothing, while reeds and other grasses were woven for mats and baskets.

The root of nodding onions was a staple food of early Indians in the San Juan Islands.

With only the most basic materials, the Coast Salish developed ingenious means of harvesting and preparing food. Nets and fishing lines were fashioned from incredibly thin strips of braided bark and plant fibers. Fishhooks, shaped from wood or horn, had hinged barbs or gates to prevent the escape of the catch. Tall poles, set up on either side of channels, supported nets to knock down flocks of low-flying birds. One such net was stretched across the 200-foot-wide channel at Pole Pass (hence the name),

EAST SOUND
Map 30

More than 7 miles long and a mile wide, the long, blunt inlet of East Sound nearly carves Orcas Island in two. Hills rise steeply along both of its sides and then suddenly drop down to the flat at the head of the bay. This is a small inland sea in itself, on which sailors can spend hours cruising about or drop in at its three diminutive ports of call, Olga, Rosario Resort, and Eastsound Village. The sound is so large that it can "make its own weather."

between Crane and Orcas Islands. Reef netting, invented by early Lummis, is still effective as a commercial fishing method today. Food was often cooked in watertight boxes made from cedar; red-hot rocks from the cookfire were dropped into the boxes to bring the contents to a boil.

Several different Coast Salish tribes fished and gathered food in the San Juans on occasion; however, the islands were primarily the tribal territory of the Swallah Indians, one of several bands of the Lummi tribe. Prior to the 1850s, large numbers of Swallahs summered throughout the islands, living in temporary shelters of wooden frameworks covered with woven mats. The mats were taken down when the group moved to another site, and the framework was left for their next visit. With the arrival of the dreary rains of fall and winter, the Indians would quit these summer shelters and repair to the protection of their established longhouses. Such permanent settlements were at Friday Harbor on San Juan Island, Fisherman Bay on Lopez Island, West Sound on Orcas Island, and two sites on Waldron Island.

The Swallahs were generally peaceful people, content with the abundance of their land. Nevertheless, they occasionally suffered at the hands of war parties from the fierce tribes to the north, and they would retaliate. Territorial acquisition was not the intent; such raids were primarily for the purpose of taking slaves who, later, were used for ceremonial sacrifices or were killed at the whim of their captors.

The most vicious raid in recorded history occurred in 1856, when a party of Haida Indians from the north swept down on the West Sound village, destroying the settlement, slaughtering most of its inhabitants, and taking those living for slaves. More than one hundred Indians were reported to have been killed. Since that time Massacre Bay has borne its lurid name. This attack, as well as earlier ones, severely reduced the tribe's numbers. The scourge of smallpox had also taken its toll. Shortly after the massacre, the San Juan Swallahs abandoned their permanent longhouses in the San Juans to join other members of the Lummi tribe who lived on the mainland, in the vicinity of today's Lummi Island.

Twenty-knot northerlies that flow over the flat at the head of the bay can become 40-knot winds by the time they reach its south end. The same effect can occur with southerlies. These "gap winds" that occur here are caused by relatively mild winds entering the channel and increasing in velocity as they are constrained by the steep hills that edge it.

With a smooth shoreline and beaches dropping off steeply along its sides, anchorages are few. Only at Buck Bay, Cascade Bay, and Fishing Bay, at the head of the sound, are the waters shallow and protected enough to permit an overnight stay.

Olga Map 30

Boating • Paddling

Facilities: Dock with float (removed in winter), guest moorage, toilet, restaurant, gifts, drinking water

Follow Orcas Road north from the ferry landing and through the town of Eastsound Village. Continue through Moran State Park and follow the road as it heads south to the village. Total distance from Orcas Landing is about 17 miles.

Olga is 5½ nautical miles from Orcas Landing and Spencer Spit, on Lopez Island, and 2½ nautical miles from Rosario Resort.

This small settlement on Buck Bay, near the mouth of East Sound, has a dock and float providing some space for visiting boaters. Although it is owned by State Parks, the dock is operated and maintained by the Olga Community Club, which charges a small fee for overnight stays. Overnight guest moorage is limited to 3 days (pay a fee at a box on the ramp); day-use is limited to 2 hours at no charge.

The Olga dock is great for a brief boating stop. Restaurants are nearby.

The dock has no power outlets, but there is a water line out to the float. The Olga store offers patrons lunch, deli goodies, and a collection of whimsical gift items. A second excellent restaurant, at the road intersection ¼ mile to the north, is open from March through December. Its nifty gift shop features the work of island artists and craftspeople.

In calm weather some anchorages are possible along the shore to the south. ✺ The lagoon at the head of the bay dries at low tide. Be cautious of a large rock in the center of the bay that is submerged at high tide.

Rosario Resort   Map 30

Boating • Paddling • Fishing • Swimming • Sights • Historical Landmarks • Scuba Diving • Nature Cruises

Facilities: Docks and floats, guest moorage with electrical and water hookups, mooring buoys (fee), restrooms, pay showers, coin-op laundry, groceries, gas, diesel, fishing tackle and bait, hotel, restaurant, coffee shop, lounge, spa, convention center, swimming pools, tennis courts, moped rental, boat rental, car rental, taxi service, dive shop, tour boats

Trail hiking distance: (Rosario Lagoon trail for registered guests only) ½ mile round trip to the park boundary at the dam

Trail elevation gain: 350 feet

🚐 Follow Orcas Road east from Eastsound Village, bearing right at an intersection 1 mile east of town. At 3 miles a prominent sign points right to Rosario Resort and Rosario Road. Follow this road downhill to the resort, 6 miles total distance from Eastsound Village, 14 miles from Orcas Landing.

🚤 By boat, Rosario lies on Cascade Bay, halfway into East Sound along the eastern shore. Rosario Point reaches out to enclose the broadly curving bay, with a small jetty-created moorage basin. Several private ferries provide passenger-only service from Anacortes, Bellingham, and Seattle.

⊥ Seaplanes can unload on the resort's float; several air services offer scheduled and chartered flights.

Unquestionably the most outstanding historical landmark of the San Juans, Rosario has gained nationwide recognition as a resort and convention center. It effectively melds the quiet grandeur of a turn-of-the-century estate with the posh of a modern marine resort.

The Rosario estate was built in 1904 by Robert Moran, a Seattle mayor who was a shipbuilder, millionaire, and man of unlimited talent and energy. Illness forced Moran to sell his shipbuilding enterprises in Seattle and retire to Orcas Island, where he purchased land enclosing Cascade Bay on East Sound and designed and supervised the building of his mansion, Rosario.

Moran built his home as solidly as he had built his ships, anchoring it on bedrock with concrete walls and inch-thick plate-glass windows. The fifty-four-room main building required six years to complete; it is said that two years alone were consumed laying the wooden parquet floor of the interior.

The care lavished on the structure was also extended to the furnishings and grounds of the estate. An organ with 1972 pipes, installed by Moran, is

The classic ketch Morning Star *is framed by lights of the Moran estate as it enters the bay.*

still played regularly, and visitors still admire an imported stained glass window. A figurehead salvaged from an old clipper ship that was wrecked in the San Juans was set up on the grounds and remains there today, a symbol for this elegant resort. Carved in 1874 from a solid pine log for the sailing ship *America*, the figure uses the motif found on the Liberty silver dollar used during this period.

Moran left his mark not only on this quiet bay but on all of Orcas Island. He purchased large quantities of property on the island and eventually donated 3600 acres of mountainous land, clothed with forests and lakes, to the State of Washington to be used as the park that today bears his name. In addition, he helped build roads, develop water systems, and provide much-needed jobs for the islanders during the Great Depression years of the 1930s.

Following the death of his wife, Moran sold Rosario in 1938. Another local ex-mayor, Gilbert Geiser of Mountlake Terrace, purchased the property in 1960. With energy and expertise possibly matching Moran's, he transformed the unique estate into a modern resort that attracts vacationers and hosts seminars and conventions year-round. The resort has changed ownership several times recently.

All of the original buildings of Rosario were named to the National Register of Historical Places in 1979, assuring their preservation in their original state with only necessary modernization. The second floor of the mansion holds an interesting museum.

Nearly any time of the year, reservations are advisable for an overnight stay at the floats or in the hotel. A fee is charged for use of buoys placed in the bay. Boats unable to secure moorage can usually find space to anchor.

Because this is private property, a landing fee is charged for coming ashore from anchored boats or buoys. The fee includes the water taxi to the resort and use of selected resort facilities. A meal in the resort's dining room makes a stop here a pleasant change for any galley slave.

Rosario Lagoon Trail • If guests at Rosario become sated with the multitude of attractions the resort offers and feel the urge to stretch their legs, a path leads up the steep hillside to the tennis courts beside Rosario Lagoon, where a trail continues to Cascade Lake, in Moran State Park. Walk past the concrete lagoon and generator building of the Rosario estate to find the trailhead opposite Discovery House—and what a trailhead! Every bit in keeping with the elegance of the resort, the rustic path is planked at its start and protected by a roof of cedar shakes. It zigzags briefly up the hillside through shadowed woods, stopping at a tiny pavilion, an ideal spot for resting, picnicking, or a romantic tryst.

From the pavilion, the path follows a road between resort villas to the Satellite Hall. Here, follow the dirt road on the uphill side of the hall to its intersection with a higher paved road near the Cascade Creek drainage. Turn left, and in 100 feet find the signed trailhead next to the steel aqueduct carrying water to the Rosario power generators. From here the trail climbs steadily, rising 350 feet in about a mile, keeping close to the aqueduct. Fragments of an older aqueduct can be seen below the trail, along with the cascading stream that gives Cascade Bay its name.

Finally the trail crosses two bridges and emerges on a road at an unmarked trailhead opposite the sluice gate of the Rosario Lagoon dam; the resort's tennis courts are to the left. Trails at either side of the dam enter Moran State Park, follow the shores of the lagoon, and reach Cascade Lake proper in about 1/2 mile. See Chapter Eight for further descriptions of the state park.

Eastsound Village   Map 33
Shopping • Sightseeing • Museum • Paddling • Hiking

Facilities: Groceries, stores, fuel, hotels, restaurants, movie theater, restrooms, dock (nearby)

Trail hiking distance: MADRONA POINT: 1/2 to 4 miles round trip

Trail elevation gain: Negligible

🚗 By land, the town is reached from the ferry landing by following the main road, Orcas Road, north to the head of the sound, a distance of 8 miles.

🚤 The village lies at the head of East Sound, 5 1/2 nautical miles from Olga, 9 1/2 nautical miles from Spencer Spit on Lopez Island, and 14 nautical miles from Friday Harbor.

✈ The Orcas Island airport, less than 1 mile due north of Eastsound Village, on North Beach Road, is reached by regular commercial flights, charter flights, and private plane.

Since the 1880s, Eastsound Village has served as the main business area for Orcas Island. At that time the few stores located here sold axes, seeds, flour, blankets, and horse collars to settlers; a blacksmith shod their horses; and a gracious inn provided meals and lodging to vacationing mainlanders. The town has not grown up much since that time—in fact, some of the original buildings are still there—but today there is a service station instead of a blacksmith shop, and the general store has a deli and is stocked like any modern grocery store. The beautiful little Emmanuel Episcopal Church, built in 1886, still opens its doors to worshippers each Sunday morning.

As in early times, stores along Main Street and North Beach Road are interspersed with private residences, although some of these homes have been converted to shops selling antiques, fine art, crafts, and gift items to visitors. Outlook Inn, which still provides overnight accommodations and fine meals, advertises that it has been in operation since 1883, making it one of the earliest such establishments in the San Juan Islands.

Eastsound Village's greatest drawback is that, even though it faces on a major waterway, it is difficult to reach by boat. The long shallow tide flat at the head of the bay makes it necessary for large boats to anchor well out in Fishing Bay and dinghy to shore. The possibility of a public dock with floats and a breakwater at the head of the bay has long been considered; unfortunately, the problems involved in building a structure that could withstand the severe storms that occasionally sweep up the long sound make the project prohibitively costly.

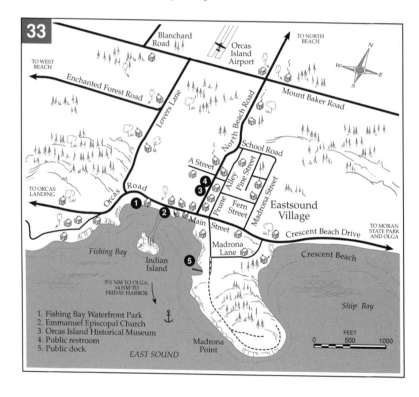

1. Fishing Bay Waterfront Park
2. Emmanuel Episcopal Church
3. Orcas Island Historical Museum
4. Public restroom
5. Public dock

Eastsound Waterfront Park • A few giant Douglas-firs provide shade to this pretty little park that sits on a low bank above the bay. The day-use park consists of only a few picnic tables in an open swath of grass; parking is along the street. Even with limited amenities, it is still a lovely site to have a beach picnic, with its unobstructed views all the way down the long fjord of East Sound. Just 200 yards offshore lies inviting little Indian Island, which is state-owned and open to the public. At minus tides a sandbar links the islet to the mainland. From the park, the beach can be walked all the way to Madrona Point, although there is no access to businesses on the bank above.

Although Eastsound Village faces on Fishing Bay, in the past it has lacked a real orientation to the water. Some of the waterfront restaurants and businesses have patio decks on their waterfront side, but public access to the waterfront is limited.

Orcas Island Historical Museum • A highlight of a visit to Eastsound Village is its interesting historical museum, located two blocks north of Main Street on North Beach Road. Six old log cabins, originally built elsewhere on the island, were brought to Eastsound Village and reassembled into the single structure that now houses the museum. Displaying a variety of construction methods ranging from massive hand-hewn, dovetailed boards to the

Morning breaks over East Sound. The inlet is so large that it sometimes makes its own weather.

The Orcas Island Historical Museum is fashioned from old log cabins.

traditional round log style, the building is nearly as interesting as the collection it houses. Only a small portion of the thousands of items owned by the museum can be shown in this facility. A major expansion is planned, once funds are available, in order to better display the historic treasures.

Each of the cabins that make up the museum is devoted to a phase of island history, such as early day farming, early medicine, the fruit industry, and lumbering. Displays rotate during the year. A totem pole, carved in traditional native style, marks the front of the museum. Behind the main structure is a shed housing antique farm machinery.

The museum has an outstanding display of Indian and pioneer artifacts and mementos from early island days. Many of the Indian objects were collected by Ethan Allen, a Waldron Island resident who was the county superintendent of schools during the early 1900s. The Allen collection, which is so valuable that it is housed in a fireproof vault, includes about twenty glass-framed wall displays containing Indian arrowheads.

Also on display is Allen's handmade boat, in which he rowed from island to island visiting the one-room schools in his district. During Allen's time there were twenty-seven such schools scattered around the San Juan Islands.

The museum, operated by the Orcas Island Historical Society, is open from 1:00 P.M. to 4:00 P.M. Monday through Saturday in the summer, and Friday and Saturday at other times. Eastsound Village Square, immediately north of the museum, has picnic tables and public restrooms (open in the summer). Summer weekends the grassy plot hosts a farmer's market. Future plans call for the addition of an amphitheater and children's play area to this heart of the village.

Madrona Point • The closest boat access to Eastsound Village is at Madrona Point. This last unspoiled peninsula on East Sound was scheduled for condominium development in 1989. However, the land was a sacred burial ground of the Lummi tribe, which lobbied heavily for federal funds to purchase the land and prevent its desecration. As bulldozers pressed at the boundaries, Congress approved a bill that authorized purchase of the point and its transfer to the Lummis as a preservation area. Although the point was once open to public use, courtesy of the tribe, littering and misuse of the area, sadly, caused it to be closed.

A day-use-only dock and float at the northwest edge of Madrona Point provides boat access to Eastsound Village. Boaters can tie up here or anchor nearby and row to the dock to visit the village, which is an easy leg-stretching ¼ mile. The road leading to the dock also makes a nice hike from Eastsound Village. The rocky, madrona-draped headlands offer spectacular views of Fishing and Ship Bays, along with occasional rock-rib accesses to stony beaches. Walk slowly and enjoy the reward of rarely seen birds and colorful flowers.

THE NORTHWEST SHORE
Map 34

On the "outer shore" of Orcas Island, the gentle uplands roll smoothly to the sea, interrupted only by small rocky points and the larger Point Doughty. Sand and gravel beaches provide some of the best recreation on Orcas Island; however, there are no public accesses, aside from a few road ends.

Small boats or canoes launched from this side of Orcas Island can spend hours investigating the shoreline, stopping at Freeman Island and Point Doughty. ❀ Sucia Island is a tempting destination, lying only 4 nautical miles to the northeast, but it is recommended only for those experienced with open-water hazards, for there are reefs and tide rips along the way.

These same reefs and tide rips make this a popular salmon fishing grounds, where many anglers troll during summer months. The offshore reefs attract scuba divers who dive from boats at Parker Reef, Point Doughty, Raccoon Point, and along President Channel, finding swimming scallops and exceptionally large lingcod and cabazon. Free diving and snorkeling are good near the docks and bays of the resorts and on a series of rocky ledges between Freeman Island and the Orcas Island shore.

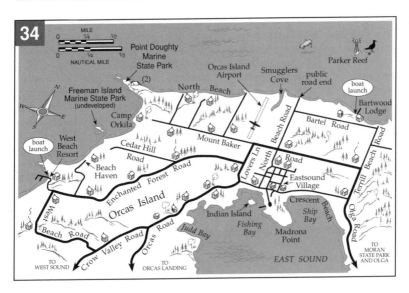

North Shore Resorts   Map 34

Boating • Paddling • Fishing • Scuba Diving • Beach Walking

Facilities: BARTWOOD LODGE: dock with float, launch ramp, restaurant, lodging; **NORTH BEACH ROAD:** boat put-in

🚐 To reach Bartwood Lodge, take North Beach Road north from Eastsound Village to Bartel Street. Here turn east and in ¾ mile reach Bartwood Estates. Resorts along the shore are reached by land from roads branching from West Beach and Mount Baker Roads. To reach the boat put-in, take North Beach Road north from Eastsound Village; ¼ mile past its intersection with Mount Baker Road, the road ends at a sand and cobble beach signed "Public shore. No overnight parking or camping."

🛥 West Beach is 10 nautical miles northeast of Roche Harbor, while North Beach is about 3 nautical miles farther.

Several commercial resorts along this side of the island have varying facilities and also have varying reactions to the wander-in public, depending on the nature of the resort. Because this shoreline provides the closest access to the popular marine state parks lying to the north, there are frequent demands on these businesses to launch boats and put in kayaks. Even though they are commercial businesses offering services to the public, they usually limit use of their land and facilities to paying customers.

On the north side of Orcas Island, the only spot that has boat launching is Bartwood Lodge. The former resort has been converted mostly to residential development; however, it has retained some of the resort facilities. Two other resorts, Smuggler's Villa and North Beach, are farther west along the shore. Facilities there are only for registered guests. Parker Reef, just offshore, and the shore east to Lawrence Point are prime fishing areas.

A public road end lies just east of the Orcas Island airport and Smuggler's Villa Resort. There is room here to park a half-dozen cars. The beach on either side of the road end is private. The gentle beach is suitable for launching hand-carried boats to explore the northern shoreline. The more skilled and adventurous can cross to Sucia Island, a scant 2 nautical miles away, beyond the menace of Parker Reef. Unfortunately, because cars may not park overnight by the roadside, kayakers must park elsewhere if they plan extended trips.

West Shore Resorts   Map 34

Camping • Boating • Paddling • Fishing • Scuba Diving • Beach Walking

Facilities: WEST BEACH RESORT: dock with float, boat launch ramp (fee), groceries, fast food, gas, fishing tackle and bait, guest moorage, cabins, campground, RV hookups, restrooms, pay showers, coin-op laundry, picnic tables, fireplaces, cabins, boat rental, scuba air

🚐 From the Orcas ferry landing, head north on Orcas Road West for 2 miles to the intersection with Deer Harbor Road. Turn left onto Deer Harbor Road, go 1 mile, and at a T-intersection, go north on Crow Valley Road. In 3½ miles, turn on

West Beach Road, which heads west and then north. As the road makes another right turn, heading east on Enchanted Forest Road, the signed side road to West Beach goes left.

🛥 West Beach is 11½ nautical miles from Friday Harbor; Sucia Island lies 5 nautical miles to the northeast.

West Beach Resort, on the west side of Orcas Island, provides facilities for boaters headed for offshore fishing grounds, scuba diving sites, or Sucia Island and points beyond.

The resort is especially popular with scuba divers, who dive north to Point Doughty and south along the shoreline to Lover's Cove. The small moorage basin is protected by a log breakwater that gives some respite from waves off President Channel.

A resort to the north, Beach Haven, has facilities only for its guests.

Freeman Island and Point Doughty Marine State Parks Map 34

Camping • Picnicking • Paddling • Fishing • Scuba Diving • Tidepools • Beach Walking

Facilities: FREEMAN ISLAND: none; **POINT DOUGHTY:** picnic tables, fire rings, 2 campsites, Cascadia Marine Trail site but no designated campsites, toilets; *no drinking water, no garbage collection*

Area: FREEMAN ISLAND: less than 1 acre; **POINT DOUGHTY:** 60 acres, 8260 feet of shoreline

🛥 Freeman Island is ¾ nautical mile north of West Beach Resort, and Point Doughty is another ¾ nautical mile; Sucia Island lies 3½ nautical miles to the northeast.

Freeman Island • Freeman Island, an undeveloped state park, is an eroded, narrow ridge of an island with a fringe of gnarled old trees. Perhaps eventually it will all wash away, but for now enjoy the meager little island, made

Freeman Island Marine State Park is a small islet.

beautiful by ravages of weather and time. The shores are very rocky; boat landing is best on the south side and west end. Scuba divers often dive in the reef extending to the west.

Freeman Island lies just 300 yards offshore of Orcas Island. Boaters frequently take day excursions to the island from West Beach Resort, Beach Haven, or Camp Orkila, all less than a mile away. Fires and overnight camping are not permitted.

Point Doughty • Point Doughty isn't an appealing anchorage, with kelp beds, tide rips, and submerged rocks in the vicinity, but for small boats that can be hauled up on the beach, it offers go-ashore camping near some of the best scuba diving to be found in the Northwest.

This State Parks-managed area is accessible to the public only by boat. A public trail from above was proposed at one time, but the idea was abandoned for fear that heavy use of such a trail would cause severe bank erosion and disturb eagles nesting in the area. Walking the beach at low tide from nearby areas is also prohibited. An overland path that reaches the point from YMCA Camp Orkila, to the south, is closed to public use.

Two campsites perch on the grassy slope above the beach, with stunning views across President Channel out to Boundary Pass. ❊ Offshore rocks can make landing boats on the beach a bit tricky; be prepared to wade. A wooden staircase leads from the beach to the bluff top.

Several generations of Northwest youngsters have had their first taste of the San Juans at YMCA Camp Orkila, which is on the west shore of Orcas Island, just south of Point Doughty. Since 1906, when the camp was founded, up to 3000 children each year have fished, swum, beach walked, sailed, canoed, hiked, and had wilderness camp-outs here, and have grown to love the islands. The camp's Marine Science Center educates campers on the local marine environment. The camp also has outstations on nearby islands, which older campers use on extended kayak and camping trips. Visitors who register at the camp's office may tour the grounds.

OBSTRUCTION AND PEAVINE PASSES
Map 35

Among an entire album of scenic treasures, Obstruction and Peavine Passes rank as sublime. On clear days ferry travelers in Harney Channel are treated to the sight of the ethereal cone of Mount Baker floating above Peavine Pass, with blue-gray layers of islands and hills stretching between.

Lying near the end of Rosario Strait, this doorway in the eastern wall of the San Juans serves boaters approaching the islands from Bellingham, which is 18 nautical miles northeast, and Vancouver, B.C., 45 nautical miles to the north. ❊ Obstruction Pass doglegs to the north around Obstruction Island and has submerged rocks lying near the edge of the channel; Peavine Pass, on the south, although narrower, is straight and easier to navigate. ❊ Currents in Obstruction and Peavine Passes can run in excess of 4 knots, and heavy tide rips occur east of Obstruction Island. Use care in small boats.

Obstruction Pass   Map 35
Boating • Paddling • Fishing

Facilities: OBSTRUCTION PASS: launch ramp; **LIEBER HAVEN RESORT:** marina, lodging, grocery store

To reach the launch ramp, follow Orcas Road toward Olga, turning east on Point Lawrence Road ¼ mile before reaching Olga; the road is signed to Doe Bay. Follow this road, turning south in another ½ mile onto Obstruction Pass Road. The road meanders down valleys and around hills, finally reaching Obstruction Pass 2 miles from the Point Lawrence Road intersection.

Obstruction Pass is 10 nautical miles northwest of Anacortes and 2 nautical miles from Olga, on Orcas Island.

A county boat launch ramp on Obstruction Pass provides the closest put-in for trailered boats seeking access to the east side of Orcas Island. A large parking lot adjacent to the fire station has a concrete ramp at its west side and an excellent county dock and float at its east side. The dock is for loading and unloading only—no overnight moorage. Property on either side of the launch facility is private, although that to the west contains a marina, resort, and small grocery store. The marina does not have guest moorages.

Boats put in here can explore westward to the state parks campground at the point and on into Buck Bay and East Sound. The small rock-walled bay immediately east of Obstruction Point is Spring Bay. The spectacular bed-and-breakfast inn gracing that shore includes guided kayak cruises as part of their accommodations package.

Spring Bay can be the starting point for excursions to Obstruction Pass and East Sound.

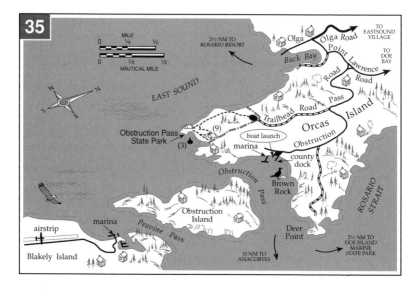

Eastward and north are Doe Island Marine State Park and Peapod Rocks. Brown Rock, lying in Obstruction Pass, is a bird sanctuary of the San Juan Islands Wilderness Area.

Obstruction Pass State Park   Map 35

Camping • Picnicking • Hiking • Boating • Paddling • Fishing • Shrimping • Beach Walking

Facilities: 9 campsites, Cascadia Marine Trail site but no designated campsites, picnic tables, fireplaces, toilets, 3 mooring buoys; *no drinking water, parking fee at trailhead*
Park area: 80 acres, 400 feet of public tidelands
Trail hiking distance: 1 mile round trip
Trail elevation gain: Negligible

To reach the trailhead to the campground, head east from Eastsound Village and turn east off Orcas Road onto Point Lawrence Road ¼ mile before reaching Olga. In ½ mile turn south on Obstruction Pass Road, which winds around an open valley, then circles a wooded hillside and heads south. As it curves east again 1 mile from the Point Lawrence Road intersection, Trailhead Road, a gravel road branching right, is signed to Obstruction Pass Recreation Site. Turn on this rough, narrow road and follow it for 1 more mile to the parking area at the trailhead. There's space here for about thirty cars (fee for parking).

By water, the park lies 1 nautical mile south of Olga on East Sound and ½ nautical mile west of the boat ramp on Obstruction Pass.

This forested point of land facing on Obstruction Pass is a favorite kayaking destination and gives backpackers and boaters alike an opportunity to camp

in seclusion above a quiet beach. The pebbled beach slopes sharply into the bay but offers a fine place to draw up small boats. At low water, explore tidepools along the rocky beaches framing either side of the bay.

From the parking area, the nearly level trail wanders for ½ mile through timber and along steep bluffs above East Sound before reaching the campground. Occasional short side spurs lead to outlooks on cliffs above the water. Campsites, picnic tables, and group sites are scattered about a timbered flat, some within view of the water. If hikers are looking for more exercise after the walk in, a loop trail circles the area through lush ferns and undergrowth. Overnight camping at the trailhead is not permitted.

A family checks out shallow rocks at Obstruction Pass State Park.

Three mooring buoys lie in the bay, and there is space for several more boats to drop anchor in the gravel bottom. It's a pleasant spot, with a nighttime view of brightly lit ferries in Harney Channel; however, during a strong southerly the anchorage might be a bit rough.

This facility, once maintained by the Department of Natural Resources, was threatened with closure in the state budget crunch of 2002. The legislature provided just enough funds for state parks to assume operation, but its future might be tenuous.

Doe Island Marine State Park Map 36

Camping • Picnicking • Boating • Paddling • Hiking • Fishing • Beach Walking • Scuba Diving

Facilities: 5 campsites, Cascadia Marine Trail site but no designated campsites, picnic tables, toilet, dock with float; *no drinking water, no garbage collection*
Park area: 6 acres, 2050 feet of shoreline on Rosario Strait
Trail hiking distance: ¼-mile loop
Trail elevation gain: 40 feet
⛴ The nearest boat launch is at Obstruction Pass, 2½ nautical miles to the south. The island a favorite stop for kayak tours.

Compared to the more spacious facilities of Sucia, Stuart, and Jones Islands, Doe Island is a "minipark," but it is a delight nonetheless. ❀ Deep-draft boats should approach the island from the east, as a tideflat extends out

Doe Island has campsites on low bluffs and a shallow cave for exploration.

from Orcas Island toward the west end of Doe Island. A dock with a 30-foot float sits on the north shore of the island. Water depth at the dock is 8 feet at mean low water, adequate for most craft except at very low tide. Buoys placed in the channel between Doe and Orcas Islands are not for public use; however, there is space to anchor. Small boats and kayaks can easily be landed behind the east point and on the gentle beaches of the park's south side, ✤ but be wary of rocks just offshore.

Campsites with fireplaces are spaced about the island—three in the timber and two in sunny clearings just above the south shore, with views across Rosario Strait to Cypress Island. A toilet is in the timber above the dock.

A trail circling the island on the bank above the beach leads to a rocky point that is festooned with flowers in spring. On the south side, the bluff has been undercut by waves, forming a high bank with an interesting cave to explore. Gulls and other seabirds often gather on the wave-washed beach rocks, flying up in startled flocks when approached too closely. The trail on the southwest side wends through trees above a high, steep bank with an understory of salal, kinnikinnick, moss, and Indian paintbrush.

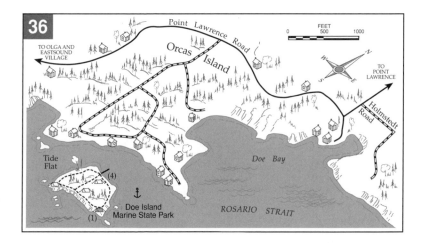

Doe Bay, ¹/₂ mile to the northeast, has, over the years, been an on-again, off-again commercial resort. In 2003 it became a private retreat center for Ayurvedic medicine, an ancient healing science. The bay's long history has included an Indian fishing village, a home for a spiritual movement called Polarity, and several incarnations of laid-back resorts.

Peapod Rocks Map 30

Wildlife Watching • Scuba Diving

Facilities: None

The rocks lie 1 nautical mile offshore from Doe Bay and 3 nautical miles from Obstruction Pass.

This mile-long chain of islets serves two "levels" of interest. Below the sea is a State Parks Underwater Recreation Area, frequently used by scuba divers. The grassy rocks protruding above water are a part of the San Juan Islands Wilderness Area, attracting flocks of seabirds who congregate and nest there. Bald eagles also frequent the rocks.

The largest of the islands is North Peapod, which has a navigational beacon. At the opposite end of the chain is, appropriately, South Peapod Rock. Stretching in between is an assortment of rocks that appear or disappear with the tide.

The underwater area from Doe Bay to Peapod Rocks is highly regarded among scuba divers for its wide range of terrain and difficulty, from the protected waters of the bay to the deep, current-swept walls of the rocks. Landing boats on the rocks is prohibited because intrusion is disturbing to nesting birds. This is a favorite haul-out area for seals and sea lions, which can often be spotted sunning on the rocks or in the water nearby. Again, too-close observation by man can startle the animals and cause them to leave their resting and warming grounds.

chapter eight

Moran State Park

Camping • Picnicking • Hiking • Fishing • Swimming • Boating • View Tower • Birdwatching • Wildflowers • Horseback Riding

Facilities: MORAN STATE PARK: 151 standard campsites, 15 primitive bicycle campsites, picnic tables, stoves, kitchen shelters, drinking water, restrooms, showers, toilets, RV dump station, 2 unguarded swimming beaches, 2 boat launches (gasoline motors are not permitted), boat rentals, interpretive displays, 31 miles of hiking trails, rental vacation home, day-use parking fee; **ENVIRONMENTAL LEARNING CENTER:** dining hall, dock, 9 cabins, restrooms with showers, infirmary

Park area: 5249 acres, 1800 feet of saltwater shoreline on the Strait of Georgia, 45,300 feet of freshwater lake shoreline

From Orcas Landing, travel north on Orcas Road to Eastsound Village, loop around the end of the sound, and head south again. The route is well signed. Distance from Orcas Landing to the park entrance is 13 miles.

Boaters who are guests at Rosario Resort can reach the park by hiking the trail from the resort, as described in Chapter Seven, Orcas Island.

DRIVE, BIKE, OR HIKE—NO MATTER HOW YOU GET THERE, Moran State Park is a "must see" for anyone touring the San Juan Islands. Oddly, though, on this water-oriented island there is no easy way for people arriving via boat to reach the park. Unless they are willing to make the steep hike up from Rosario or rent cars or motor scooters at the resort, they must be content with the many magnificent views of Mount Constitution visible from the waterways. From the northern reaches of Rosario Strait, the lookout tower on the 2407-foot-high summit is visible to the naked eye. Boaters can gaze up and admire the scenic mountain and realize that landlubbers in the tower are admiring their scenic craft cutting the blue waters.

Moran is the fourth largest Washington State park. Thirty-six hundred acres of park land was a gift to the state in 1920 by wealthy shipbuilder Robert Moran, who built his lavish estate, Rosario, on Cascade Bay, just below. Over time, additional property was acquired until today the park contains more than 5000 acres. Much of the park development, including the picturesque old timber and stone picnic shelters, was accomplished in the 1930s by the Depression-era Civilian Conservation Corps (CCC).

Camping • Four pleasant car-camping areas, with a total of 151 campsites, are located on Cascade and Mountain Lakes; an additional fifteen sites are

Opposite: The Mount Constitution lookout tower has views of the park's forested slopes and distant Rosario Strait.

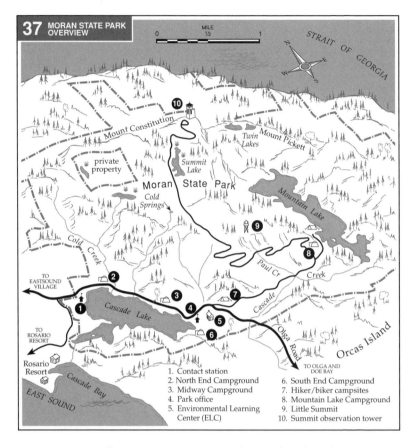

37 MORAN STATE PARK OVERVIEW

1. Contact station
2. North End Campground
3. Midway Campground
4. Park office
5. Environmental Learning Center (ELC)
6. South End Campground
7. Hiker/biker campsites
8. Mountain Lake Campground
9. Little Summit
10. Summit observation tower

in a primitive walk-in camping area east of Cascade Lake. The maximum site length is 45 feet, and some areas and campsites will not accommodate large RVs.

Because of the ferry trip, many visitors stay several days, and campgrounds are often filled every night throughout the summer. Campsites can be reserved from Memorial Day to Labor Day. With more than 60,000 campers per month in prime season, chances of finding an empty campsite without a reservation during this period are slim.

Information regarding state park reservations can be obtained online at the parks website, *www.parks.wa.gov*, or by calling (888) 226-7688 (CAMPOUT). When park campgrounds are full, a notice is usually posted at the Anacortes ferry terminal. If this occurs, go elsewhere on the mainland, or telephone ahead from the ferry terminal to find accommodations at commercial campgrounds or motels on one of the islands.

A group camp, the Environmental Learning Center (ELC), near the south end of Cascade Lake, is available for large organized parties, by reservation.

This camp can accommodate up to 155 persons; a fee is charged for its use. The ELC has a kitchen, dining hall, restrooms, showers, cabins with bunks, and its own stretch of beach with a dock on the lake, making it ideal for church or scout groups or family get-togethers. A fully equipped rental vacation home, available for rent separately, has two bedrooms and two baths. It shares the ELC dock and beach.

Bicycles and Horses in the Park • Moran State Park is popular with bicyclists. Although the steep Mount Constitution road would severely tax someone who's out of shape, many cyclists do make the trip to the top and ride down from there (some cheat a bit by having a truck tote the cycles to the summit). Brakes must (repeat, MUST) be in good shape for the downhill run on either road or trails. Drinking water is available at Cascade Lake, Mountain Lake Landing, and the summit. Check with park rangers for current restrictions on mountain bike and equestrian use of the trails. None of the park campsites accommodate horses.

Park Wildlife • More than twenty different mammals and a hundred species of birds are found in the state park. Rabbits, raccoons, or wild turkeys (which are not native, but were introduced) might be seen near the roads, campgrounds, and lakes. Black-tailed deer occasionally cross roads; drive carefully to avoid hitting them.

For the best wildlife viewing, take to the trails and walk quietly, watching and listening for telltale movement, the chattering of squirrels, and the calls of birds. There are no bears, wolves, or poisonous snakes, although bears and elk once did roam here. Lakeshore trails are excellent places to spot river otter, muskrat, and mink, especially at dusk. Watch for burrows, tunnels, and otter slides at the water's edge.

For the safety of wildlife and the convenience of other park visitors, pets must be on leashes no longer than 8 feet and must be under control at all times while in the park, including in the backcountry. Pets illegally unleashed on trails have killed fawns and other wild animals. It is best to leave your pet at home and improve the outdoor experience for everyone.

Hiking Trails • More than 30 miles of trails lace Moran State Park. Most are enclosed by forest, but at times, especially on the upper trails, the timber opens and rocky, moss-covered bluffs protrude to give superb

Black-tailed deer are often seen in Moran State Park.

views north, west, or south. Matia, Barnes, Clark, Lummi, Cypress, Blakely, and Lopez Islands lie below, and on clear days the snowy mass of Mount Baker rises in the distance. All trails in the park are described in this chapter under the area in which they originate. *Note:* Trail numbers in the hike descriptions are keyed to maps.

Trail maintenance at Moran State Park is sporadic on the less popular trails. In marshy areas, brush and nettles might overgrow the path and in some spots hikers might encounter downed timber. Before hiking the more remote trail segments, check with park rangers on trail conditions.

Most hikes are described the easy way—beginning at the top and going downhill. Many variations are possible, with side trails leading to alternate

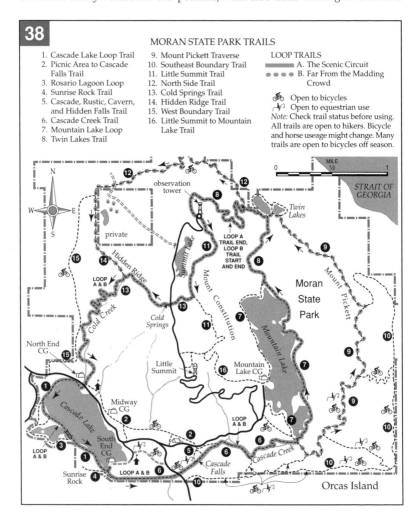

38

MORAN STATE PARK TRAILS

1. Cascade Lake Loop Trail
2. Picnic Area to Cascade Falls Trail
3. Rosario Lagoon Loop
4. Sunrise Rock Trail
5. Cascade, Rustic, Cavern, and Hidden Falls Trail
6. Cascade Creek Trail
7. Mountain Lake Loop
8. Twin Lakes Trail
9. Mount Pickett Traverse
10. Southeast Boundary Trail
11. Little Summit Trail
12. North Side Trail
13. Cold Springs Trail
14. Hidden Ridge Trail
15. West Boundary Trail
16. Little Summit to Mountain Lake Trail

LOOP TRAILS
A. The Scenic Circuit
B. Far From the Madding Crowd

Open to bicycles
Open to equestrian use
Note: Check trail status before using. All trails are open to hikers. Bicycle and horse useage might change. Many trails are open to bicycles off season.

destinations. One nice advantage of trails in the park is that groups of hikers with varied stamina, such as families with several children, can hike together for a distance, then some can choose an easy exit back to civilization while those with more endurance can continue on a more demanding route. A "designated driver" can drop off hikers at the top and pick them up at points along the way.

Many trips described here are one way, beginning at one point on the road and emerging farther along. The lower park road between the two park entrances also serves as a main Orcas Island county road, connecting Eastsound Village with Olga and Doe Bay. Traffic on the county road travels fast, even during busy summer times; use care when walking alongside the road or crossing it.

Overnight camping is not permitted anywhere in the park except at established campgrounds. On long hikes carry water; stream and lake water might contain harmful bacteria or microorganisms. When nettles and brushbeating are anticipated, wear long pants and carry a stick to push vegetation aside.

The fire hazard can be extreme, especially in open meadows; be sure all cigarettes are properly extinguished, do not smoke while moving on trails, and do not toss cigarettes from cars.

More than 30 miles of trails lace Moran State Park. Some are open for bicycle and equestrian use.

CASCADE LAKE
Map 39

Usually the busiest place in Moran State Park, Cascade Lake boasts the park's three largest campgrounds (North End, Midway, and South End) and a day-use recreation center. All the campgrounds have spacious, level campsites with fire grates and picnic tables. Restrooms and water faucets are centrally located; Midway and North End campgrounds have showers in the restrooms.

Just inside the park entrance is a booth where campground reservations can be confirmed. If the entry registration booth is not open, self-register at whichever campgrounds are open.

North End Campground, with fifty-two campsites, is ¼ mile inside the park's west entrance on a rise above the road and lake. A few hundred feet down the road from North End Campground, facing on Cascade Lake, are the picnic area and recreation center, where there are picnic tables, children's play equipment, and rustic picnic shelters with wood-burning stoves. Because it is so shallow, only 15 feet at its deepest, in summer the 170-acre lake warms enough for comfortable swimming. A beach has roped-off sections for wading and swimming, although there are no lifeguards. On hot summer days the swimming area is crowded, and parking in the vicinity can be difficult.

Rowboats and foot-operated paddle boats are rented at Cascade Lake in summer. Private boats may be launched at a ramp at lower Midway Campground;

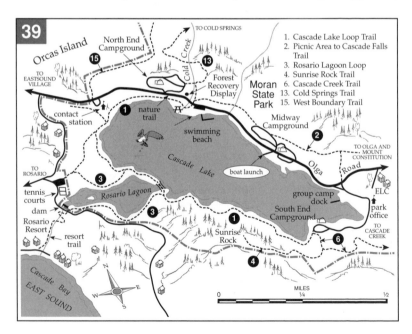

1. Cascade Lake Loop Trail
2. Picnic Area to Cascade Falls Trail
3. Rosario Lagoon Loop
4. Sunrise Rock Trail
6. Cascade Creek Trail
13. Cold Springs Trail
15. West Boundary Trail

In summer, shallow Cascade Lake warms enough for swimming and wading.

gasoline motors are banned. Visitors enjoy an exploratory paddle of the lake, peeking into tiny bays and gazing up at the heights of surrounding cliffs. Trout fishing is popular, from either boat or shore; the bridge across Rosario Lagoon, reached by trail from either end of Cascade Lake, is sometimes a successful spot. The lake is stocked with rainbows, cutthroats, and silvers every June. Observe state Department of Fish and Wildlife regulations on licenses, season, and limits.

Midway Campground, ¾ mile farther south along the lake, has forty-nine campsites lining both sides of the road, with some on the shore. Smaller South End Campground, located on a spur road around the far end of the lake, has seventeen campsites, some of them walk-in for bicyclists and backpackers.

A primitive camp area, with fifteen informal sites for bicycle and walk-in camping, is situated away from the lake on the north side of the Mount Constitution road, ¼ mile east of the county road intersection. This campground has only toilets, and has no drinking water.

FOREST RECOVERY DISPLAY. On January 24, 1972, a violent storm with winds up to 100 mph wracked the San Juan Islands. At Moran State Park, hundreds of trees were downed, some of them century-old patriarchs. Park personnel spent months in clean-up and repair of facilities and trails. Near Cascade Lake, a 200-foot, 200-year-old western red cedar toppled by the winds has been left undisturbed as a reminder of the storm and an illustration of forest recovery.

Find the interpretive exhibit behind the information booth and north of the large picnic shelter. A billboard display describes the storm. The giant tree is a progressive exhibit; witness how nature, the original "ecological recycler," reclaims its own products.

Cascade Lake Loop Trail *(1)* Maps 38 and 39
Trail hiking distance: 2³/₄-mile loop via South End Campground; 4-mile loop via Cascade Falls
Trail elevation gain: negligible via South End Campground; 50 feet via Cascade Falls

This nearly level hike, with ever-changing perspectives of the lake and mountain, is enjoyable whether done only in part or walked as a 2³/₄-mile trail and road circuit. The trail circles the southwest side of the lake on a bank 30 feet above the water, with very few accesses to the lake itself.

Begin the hike west of the picnic area at Cascade Lake, passing through a marshy area bordered by a picturesque split-rail fence. The trail wanders along a rocky bluff where weathered Douglas-firs frame the lake views and droop low over the water. At a fork in a few hundred yards, a spur heads west to the Rosario Resort tennis courts. At another fork less than 1¹/₄ miles beyond, the right-hand trail (3) goes along the edge of Rosario Lagoon.

Another 300 yards down the lakeshore, a rustic log bridge spans the mouth of the lagoon, and farther south along the lake are good views of the mountain summit. Belted kingfishers and shy, long-legged great blue herons might be spotted along the shore; watch also for signs of muskrat and otter. Muskrat burrows, which resemble those of a beaver, can be seen in the water. A species of large snails found in abundance along the shores of Cascade Lake is a dietary staple for these muskrats; look for piles of empty shells.

Reach South End Campground 1¹/₂ miles from the trailhead. Follow the road past the ELC and service buildings to the junction with the paved county road. Here a short spur trail heads uphill to meet the Picnic Area to Cascade Falls Trail (2). Follow this trail west to return to the picnic area.

For a slightly longer loop hike, pick up the Cascade Creek Trail (6) by campsite 17 of South End Campground and follow it for about ³/₄ mile until it emerges at Olga Road. Cross the road and catch the trail that continues uphill for an additional ¹/₄ mile to Cascade Falls. Follow the left-hand fork, which leads to the Cascade Falls parking area.

At the parking area, cross the Mount Constitution road and pick up the east end of the Picnic Area to Cascade Falls Trail (2) as it heads west, traverses a steep sidehill past the primitive camping area, and continues on to Midway Campground. From here the trail proceeds west to reach the road near the information display opposite the picnic area.

Rosario Lagoon Loop *(3)* Maps 38 and 39
Trail hiking distance: ³/₄-mile loop from Cascade Lake Loop intersection
Trail elevation gain: Negligible

Detour from the Cascade Lake Loop onto a path by the quiet arm of the lake that includes probably the best birdwatching in the park, as waterfowl often congregate on the peaceful lagoon. To reach it, hike the Cascade Lake Trail around the north end of the lake to a fork ³/₄ mile from the picnic area. Rosario Lagoon can be seen through the trees on the right.

The right-hand fork of the trail leads along the north edge of the lagoon.

A nearly level trail edges Cascade Lake.

The quiet water is a popular stopover for migratory waterfowl; mergansers, goldeneyes, buffleheads, and ring-necked ducks are but a few of the many birds that call at the lagoon in fall, winter, and spring.

The trail touches the edge of the lagoon and then wanders away through thick woods, terminating in a parking lot north of the Rosario Resort tennis courts. Many years ago Cascade Lake was only a large marshy area. Before the turn of the century, the dam that created the lake was built to provide hydroelectric power for Rosario, below.

From the tennis court parking lot, take the paved road south, past the courts, to the east side of the dam. On the right a trail can be seen dropping down the steep slope to Rosario. Look for a small sign to the left of the road that points to the trail that continues around the lagoon. If the route is lost in the brush at the outlet of the lagoon, follow close to the water's edge until it again becomes clear. Lake water laps at the hiker's boots; salal and sword fern crowd the trail. Rejoin the Cascade Lake Trail at the log bridge.

Sunrise Rock Trail *(4)* Maps 38 and 39
Trail hiking distance: 1½ miles round trip
Trail elevation gain: 500 feet

A short but steep climb leads to views down to the shimmering water of Cascade Lake and across to the lookout tower of Little Summit. This trail receives only sporadic maintenance and might require some routefinding.

Find the Cascade Creek Trail (6) by campsite 17 of South End Campground and follow it out of South End Campground. In ¼ mile the Sunrise Rock Trail branches right, drops slightly downhill, and then begins the climb to the viewpoint, gaining 350 feet in ¼ mile. In cool, virgin forest the trail passes several ancient Douglas-firs nearly 6 feet in diameter, showing the ravages of forest fires, lightning, and woodpeckers.

Where the trail becomes sketchy, look for an apparent clearing in the trees around the hill on the right. A mossy ledge provides views of the lake and mountain.

Sunrise Rock affords high views of Cascade Lake and small sailboats breaking its surface.

CASCADE CREEK
Map 40

Cascade Creek, the outlet of Mountain Lake, offers scenic waterfalls, woodland flowers, and (perhaps) wildlife just a short distance from the road. Even novice hikers can negotiate the easy trails; however, they are often muddy, so wear sturdy shoes. The stream is closed to fishing.

The odd little American dipper, or "water ouzel," might be seen here from September through April along the banks of the stream. The plump, slate-gray bird, slightly larger than a wren, dives into the swift-flowing water and walks along the creek bottom to catch aquatic insects, invertebrates, and small fish. A unique adaptation—flaps covering its nostrils—enables it to survive underwater.

Cascade, Rustic, Cavern, and Hidden Falls Trail (5) Maps 38 and 40
Trail hiking distance: ¹/₂- to 1-mile loop, depending on destination
Trail elevation gain: 200 feet

A chain of waterfalls on Cascade Creek can be reached by a short spur trail from the road, or they can be viewed as part of a longer scenic jaunt from Mountain Lake to Cascade Lake. For the shorter trip, park at the trailhead on the south side of Olga Road, ¹/₂ mile from the Mount Constitution road intersection. Be careful not to block the service road that goes straight ahead. The trail sign directs hikers first to Rustic Falls; however, the unmarked, abandoned road to the right of the trail sign can be followed directly to Cascade Falls in ¹/₄ mile, with 130 feet of elevation loss. Here it meets the Cascade Creek Trail (6).

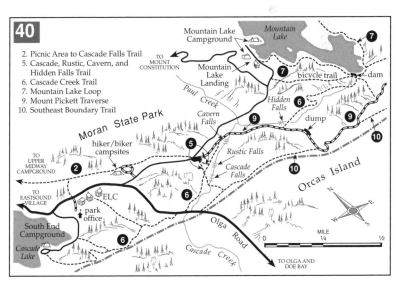

40

2. Picnic Area to Cascade Falls Trail
5. Cascade, Rustic, Cavern, and Hidden Falls Trail
6. Cascade Creek Trail
7. Mountain Lake Loop
9. Mount Pickett Traverse
10. Southeast Boundary Trail

Mountain Lake Campground
Mountain Lake
TO MOUNT CONSTITUTION
Mountain Lake Landing
Paul Creek
bicycle trail
dam
Hidden Falls
Moran State Park
Cavern Falls
dump
hiker/biker campsites
TO UPPER MIDWAY CAMPGROUND
Rustic Falls
Cascade Falls
Orcas Island
TO EASTSOUND VILLAGE
ELC
park office
South End Campground
Olga Road
Cascade Lake
Cascade Creek
TO OLGA AND DOE BAY
MILE
0   ¹/₄   ¹/₂

Cascade Falls fans across a cliff and then drops into a shallow pool.

Although the hike is worthwhile any time of the year, the waterfalls are at their best in winter and spring when rainfall swells the lakes and streams. By late summer of a dry year they might be reduced to a trickle. At Cascade Falls, the most spectacular of the four, the water fans widely across a 100-foot-high cliff, dropping into a tiny pool at its base. For a head-on view of the cataract, cross the stream cautiously on slanting (and slippery) downed logs.

The trail switchbacks to the top of the falls, then levels out in the brushy valley of Cascade Creek, where salal and salmonberry overhang the stream. In spring you might find mushrooms and wildflowers along the trail, but by summer dense patches of nettles discourage off-trail wandering.

The upper falls are much smaller than Cascade Falls but lovely nonetheless. Rustic Falls is about 500 feet from Cascade Falls, and ¼ mile farther is the narrow plume of Cavern Falls. Just beyond Cavern Falls, the trail merges with the dirt service road; continue on for ¼ mile to Hidden Falls, located below the footbridge at the Mountain Lake Loop (7) intersection. You can follow the service road back to the parking area on the return trip.

Cascade Creek Trail (6) Maps 38 and 40
Trail hiking distance: 2¾ miles one way to South End Campground; 4¼ miles one way via Cascade Lake
Trail elevation loss: Either trail, 500 feet

For the longer hike from Mountain Lake to Cascade Lake, find the signed trailhead at Mountain Lake Landing, across from the park cabin. The level path heads south along the lakeshore and passes a spur trail from Mountain Lake Road.

Reach the concrete dam at the lake outlet ½ mile from the trailhead; drop down the side of the dam to the wooden footbridge crossing Cascade Creek and turn right at a signed trail intersection at the end of the bridge. Downstream 200 yards is a pretty spot where the water cascades in foamy white rivulets and an unusual L-shaped bridge crosses the creek. From here the trail occasionally leaves the creek for short distances only to switchback steeply down the drainage and rejoin the creek. At a third bridge, at Hidden Falls, 1½ miles from Mountain Lake Landing, join the Mount Pickett service road, then leave it in another ½ mile where the main trail branches left.

Pause to enjoy scenic Cavern, Rustic, and Cascade Falls tumbling down the slope. Sections of an old wooden aqueduct, still in evidence at spots along the trail, are part of the park's original water system. The route crosses the county road near the south park entrance, 2 miles via trail from Mountain Lake Landing. Find the continuation of the trail, which might be unsigned, slightly up the road to the west.

Cascade Creek heads south out of the park, paralleled by the county road, but the trail continues west through a timbered flat, passing giant, century-old Douglas-firs. Walk quietly and watch for Douglas squirrels, pileated woodpeckers, and black-tailed deer in the open forest.

Avoid an unmarked spur trail to the right leading to the group camp and continue on the left fork through brush and, in spring, colorful displays of wildflowers. A short distance before reaching the lake, signs at another trail intersection point left to Sunrise Rock (4), straight ahead to the Cascade Lake Loop Trail (1), and right to South End Campground. By taking the right-hand spur, you soon will see the inviting blue water of Cascade Lake and then shortly reach the campground.

Energetic hikers might wish to extend the hike by continuing straight ahead at the last intersection and following the trail on the south side of Cascade Lake, arriving at the picnic area at the north end of the lake in another 1½ miles.

MOUNTAIN LAKE LANDING
Map 41

Lying a bit off the main thoroughfare, Mountain Lake does not receive as much tourist attention as popular Cascade Lake. It therefore offers more solitude to those who are willing to leave their cars to enjoy its crystal waters and level, tree-cloaked shoreline.

To reach the lake, head east in the park on the county road to the Olga–Mount Constitution road intersection and go left toward Mount Constitution; 2 miles from the intersection take a right-hand fork, which is signed to Mountain Lake Landing. The road ends in ½ mile at a small parking lot. A vehicle-accessible campground with seven campsites lies in a hollow immediately west of the parking area; eleven additional walk-in sites are a short distance from the road, on a small peninsula overlooking the lake.

The long, 198-acre lake fills a narrow green valley trough between Mount Pickett and Mount Constitution. Rainbow, cutthroat, silver, and Eastern brook trout stocked in this deep, cold lake each spring make it a popular fishing spot. The best fishing is from boats; they can be rented at a boat dock below the parking area. Or bring your own for fishing—or just for a tranquil paddle and magnificent views of Mount Constitution. Launch boats on the north side of the peninsula at Mountain Lake Campground; gasoline motors are not permitted. Pack a lunch and go ashore on one of four miniature islands in the lake for an hour of quiet reverie.

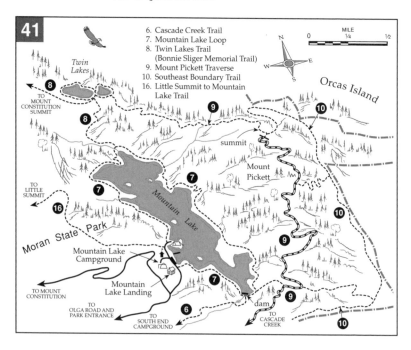

Mountain Lake Loop (7) Maps 38 and 41
Trail hiking distance: 3½-mile loop
Trail elevation gain: 50 feet

A nearly level hike that circles the shore of Mountain Lake is highlighted by a unique view of the summit of Mount Constitution. A counterclockwise route around the lake is recommended so the prime views of the mountain are ahead, rather than at your back.

The trail begins south of Mountain Lake Campground, contours the lakeside, and in ½ mile crosses the outlet of the lake on a bridge below a concrete dam. Just beyond the dam a right-hand fork of the trail turns down Cascade Creek (6), while the main trail continues straight ahead along the shore. Avoid a spur, branching to the right a few hundred feet east of the dam, that joins the Mount Pickett Traverse (9).

The long summit ridge of Mount Constitution rises above the lake. Little Summit can be seen on the left and the stone observation tower of the main summit far on the right. Below the summit, precipitous 1000-foot cliffs show their dramatic profile.

Look for bald and golden eagles, hawks, and ospreys soaring in the updrafts near the mountain. Several pairs of ospreys are believed to nest in the vicinity, although others summer here. The same factors of population, pollution, and pesticides that threaten bald eagles have severely reduced the osprey population. In addition, bald eagles frequently steal fish ospreys have caught and generally harass them, at times causing them to leave. Ospreys, or sea hawks, which resemble small white-breasted eagles, favor the heights of Mount Constitution, with its remote nesting sites and fish-filled lakes.

At the north end of Mountain Lake, 2¼ miles from the trailhead, a trail branch goes right, to Twin Lakes (8). Continue along the Mountain Lake shore, with views across the lake to wooded Mount Pickett, named for the commander of U.S. forces in the San Juans during the Pig War boundary dispute of 1859 to 1872.

Trail's end is reached at the parking lot at Mountain Lake Landing, 1¼ miles from the Twin Lakes Trail intersection. The only appreciable

Ospreys, known in the football crowd as seahawks, frequent the heights of Mount Constitution. Photo: Bob and Ira Spring elevation gain of the hike is midway around the lake, where the trail climbs 50 feet above the water to skirt a rocky cliff.

Twin Lakes Trail (from Mountain Lake) (8)   Maps 38 and 41
Trail hiking distance: 2½ miles one way to Twin Lakes, 4 miles one way to summit
Trail elevation gain: 190 feet to lakes, 1490 feet to summit

Tucked away on a timbered shoulder of Mount Constitution, a pair of small lakes is the destination for one of the park's most pleasant hikes. During fishing season, anglers will want to take a fly rod to try for rainbow and cutthroat in the chilly spring-fed waters of the larger of the two lakes. The smaller lake is not stocked, and the stream joining the two lakes is too small for trout to navigate.

This trail and its continuation from Twin Lakes to the summit of Mount Constitution have been designated as the Bonnie Sliger Memorial Trail, to honor a young woman who died in 1977 in a tragic fall at Doe Bay. She was a popular Youth Conservation Corps supervisor who had spent much time working with youngsters on trail maintenance in the park. The more strenuous trail from the lakes to the summit is described in the Mount Constitution section.

From the trailhead by the park cabin north of Mountain Lake Campground, the wide, level path (7) meanders along the lakeshore for 1¼ miles to the north end of the lake. Leave the lake at a signed trail junction, following the Twin Lakes Trail (8) along a brook. In a stand of alder you might find scattered remains of an ancient log cabin, possibly built by Civil War draft dodgers who are said to have lived in the area. Big Twin Lake is reached just short of a mile from the trail intersection.

Trails circle the shores of both lakes. The edges of the lakes are fairly overgrown with trees to the waterline, with only a few spots where the lakeshore itself is easily accessible. Breaks in the enclosing timber permit glimpses of the summit of Mount Constitution. The distance around Big Twin Lake is about ½ mile; around Little Twin Lake is slightly less. The branch of the trail headed to the summit goes west on the south side of Big Twin Lake.

Mountain Lake lies in a valley below the summit of Mount Constitution.

Mount Pickett Traverse *(9)* Maps 38 and 41
Trail hiking distance: 5 miles one way
Trail elevation gain: 1250 feet

A long trek combining a trail and an abandoned road can be used as part of an ambitious around-the-park excursion. Begin the hike at the Cascade Falls pullout on the Mount Constitution road, ½ mile east of Orcas Road intersection. Follow the dirt service road east past Hidden Falls and the intersection of the Cascade Creek Trail (6). The road first climbs gradually but steadily, then levels a bit at a flat near Mountain Lake, where a spur heads left to the Mountain Lake Loop (7). Here the road begins to climb in earnest, switchbacking up the steep arm of the mountain. Tall second-growth timber limits views to a few tantalizing glimpses between the trees of distant blue water.

The road again levels somewhat at 1600 feet elevation and near a large marsh on the left, a spur of the Southeast Boundary Trail (10) branches east. The 1750-foot summit of Mount Pickett is finally reached 3½ miles from the Cascade Falls trailhead. Now the road continues steadily downhill to the northwest for another mile before narrowing into a footpath. The trail continues for ½ mile farther to the shore of Little Twin Lake.

The nature of the forest changes dramatically upon crossing the Mount Pickett summit. The south slope consists mainly of second-growth fir and cedar, with typical Cascades-type underbrush. North of the summit a verdant carpet of moss coats the open ground between huge trunks of towering old-growth cedar spanning overhead in cathedral-like arches, with stands of alder around marshy areas.

Total distance from Cascade Falls to Twin Lakes is 5 miles; elevation gain from the falls to the summit is 1250 feet, with 650 feet lost on the descent to Twin Lakes. From Twin Lakes, hikers can return to the road via the short but very steep trail to the summit of Mount Constitution (8), 1½ miles more, or the gentle, 2¼-mile longer way, which follows the Twin Lakes Trail (8) to Mountain Lake and then continues on the trail along the west shore of Mountain Lake (7) to the road. For those who prefer more downhill and less uphill, hike the trail in the opposite direction, starting at either Mountain Lake or the summit of Mount Constitution.

Southeast Boundary Trail *(10)* Maps 38 and 41
Trail hiking distance: 8½ miles one way
Trail elevation gain: 1300 feet with many ups and downs

One of the longest and most strenuous trails was originally built during the 1930s by the CCC; after many years of disuse it was reclaimed by trail crews in 1987. The upper trailhead for the Southeast Boundary Trail heads east from the Mount Pickett Traverse (9) at a switchback 100 yards south of the top of Mount Pickett, as described previously. The path curves around the east side of the mountain summit, dropping through a forest of open old-growth cedar. In ½ mile the route swings to the southeast and begins a long traverse south, descending gradually at first, then more abruptly as it crosses steep sidehills supporting thick stands of western hemlock. Splendid views north and east at a few outcroppings reveal a scattering of islands below and Mount Baker towering in the distance.

In a clearing at the head of a drainage, 1¾ miles from the trailhead, the trail meets a short spur descending from the Mount Pickett road (9). This spur leaves the Mount Pickett road near a large marsh on the lower shoulder south of the summit and then picks its way down a precipitous hillside to join the main Southeast Boundary Trail. Total length of the spur trail is ½ mile; elevation loss is 600 feet.

From this junction, the Southeast Boundary Trail continues south through a series of ups and downs (mainly downs) to arrive at the park's southeast boundary, 1¼ miles from the spur trail intersection. Here is a choice, as the trail offers two forks; unfortunately, both climb relentlessly uphill. The right fork ascends 550 feet in little more than a mile to join the Mount Pickett service road (9) 100 yards uphill from its intersection with the Mountain Lake spur trail.

The left fork climbs west along the southern boundary of the park. At 1¾ miles from the trail fork it reaches a junction with a short path leading north to the Cascade Falls parking area. In another ¼ mile the trail reaches its southern terminus at the county road, at the park's east boundary.

The Name Game

The U.S. Exploration Expedition of 1838–1842, commanded by Lieutenant Charles Wilkes, named Mount Constitution after the famous American frigate. In a fit of patriotism, Wilkes chose to name all of the San Juan Islands "the Navy Archipelago," and began flinging names commemorating the officers and ships of the War of 1812 at every bit of land and water in sight. It might be that he was unaware of the Spanish and British names already given to many of the landmarks, or (more likely) he felt American names were more suitable, because the United States was attempting to establish claim to the region.

In Wilkes's scheme, Lopez and Orcas Islands were named Chauncy and Hull Islands, in honor of two U.S. Navy commodores. East Sound was designated Old Ironside Inlet, the nickname of the USS *Constitution*, which Hull commanded, and West Sound was Guerrier Bay, for the British warship that Hull defeated. The Wasp Islands were named for an American warship that distinguished itself during the War of 1812, and Jones Island to the north was named for the ship's commander, Jacob Jones.

Five years later a British surveying expedition, led by Captain Henry Kellett, restored many of the original Spanish and British names. A number of Wilkes's names were retained, however, including Blakely, Decatur, James, Jones, Frost, Shaw, Clark, and Watmough (all honoring U.S. naval officers)—and also, of course, Mount Constitution. Old Ironside Inlet, fortunately, did not survive.

Total distance of the longest trail choice is 5 miles, not including the 3¹/₂-mile hike up the Mount Pickett Trail to reach the Southeast Boundary trailhead. Elevation difference is 1300 feet, with much more elevation gained and lost en route because of trail ups and downs.

MOUNT CONSTITUTION
Map 42

Rising nearly ¹/₂ mile above the surrounding sea, Mount Constitution is a dramatic landmark recognizable from many points throughout the San Juan Islands. The expansive view from the summit and the fascinating old stone tower make it the culmination of most tourists' visits to the San Juans.

From October to April the road to the top of the mountain is gated at the Olga Road intersection at 5:00 P.M., except during fishing season, when it is blocked above Mountain Lake, allowing early morning access to the lake for anglers. From June through August, the road is kept open until 10:00 P.M. to accommodate late-day hikers and tourists who stay on the mountain to enjoy spectacular sunsets from the summit.

The Mount Constitution road leaves the county road 1¹/₄ miles east of the main park entrance; in another mile it begins the upward climb to the top of the mountain. Narrow, with steep switchbacks and hairpin curves, it is not recommended for trailers, buses, or large mobile homes. Halfway up, at the end of a switchback, is a small pullout space with dramatic views down to Cascade Lake, the twin summits of Entrance Mountain, East Sound, and Spencer Spit, on Lopez Island.

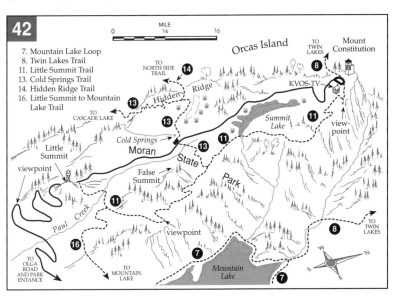

7. Mountain Lake Loop
8. Twin Lakes Trail
11. Little Summit Trail
13. Cold Springs Trail
14. Hidden Ridge Trail
16. Little Summit to Mountain Lake Trail

At Little Summit the road levels out and traverses the long plateau leading to the true summit. Total distance from the park entrance to the summit parking lot is 6 miles. Buildings and radio towers just below the observation tower are relay facilities for KVOS-TV, Bellingham.

LITTLE SUMMIT. Views rivaling those from the observation tower on the higher main summit look down to Cascade Lake and Rosario Resort and out to the symmetrical humps of Entrance Mountain. Beyond are Shaw, San Juan, and Lopez Islands, and, in the far distance, above the Strait of Juan de Fuca, the white peaks of the Olympic Mountains.

As the Mount Constitution road completes its last switchback and reaches the summit plateau, a pullout on the east side of the road provides parking space for a few cars. Walk 500 feet up the trail to an open viewpoint.

A toilet and a few picnic tables are situated in the adjacent meadow. Rest on the stone and log bench and enjoy the scene, or wander across the open slopes for ever-widening perspectives—lovely even on foggy days when the mists swirl around the islands, encompassing, then suddenly revealing, bits of the marine view.

SUMMIT LAKE. This long marshy lake near the mountain's summit is only about 10 feet deep at its maximum. During winter it sometimes freezes over and islanders go ice-skating here. There is only enough space to park two or three cars along the road where it meets the lake; be careful not to block the road or obstruct the vision of drivers.

Drop a canoe or inflatable boat into the water to commune with the frogs and explore the 1/2-mile-long lake, or drift quietly and watch for eagles, hawks, and waterfowl. There are no fish. The marshy shoreline makes hiking around the lake impossible.

SUMMIT OBSERVATION TOWER. Perched atop the hard-rock, 2407-foot summit of Mount Constitution, the stone lookout tower is one of the most unusual and interesting features of Moran State Park. Children especially delight in climbing the many flights of stairs inside the tower, exploring the cell-like rooms, peering out the narrow window slits barred with wrought iron, and firing imaginary crossbows at imaginary armored knights (or laser guns at alien intruders) in the forest below.

Originally designed as both a fire lookout and a public observation tower, the 50-foot-high structure is a facsimile of the military fortifications built by mountain tribes in the Caucasus Mountains of Russia during the twelfth century. Orcas Island quarries supplied the sandstone blocks for the CCC crews that erected the tower in 1936. A display just inside the tower tells of its history, and that of Robert Moran, the donor of the park property.

From the top, the highest point in the San Juan Islands, views spread in all directions; displays identify visible landmarks. Look down to Twin and Mountain Lakes shimmering below, surrounded by dense green forest. Look out in all directions to the array of green and brown islands scattered in the azure fabric of the sound. Especially striking is the stratified geological pattern of the northern San Juan and Canadian Gulf Islands. Toylike boats, ferries, and large tankers dot the water, their silver wakes remaining as long streaks on the smooth surface. To the east, massive Mount Baker looms,

The observation tower on Mount Constitution is patterned after a fortification in Russia's Caucasus Mountains.

and to the south, through the smog of civilization, Mount Rainier rises.

From the viewing area at the base of the tower, peer over the stone railing for an added thrill—a dizzying view straight down the precipitous 1000-foot-high face of the mountain. From vantage points such as this, look for eagles and ospreys circling on updrafts and swallows and flocks of swifts performing high-speed aerial acrobatics. Common nighthawks, which dart about at dusk capturing night-flying insects, nest in thickets along the top of the summit.

Little Summit Trail (11) Maps 38 and 42
Trail hiking distance: 2¼ miles one way
Trail elevation loss: 400 feet

Hike from north to south along the mountain rim, looking downward into lakes and forest, outward to islands and sea—but take time to enjoy the quiet forest, too. The character of the vegetation changes rapidly as the trail traverses the gradually sloping summit plateau. It is thought the abrupt changes in the timber are caused by localized variations in the depth and permeability of the soil.

Entrance Mountain is seen from the roadside near Little Summit.

At one time a number of small ponds dotted the summit; many of these filled in with organic material and are now meadows. Hemlock and fir edge these former marshes, sustained by water seeping in the soft peat. In areas where sandy soil covers the hard summit rock, crowded stands of lodgepole pine with shallow root systems grow, but most reach only 15 feet in height and 2 to 3 inches in diameter. Thickets of manzanita growing in the loose sandy soil attract birds that feast on their tiny applelike fruit.

Near the brow of the plateau, where dirt lodges in the spaces between rock outcroppings, mountain hemlock and Rocky Mountain juniper with tenacious roots grow. Strong winds buffeting the face of the mountain twist these trees into beautiful shapes resembling bonsai. In the valley of Paul Creek near Little Summit, moistness creates another forest type—the soaring, big-trunked timber of western red cedar and western hemlock.

The signed trail departs from the summit behind the KVOS-TV buildings. Watch the route carefully at the beginning, as there are several confusing side trails. After two downhill switchbacks and a short traverse, a spur trail leads to an open rock with limited views to the south. The main trail descends steeply to a larger moss-covered rock, ¼ mile from the start, with a 180-degree outlook encompassing the nearby summit cliffs and the distant shores of the mainland.

Views change as the route edges along the brow of the summit. The final open vista is southeast down to Mountain Lake, then the route turns southwest into the forest. At about ¾ mile the trail crosses a trickling stream on a crude log bridge; the dam at the outlet of Summit Lake can be seen through the trees on the right. The Cold Springs Trail (13) intersects in another ¼ mile, 1 mile from the summit trailhead.

Continuing southeast toward Little Summit, the trail passes east of False Summit, barely noticeable through the trees, and then descends for some distance to a grassy knoll with an eagle's-eye view down to Mountain Lake. Here the lowest point of the trail is reached, some 400 feet in elevation below the summit.

The trail continues on, traversing a sidehill and climbing slightly. In ¼ mile watch carefully for another trail intersection that is signed, but easily could be missed. To the left, the Little Summit to Mountain Lake Trail (16) heads downhill above the gully of Paul Creek, following the path of an old telephone line through heavy timber to emerge at the kitchen shelter at Mountain Lake Campground. The desired route to Little Summit turns right sharply at the intersection, contouring the slope. The path, almost a road now, crosses Paul Creek and in a short distance reaches Little Summit.

Twin Lakes Trail (from summit) (8)   Maps 38 and 43

Trail hiking distance: 1½ miles one way to lakes, 4 miles one way to Mountain Lake Landing

Trail elevation loss: 1300 feet to lakes, 1490 to Mountain Lake Landing

Here's one of the steepest trails in the park, losing more than 1000 feet in a mile—but what scenery! Leave the hoards of car-bound tourists at the summit for challenging trails and rugged vistas. The longer but easier section of the trail, between the lakes and Mountain Lake Landing, is described in the Mountain Lake section.

Find the signed trail on the north side of the turn-around loop at the summit. After a few switchbacks it crosses a wooded flat and zigzags down again to the end of a switchback, where an opening looks north to Matia Island and Canada. The trail now turns eastward, traversing a saddle. Occasional glimpses through the trees reveal the craggy face of Mount Constitution rising above.

At ¾ mile a short side trail on the right leads to an east-oriented rock outcropping, with views to the long outlines of Barnes and Clark Islands just below, Lummi Island farther in the distance, and Mount Baker on the horizon. Another ¼ mile down the main route, a second spur trail leads right, to the last viewpoint, the most spectacular of all. There is space here to rest and picnic, enjoying the wide views east and south—Mountain Lake, Obstruction Pass at the tip of Orcas Island, the midchannel hump of Obstruction Island, thickly forested Blakely Island beyond, and to the far right an impressive view upward of the vertical summit cliffs.

More switchbacks reach a gully and a signed trail junction with the North Side Trail (12). Take the fork on the right, arriving at Big Twin Lake in another 500 yards. The continuation of the trail to Mountain Lake branches south, on the south side of Big Twin Lake.

North Side Trail (12) Maps 38 and 43
   Trail hiking distance: 4¾ miles one way
   Trail elevation loss: 1000 feet to Twin Lakes; elevation gain: 650 feet to Cold Springs

Swing wide around the north flank of Mount Constitution through cool forest, past marshes and ponds. Views are few, but majestic eagles and hawks frequently can be seen in this oft-ignored section of the park. The trail is not heavily used and not regularly maintained; in brushy areas routefinding might pose a problem.

Begin the hike on the Twin Lakes Trail (8) from the top of the mountain. At the trail junction 1¼ miles below the summit, turn left onto the North Side Trail (13), which is signed to Cold Springs. The route heads northwest through open second growth, maintaining a gradual but steady ascent. As it swings over a ridge line and heads west, watch for an impressive grove of cedar below, along a stream bed. The trail then switchbacks uphill, occasionally obscured by growths of short fir.

Just beyond a marsh on the right, the trail is clear again and a long traverse begins. Suddenly, an incongruous sight beside the trail: a deteriorating park bench of hewn logs. Perhaps Robin Hood and his merry men gather here to plot their next foray against the Sheriff of Nottingham!

The trail slowly climbs, traversing steep slopes covered with an open stand of tall hemlock, and 2 miles from the Mount Constitution/Twin Lakes intersection it crosses a rough jeep road that can be followed downhill (for no particular reason) to the park boundary; private property lies beyond.

The trail continues its traverse and in 300 yards crosses a powerline right-of-way that is the north end of the West Boundary Trail (15). At this point the trail becomes the Hidden Ridge Trail (14), which shortly joins the Cold SpringsTrail (13) and reaches the road.

For a mostly downhill trip, reverse the route, starting at Cold Springs (13); at the lower intersection continue downhill to Twin Lakes (8) and then on to Mountain Lake Landing (8). Total distance is 5½ miles; elevation loss is 1130 feet.

COLD SPRINGS AND HIDDEN RIDGE
Map 44

An isolated picnic area in open forest is reached by driving 3¾ miles up the mountain from Orcas Road–Mount Constitution road intersection to a gate at an old service road. There is parking space for a couple of cars at the gate and along the roadside. Just inside the barrier is a rustic shelter with picnic tables and a stove, and downhill, south of the shelter, a log gazebo roofed with cedar shakes protects what was once Cold Springs. At one time this area was a campground, but it has been closed to overnight use for some time. The old-fashioned hand pump that supplied spring water was so frequently vandalized that park rangers gave up efforts to keep it operational and capped the spring. Picnickers must now supply their own water.

Cold Springs Trail *(13)* Maps 38 and 44
Trail hiking distance: 2¾ miles one way
Trail elevation loss: 1700 feet

The east branch of this trail begins at the Cold Springs parking lot, crosses the road, and in ⅓ mile intersects with the Little Summit Trail (11). From this junction, hikers can go south to Little Summit or north to the Mount Constitution summit. Walk the road back to your start point for a nice loop hike, or arrange for car pickup at either destination.

For the Cold Creek route, head west from the Cold Springs shelter on the south side of the picnic area. Hike through the swampy flat to a trail intersection in ½ mile, and bear left on the trail signed to Cascade Lake. The trail zigzags downhill, crossing and recrossing branches of Cold Creek.

As the steep descent begins, the vegetation immediately changes from wetland to dry, open forest. Curious squirrels edge headfirst down trees, circling out of sight around the trunk when hikers approach. An open, moss-covered bluff ½ mile from the trail intersection is a good place to rest, break out the chocolate bars, and enjoy the view of Cascade Lake, Rosario Resort, and points beyond. Aside from occasional glimpses of scenery through the trees while on the trail, this is the only viewpoint along the route.

In about 1¼ miles the trail crosses two branches of Cold Creek on log bridges. A traverse begins and the trailside growth changes from open forest to tangled vine maple, berry bushes, and nettles. At the end of the final

The gazebo at Cold Springs covers the now capped-over spring.

switchback, just below the North End Campground, the creek cascades prettily over water-worn boulders overhung with ferns. Cold Creek is a natural spawning ground for native trout; fishing is not permitted.

The trail ends at the Cascade Lake recreation center. For a real workout, begin at Cascade Lake and hike uphill, gaining 1700 feet of elevation in 2 miles.

Hidden Ridge Trail (14) Maps 38 and 44
Trail hiking distance: 1¼ mile one way
Trail elevation loss: 1500 feet

West of Cold Springs a trail wanders out to Hidden Ridge (14) through a cool marsh with cedar, hemlock, alder, and maple. Ferns thickly cover the forest floor, and, in season, trilliums, skunk cabbage, and marsh marigolds brighten the green carpet with their blossoms. Several ponds along the way are nearly dry in summer, but during the wet season they offer sanctuary for migrating waterfowl. In the forest look for varied thrush and several species of warblers.

From Cold Springs, follow the Cold Springs Trail (13) west to a fork. The left-hand fork switchbacks steeply down to Cascade Lake. Bear right here,

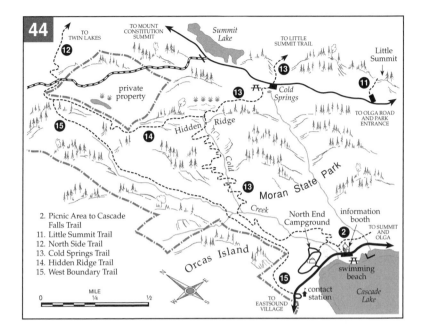

continuing along the plateau of Hidden Ridge. The virtually flat route wanders through alder, fir, and sword fern and reaches a concrete post marking the corner of private land. The path turns north, takes a short switchback down a rise, and passes a lake and marsh. It reaches its end at the junction of North Side Trail (12) and West Boundary Trail (15).

West Boundary Trail (15) Maps 38 and 44
Trail hiking distance: 4¹/₂ miles one way
Trail elevation loss: 1700 feet

This is not really a trail per se, but a jeep road along a power line going up to the radio towers at the summit of Mount Constitution. The West Boundary Trail is extremely steep throughout its length, with little in the way of scenery except glimpses northwest through trees. Its primary appeal is to hard-core hikers seeking a remote wilderness experience in the heart of civilized Orcas Island.

The upper end of the trail starts at the intersection of the North Side Trail (12) and the Hidden Ridge Trail (14), 1³/₄ miles north of Cold Springs. The powerline drops briefly to the west, then heads south near the top of a 600-foot-high cliff. In ¹/₂ mile the head of the west fork of Cold Creek is reached, and the road and power line start an uninterrupted 1-mile drop down the drainage—very steep in places.

In another 1¹/₄ miles the trail heads west, then south another ¹/₄ mile, to meet the county road at the northwest park entrance.

AROUND THE MOUNTAIN
Map 38

Although Moran State Park's trails were designed for day hikes, and back-country camping restrictions preclude tenting along the trail, a determined hiker can complete a circuit of the park by planning ahead to stay in one of the established campgrounds where the trail meets the road. In summer make reservations in advance for campsites, and check in with the ranger. Remember that dogs must be kept on leashes, even in the backcountry, so it is a good idea to leave your best friend at home.

Two possible routes are listed here, although a number of variations can be worked out. Hikers can choose the shorter, somewhat easier scenic route, or opt for the more challenging, less-traveled outer loop, which might involve some brush beating and trailfinding problems and, along with it, more solitude. Either circuit could be completed in one day by a seasoned hiker,

Sunlight filters through lodgepole pines near the summit of Mount Constitution.

with little time taken for sightseeing. Specific sections of trail are described earlier in this chapter.

Both hikes described here begin and end at the top of the mountain, with overnight stops at South End Campground on Cascade Lake. Cars may not be left overnight at the summit, so hikers must park at the campground and prearrange transportation up and down the road with a friend, or resort to the expedience of an extended thumb.

Route A: The Scenic Circuit Map 38
Trail hiking distance: 11¼-mile loop
Trail elevation loss and gain: 2050 feet, with some ups and downs, all lost the first day and regained the second day

From the parking lot below the observation tower, take the Little Summit Trail (11) south and turn right onto the Cold Springs Trail (13). Follow the trail along Hidden Ridge and in ½ mile head downhill, following the Cold Springs Trail to the Cascade Lake recreation center. Cross the road and turn right onto the Cascade Lake Loop Trail (1), which circles the north and west sides of Cascade Lake, finally reaching South End Campground, the first night's destination. Total day's distance is 5¾ miles.

Begin the second day with a hike along Cascade Creek from Cascade Lake to Mountain Lake (6), reaching the dam at the outlet of Mountain Lake. At the trail intersection turn right along the east side of the lake (7), and at the north end head up-valley to Twin Lakes (8). From Twin Lakes, climb the trail back to Mount Constitution's summit (8). Total day's distance is 5½ miles.

Route B: Far from the Madding Crowd Map 38
Trail hiking distance: 15¼ mile loop
Trail elevation loss and gain: 2050 feet, with some ups and downs, all lost the first day and regained the second day

Begin the hike on the trail descending to Twin Lakes (8) from the summit parking lot below the observation tower. Just before reaching the lakes turn left onto the North Side Trail (12), which is signed to Cold Springs. The route swings around the northwest corner of the park, reaching the intersection with the Hidden Ridge Trail (14), which eventually joins the Cold Springs Trail (13). From here hike downhill, following the Cold Springs Trail to Cascade Lake. Turn right onto the trail around the north and west shores of the lake (1), arriving at the night's destination, at South End Campground. Total day's distance is 7½ miles.

On the second day, take the trail on the west side of the campground, signed to Mountain Lake (6), and follow it along Cascade Creek to the point where it joins the dirt service road. Take the road over the top of Mount Pickett (9). Beyond Mount Pickett the road narrows to a trail as it approaches Twin Lakes. End the day by returning to the main road via the steep trail from Twin Lakes up to the summit (8). Total day's distance is 7¾ miles.

chapter nine

The Northern Boundary

DOTTING THE SEA LIKE SCATTERED GEMS of a broken necklace, a scenic string of islands—Patos, Sucia, Matia, Clark, Barnes, and their attendant smaller islets and rocks—form the northern boundary of the San Juans. Although early settlers lived on the larger of these islands from time to time, none were ever officially opened for homesteading. In early days, cobblestones for Seattle streets were quarried on Sucia, and later foxes were commercially raised there and on Matia Island.

During the late 1800s, after the settlement of the boundary dispute with Britain, the U.S. government set aside some of the islands as lighthouse reservations or military reserves for coastal defense. When modern warfare made the concept of fixed coastal defense fortifications obsolete, many of the islands were converted to wildlife sanctuaries and state marine parks. Sucia was made available for private development in the 1950s. Over a twenty-year period, beginning in 1952, portions of the present park land were purchased by the state for recreational use. During the 1960s, 319 acres were bought by the Puget Sound Interclub Association, an organization of boaters,

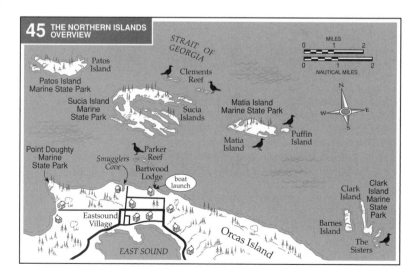

45 THE NORTHERN ISLANDS OVERVIEW

Opposite: *Kayakers navigate around one of the slender islands in Sucia Island's Echo Bay.*

233

Sucia Sandstone

The two dozen islands and rocks of the Sucia group, along with Stuart and Waldron Islands to the southwest and British Columbia's Gulf Islands to the north, share a common geological history. Rocks exposed here are more recent than those of islands farther south.

Geologists theorize that in this area the San Juan Islands deposits, described in the Introduction, were covered by sand and silt laid down in a river estuary during the Cretaceous period, around 75 million years ago. When the Juan de Fuca Plate arrived some 50 to 40 million years ago, bearing a huge subcontinent, it subducted and scraped off the landmass into an enormous mound—Vancouver Island. The pressure of this gigantic mass compressed the basin of the river estuary, folding and tilting the sedimentary deposits of shale and sandstone. Sea animals such as clams, snails, and ammonites that were buried in the sediment of the estuary became the well-known fossils found in Sucia's Fossil Bay. More recently, these rocks were covered by layers of gravelly till from glaciers that at least twice covered this region. Erosion of the folded beds of alternating hard and soft material accounts for the long parallel ridges enclosing slender bays.

Sucia Island has some of the finest examples of the eroded cliffs that are typical of these northern San Juan Islands. Sandstone beds exposed on the uptilted edges of the islands have been eroded to fantastic shapes and patterns, ranging from a fine honeycombing to body-size caves, lovely enough to make a sculptor envious. Caves formed here were used by early day smugglers and today delight beach explorers. The rocks are sculpted by the chemical action of salt water on sandstone, assisted by the wearing action of wind and waves. Low-level wearing of the beaches here and on many of the other San Juan Islands is limited by tide rips offshore; only at high tide do storm waves reach shore without being broken up by tide rips, thus beaches at the high tide level demonstrate the cutting action of the waves. Trails on some of the islands are on sandstone that shows the same pock-marking of saltwater erosion as does the beach a hundred feet below, indicating it was once at water level and, over time, has been uplifted. This is especially evident along the Ewing Cove trail on Sucia Island.

At Rolfe Cove on Matia Island, the rock cliff just west of the trail illustrates the geological origins of the island. Two wide, dark bands of conglomerate are sandwiched between bands of sandstone, and the whole layer cake is tilted upward at about a 60-degree angle, clearly demonstrating the upthrusting that created the island.

Glacial till overlaying the sandstone provides good support for vegetation, thus the larger islands are thickly covered with brush and trees. One of the most common is the Pacific madrona (arbutus to our Canadian friends), with broad evergreen leaves and peeling red bark. Its gracefully twisted trunks overhang many of the islands' shores, picturesquely framing marine views.

under the leadership of Ev G. Henry, and entrusted to the care of the State Parks and Recreation Commission for use as a marine park.

All or part of Patos, Sucia, Matia, and Clark Islands are now state parks, with mooring and camping facilities for visiting boaters. Camping is permitted only in designated sites; a fine might result for those who pitch tents in unauthorized areas. There is no garbage collection at Patos, Matia, and Clark Islands. Although Sucia does have containers, visitors are encouraged to take their trash with them to ease the problem of garbage disposal.

The nearest put-in for small craft is at Bartwood Lodge, 2 nautical miles from Sucia Island on the north shore of Orcas Island; a fee is charged for launching. ❀ Tidal current in the channel can be strong, and rough water might occur near the middle at Parker Reef. In a small or unpowered

A honeycomb pattern, caused by water and wind erosion, is frequently found in sandstone rocks of the Sucia Islands.

boat, crossing at slack tide is recommended, with a careful eye to the weather, as the crossing can be quite risky when the direction of the wind opposes that of the current. Once Sucia is reached, small boats can island-hop, timing their open-water adventures for favorable tides. ❀ Strong tidal currents and tide rips occur at many points on these passages; kayakers should not attempt these trips unless trained and experienced in open-water paddling.

Patos Island Marine State Park Map 46

Boating • Paddling • Camping • Picnicking • Fishing • Hiking • Beach Walking • Tidepools

Facilities: 7 primitive campsites, picnic tables, fireplaces, toilets, 2 mooring buoys, 1½ miles of hiking trail; *no drinking water, no garbage collection*
Area: ISLAND: 209 acres; **PARK:** 207½ acres, 4⁴⁄₅ miles of shoreline on the Strait of Georgia
🛥️ The nearest boat launch is at West Beach Resort, on the north side of Orcas Island, 5 nautical miles across President Channel. Active Cove is 2½ nautical miles northwest of Sucia Island's Shallow Bay.

Patos Island, the northern outpost of the San Juan Islands, commands sweeping views of Canadian lands and of boundary waters heavily plied by commercial vessels. A lighthouse occupies 2 acres of the western tip, at Alden

Active Cove is one of the most scenic moorages in the San Juans.

Point; the remainder of the 1-mile-long island is a marine state park. On the eastern end, parallel ridges of erosion-resistant rock extend far out into the water like toes on a foot, thus the name Toe Point. Slightly removed from the pleasure-boating mainstream and lacking the many protected anchorages of Sucia and Stuart, Patos attracts few boaters, and the beaches are uncrowded.

❄ Heavy tide rips occur off Alden Point, along the north side of the island, and around Toe Point. The east entrance to Active Cove, the only protected harbor on the island, is narrow, shallow, and filled with large rocks, so entry should be made from the west. The deep, narrow cove holds two mooring buoys and has room for a few additional boats to drop anchor. There is also a reasonably well protected anchorage (except in northerlies)

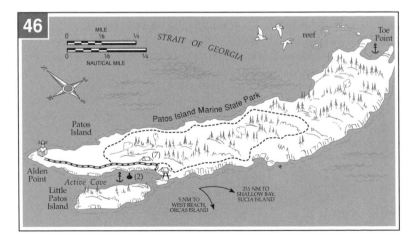

in the cove at Toe Point; however, there are no onshore facilities.

At the head of Active Cove, on a grassy spit, are three campsites and a few picnic tables; two more sites are farther back in the trees. Two "penthouse" campsites are perched on a cleared flat area on the bluff west of the beach, just off of the island loop trail.

Patos Light was established in 1893; the present structure was built fifteen years later. The light is now automated, as are all such navigational warning devices throughout the San Juans. Patos Island is the setting for Helene Glidden's book, *The Light on the Island*. Glidden lived here as a child at the turn of the century when her father was lighthouse keeper; her book is based on her childhood adventures and the early history of the San Juan Islands. The vivid accounts of smugglers, Indians, visits by Col. Teddy Roosevelt, rowing to Bellingham in a skiff, and the day-to-day routine on this far outpost give readers insight into early life in the islands. The book has recently been reprinted.

Eagles seem to have become quite accustomed to visitors at Patos Island and sometimes can be seen sitting on rocky points as they calmly watch passing boaters. Such apparent acceptance of humans should not be interpreted as domesticity, however. The birds are very susceptible to disturbance during nesting season and should not be harassed, even in the spirit of curiosity.

Beaches and Trail
Trail hiking distance: 1½-mile loop
Trail elevation gain: Negligible

Eroded sandstone cliffs 10 to 20 feet high edge the south side of the island, making beach walking there difficult except on the rock benches immediately east of Active Cove. In contrast, the north-side beaches are a true delight and can be walked at all but extreme high tides, when the headlands have to be crossed by short inland scrambles. At the west end of the north shore, eroded, kelp-covered rock beaches offer tidepools; eastward, gravel beaches separated by small headlands of sandstone and conglomerate stretch along the shore to Toe Point. Watch for seals fishing the turbulent waters of tide rips or resting on offshore rocks.

Beaches on the north side of the island can be reached from a loop trail that heads east from the campground along the bluff edge above the south shore. In ¼ mile the trail turns inland, continuing east through dense alder, fir, cedar, and shoulder-high sword fern. The nearly level trail skirts east of the highest point of Patos (100 feet), then swings north and west, as wild rose and thimbleberry crowd its edges. The path finally emerges near mid-island at north beach accesses. After paralleling the north shore, sometimes making short inland digressions, the trail completes its loop with a short climb over the west end of the center island rib. Here it reaches an unmarked intersection with an overgrown service road. The road left goes to the lighthouse area; follow the branch to the right to reach the campground at the head of Active Cove.

Sucia Island Marine State Park   Map 47

Boating • Paddling • Camping • Picnicking • Hiking • Swimming • Beach Walking • Fossils • Clam Digging • Crabbing • Fishing • Scuba Diving • Birdwatching • Wildlife Watching

Facilities: 55 campsites, 16 picnic tables, 2 group camps, 2 Adirondack shelters, 3 picnic shelters, fireplaces, drinking water, composting toilets, toilets, underwater marine park, 2 docks with floats, 52 mooring buoys (including oil spill buoys), 2 lineal mooring systems, 6¼ miles of trail and 3½ miles of service road, portable-toilet dump

Area: ISLANDS: 749 acres; **PARK:** 564 acres, 13¾ miles of shoreline on the Strait of Georgia

🚤 Sucia Island, which generally is the major destination for boaters, lies 2 nautical miles north of the north shore of Orcas Island, the nearest point where boats can be rented or launched, and 4½ miles from Orcas's West Beach Resort.

Mile-long rocky fingers protecting shallow bays form the group of eleven islands known as the Sucias. All of Sucia Island, Little Sucia, Ewing, and the Cluster Islands are park property. The two large, long, forested islands in Echo Bay, appropriately named North Finger and South Finger, are privately owned.

Snowy Mount Baker overlooks boats moored in Echo Bay.

With nearly 9 miles of shoreline, six bays, and extensive boat and camping accommodations, Sucia Island State Park provides one of the best public marine recreational facilities in the San Juans. Just 2 nautical miles north of Orcas Island, Sucia is inviting to boaters in vessels ranging from kayaks to luxury yachts. The fifty-two mooring buoys scattered around the island are heavily used; five of these buoys, sitting near the entrances to Echo and Fossil Bays and Fox Cove, were installed as anchor points for oil-spill protection booms. Recreational boaters may use them when they are not needed for an emergency. Additional moorage is on two docks with floats in Fossil Bay; small boats can be beached at the head of any of the bays.

❁ Boaters in small craft will need to exercise caution en route to Sucia from Orcas Island or points beyond, carefully considering the weather and tidal currents. Heavy summer traffic and larger boats can also be hazards. The trip is recommended only for experienced sea kayakers and canoeists.

During summer, facilities can be very crowded at Sucia, with well over 100,000 visits by boaters annually. Be prepared to anchor if necessary. Buoys and floats are first-come, first-served, and the practice of "reserving" a buoy or float space by tying a dinghy to it for the later arrival of a friend or for the return of the mother craft is neither courteous nor legal; it can result in

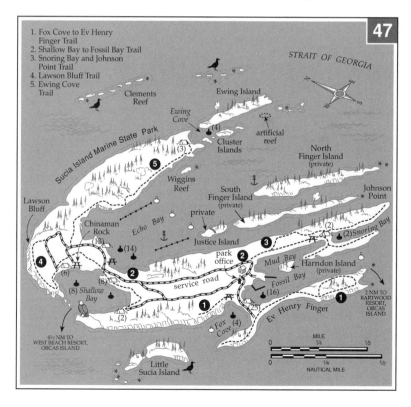

Sucia Wildlife

The pitted sandstone that makes the islands such a scenic delight provides nesting areas for a variety of marine birds, such as pelagic cormorants and pigeon guillemots, while seals and sea lions haul out on the smooth, sun-warmed rocks of the more secluded beaches and nearby reefs.

Birdwatchers can often spot bald eagles, ospreys, or turkey vultures perched atop scraggly fir trees or soaring the skies above them. Although rare, brown pelicans have been seen here, foraging the shores. Cormorants, known colloquially as "shags," sit on rocks or vacant buoys, overseeing the harbors. Cormorants are not completely waterproof, thus they must perch with wings hanging loosely or slightly outspread to dry their "sails." Their lack of oily waterproofing makes them less buoyant, enabling them to dive underwater to depths of several hundred feet to capture food. When winds are high, pelagic cormorants can be seen with their long black bodies plastered against sandstone cliffs; in good weather they frequently fly as flocks in sinuous V-formations.

Observant visitors might spot otters swimming along the shores. One evening in early June, we watched an otter diligently foraging for seafood in Sucia Island's Shallow Bay. With its stomach finally filled, the otter scrambled up the beach and rolled in the soft sand like an ecstatic puppy before finally sauntering into the forest. The following day we watched a pair of otters fishing along the shore in Fossil Bay.

Although this is the ocean, the animals seen in the San Juans are river otters, ranging 2 to 3 feet long (with another 1 to 1½ feet of length for their tail) and weighing ten to twenty-five pounds. Sea otters have a larger, heavier body (but proportionally shorter tail) and weigh thirty to eighty-five pounds. Sea otters were so heavily hunted for their fur during the late 1800s that they nearly became extinct in the Pacific Northwest; they are making a slow comeback along the Pacific Coast.

A sleek river otter forages for goodies on a Sucia Island shore.

The sun sets at Shallow Bay.

your tender being cast adrift. A fee is charged for on-shore camping and for moorage on floats, buoys, or lineal moorage after 3:00 P.M.

Camping areas, connected by trails or service roads, are situated around Sucia Island at Fossil Bay, Echo Bay, Shallow Bay, Snoring Bay, and Ewing Cove, for a grand total of fifty-five sites. Camping is permitted only in designated sites. In the summer, drinking water is available at Fossil Bay, Fox Cove, and Shallow Bay; however, from November through March all water pipes except those at Fossil Bay are shut off.

The Spanish name "Sucia" is correctly pronounced Su-SEE-uh, although few people (even residents) say it that way. The common pronunciation is SOO-shuh—not as melodious, but perhaps more logical to an Anglicized tongue. The name, meaning "dirty water," was given to the island by early explorers who noted the dangerous rocks and reefs near the shores. ✹ Boaters should take warning from the name and be wary of submerged rocks offshore and in the bays. Deep draft boats should be especially careful that they have enough depth throughout the swing of their anchorage during low tide. Fierce wave action can occasionally present problems to boaters at Sucia. When a southeaster blows into any of the bays on the southeast side of the island, the anchorages are at best uncomfortable and possibly dangerous. West-facing Shallow Bay offers the best protection during these conditions. It might be necessary to go elsewhere if it is not possible to secure a safe moorage.

The fashion once was to spray-paint the name of visiting boats on the sandstone cliffs of the island. All this graffiti has been cleaned from the rocks, and the fad hopefully is now past, so that today's visitors can enjoy the natural beauty rather than the ugly scrawls of insensitive visitors.

Sucia Bays

FOSSIL AND MUD BAYS. Fossil Bay is the hub of park activity, with its two floats and seventeen buoys filled nearly every night of the summer season. From the dock, hard-surfaced trails lead to a disabled-accessible picnic shelter and two Adirondack shelters in the sparse trees near the docks. More campsites are nearby on the sandspit between Fossil Bay and Fox Cove and on the finger on the south side of the cove.

Mud Bay, offset from Fossil Bay, nearly empties at low tide; other times the water is just deep enough for dinghying. Harndon Island, at the entrance to Mud Bay, is private property.

FOX COVE. Separated from Fossil Bay by a low sandspit, Fox Cove faces westward, sheltered by Little Sucia Island. Worn cliffs on the north side of the bay form marvelous shapes, including an 8-foot-high rock mushroom where children can pretend to be in Alice's Wonderland. There are five mooring buoys in Fox Cove. ❃It can be entered via either a narrow rocky channel on the south end of Little Sucia or a much wider and safer passageway on the east side of that island; nervous skippers should choose the latter. The sandy beach at the head of the cove is one of the best on the island for wading and swimming.

Off-season, row out to Little Sucia Island from Fox Cove for a private picnic and evening views of blazing sunsets. ❃Currents in the channel between the islands can be strong; use care. Little Sucia is a designated wildlife refuge and is closed to public use from January 1 through August 15. It is open only for day use the rest of the year.

SHALLOW BAY. Indenting the western end of the horseshoe-shaped island, Shallow Bay has three distinct sandy beaches with a campground on each, separated by rocky headlands. ❃Enter the bay with care, as submerged rocks extend out from the points at either side of the entrance. The channel is marked by daybeacons. Eight buoys and numerous good anchorages attract boaters. However, the bay is extremely shallow; check water depth and the predicted tides before settling down for the night.

Shallow Bay offers driftwood, clams, and crabs to beach walkers. Large cockles might be picked up right on the surface at low tide, while other clams hide deeper in the sand. Dungeness crabs lurking in the eelgrass of the cove might be trapped with crab pots in deep water or routed out of the seaweed (carefully) during a minus tide. Refer to the Introduction for regulations on shellfish harvesting.

Chinaman Rock, on the northeast side of Shallow Bay, is a striking example of the wave- and chemical-eroded sandstone and subsequent uplifting so characteristic of these northern isles. The rock is mostly obscured by a growth of trees but can be found by going to the east end of the northernmost beach, then walking into the trees at the edge of the cliff.

Body-size hollows have obviously been geologically uplifted at least 30 feet since they were formed. Legend is that during the late 1800s, Chinese aliens smuggled into the United States from Canada often hid in the recesses from patrolling immigration officials. Do not deface the rock, so that others can enjoy this fascinating spot in its natural state.

A mushroom-shaped rock is a shoreline attraction at Fox Cove.

ECHO BAY. The largest bay on the island, Echo contains twelve mooring buoys and two lineal mooring systems and has ample space for many more boats to swing at anchor. The large, blue-striped buoy in the center of the bay is reserved for Coast Guard boats when they are stationed in the area. Because this is the most open of Sucia's anchorages and is exposed to waves and surges, it can be uncomfortable during some wind and tide conditions.

The eastern half of the tiny island at the western tip of South Finger Island is a recent park addition. The property was turned over to the state in 1986 after previously being confiscated by U.S. marshals when the owner was convicted of running a drug-smuggling operation there. When the would-be smuggler scouted and purchased the island in winter, the deserted spot seemed perfect for clandestine activities. He didn't realize it was smack-dab in the middle of the state's most popular marine state park. Surprise!

The 2-acre island, now appropriately called "Justice Island," is a nesting area for bald eagles and pupping ground for seals, so public use is prohibited. The western half of the island is privately owned.

SNORING BAY. Tiny Snoring Bay lies on the south side of Johnson Point. Although the inlet generally is scorned by powerboaters, it is a haven for kayakers seeking refuge from the noise and fumes of motors. The story goes that the bay received its name when park officials visiting the island discovered a ranger there enjoying a siesta. Snoring Bay has two mooring buoys and two campsites.

EWING COVE. Boaters seeking privacy might find it in Ewing Cove, on the north side of Echo Bay, snuggled between Ewing Island and the Cluster Islands. The long, narrow cove boasts sandy beaches and exquisite examples of the worn sandstone that makes the rest of the island so popular. ❄Approach the cove from the east, favoring the Ewing Island side of the channel, where the shore drops off rapidly to 50 to 75 feet of water; avoid rocks and shoals that extend out from Cluster Islands. Do not try to enter via the narrow channel on the west end of Ewing Island; it is shoal, laced with rocks, and suffers from fast and unpredictable tidal currents. When entering the cove, stay reasonably close to Ewing Island (within 100 yards or so), and keep a sharp eye out for submerged rocks and reefs that lie on the southwest side of the channel.

Four mooring buoys are available in 25 feet of water, and three campsites and a toilet are located above the beach at the west end of the cove. A buoy near the east end of the cove marks the site of an underwater marine park area, a favorite of scuba divers. Three sunken vessels are below the buoy and several yards to the east, in 45 feet of water.

At Ewing Cove, an added bonus for birdwatchers is Clements Reef and adjoining rocks, part of the San Juan Islands Wilderness Area, lying less than 1/2 mile to the north. Hundreds of seabirds congregate here, some of them nesting on Sucia and Matia, others merely resting on their migratory flights. ❄Be content to identify them with strong binoculars from shore, for waters around the reef can be treacherous and any approach by man disturbs the birds. Seals and sea lions, too, can be seen on the reefs in large numbers, snoozing in the sun or warily eyeing passing boaters.

Hiking Trails

A dirt service road loops through the wooded main section of the island, with branch trails stretching from it to all ends of the island fingers. Some of the major destinations are described here. Because of the many possible starts and variations, specific distances are not given. The elevation gain is never greater than 100 feet, but there might be many ups and downs.

Except for park service equipment, motorized vehicles and bicycles are prohibited on park roads and trails. The rock quarry near the head of one dock at Fossil Bay is particularly dangerous; stay out of the area. Wear sturdy shoes on any long hike; deck "tennies" or sandals do not provide adequate footing on steep, slippery trails.

FOX COVE AND EV HENRY FINGER. The trail around the north side of Fox Cove follows the high edge of the bluff above the bay, while paths on Ev Henry Finger, Johnson Point, and the northern edge of Echo Bay skirt the water. Search shoreline rocks, especially on Ev Henry Finger, for fossilized clams, snails, and ammonites 75 million years old. Such specimens may be collected if they are lying loose, but digging in the banks is illegal.

SHALLOW BAY TO FOSSIL BAY. This trail is a service road that leaves the Shallow/Echo Bay spit, passes a branch to the Shallow Bay campground, then heads southeast in a continuous series of ups and downs, all in the woods, with no views. It finally arrives at a steep descent to the marshes behind Harndon Island and the ranger's residence. Here a spur trail heads steeply uphill to the southeast, to Snoring Bay (3/4 mile) and Johnson Point (1 1/2 miles). The main road continues over an intervening rib to Fossil Bay, after first passing a track northwest to the Shallow Bay campground. This route is flat, except for a short switchback up to its junction with the Shallow Bay-Fossil Bay road, which is definitely a superior way to get to Fossil Bay.

LAWSON BLUFF. A short but very scenic loop skirts the edge of Lawson Bluff on the northwest side of Sucia Island. Find the signed trail out of the northernmost campsite at Shallow Bay, near the toilets. A network of side paths leading to open viewpoints confuses the route as it rounds the point north of the Shallow Bay entrance. All paths eventually lead back to the main route along the edge of the bluff. The way climbs gradually, staying just above the precipitous cliffs of Lawson Bluff. Keep a hand on the kids—the trail is easy enough, but in places it is so near the edge that a misstep could cause a bad fall.

Aerial views stretch down the sheer cliff to the ocean glimmering 100 feet below and north to the long stretches of Patos Island and the rugged outlines of Canada's Gulf Islands. After about 1/2 mile the trail turns inland, joining the northernmost loop of the service road at a signed trailhead in another 200 yards. Turn right to return to Shallow Bay, left to reach the head of Echo Bay (the easiest return to Fossil Bay). Total distance of the loop hike from Shallow Bay is about 3/4 mile.

Madrona branches form a delicate tracery along the trail to Ewing Bay.

EWING COVE. The most beautiful hike on Sucia, and possibly in the entire San Juans Islands, is the 2-mile-long trail running along the north side of Echo Bay to Ewing Cove. This is a "three-or-more rolls of film" hike for photography buffs. The signed trailhead leaves the park service road about 300 yards east of its spur to Chinaman Rock.

After a few hundred yards of meandering through thick brush, the path breaks out to the edge of the bluff above Echo Bay, which it follows for the remainder of the hike. At a few points inland, detours have been created to avoid dangerously eroded sections of trail falling off the bluff above 75-foot cliffs—take the detours.

There is no beach access at first, as the trail winds along the 100-foot-high cliffs, whose eroded sandstone cavities are used as nesting sites by darting swallows. In ¼ mile a grassy knob, so tempting it needs to be signed "No Camping," provides views down the sinuous waterways between the Finger Islands.

Pocket coves have steep, somewhat hazardous scrambles down to beaches framed by wave-sculpted sandstone. Graceful madronas and gnarled, silver, long-dead junipers frame pictures of the myriad shapes and forms carved in the rock. Small rocks and islets just offshore await the visit of kayakers.

Where the tread is on sandstone, note that this rock shows the same pock-marking of saltwater erosion as does the beach 70 feet below, indicating it was once at water level and has, over time, been uplifted.

Cawing crows warn eagles, woodpeckers, and gulls of a hiker's pending arrival. As the trail nears its destination at Ewing Cove, the cliffs moderate and ready beach access is available. Not moderated, however, is the fantasy of wave-carved sandstone forms continuing out along the Cluster Island chain. The cove itself is a remote and peaceful retreat—difficult to leave for the trip back to the hubbub of the main island campgrounds.

Matia Island Marine State Park and Wildlife Refuge   Map 48
Boating • Paddling • Camping • Picnicking • Hiking • Birdwatching • Clam Digging • Crabbing • Tidepools • Fishing • Beach Walking

Facilities: 6 campsites, dock with float (float removed in winter), 2 mooring buoys, picnic tables, fire braziers, composting toilet, trail; *no drinking water*
Area: ISLAND: 145 acres, 3³/₄ miles of shoreline on the Strait of Georgia; **PARK:** 5 acres
Trail hiking distance: 1-mile loop
Trail elevation gain: Negligible
Matia Island lies 2¹/₄ nautical miles east of Fossil Bay on Sucia Island; 2¹/₂ nautical miles northeast of Bartwood Lodge, on the north shore of Orcas Island, where boats may be launched for a fee; and approximately 14 nautical miles from launch ramps at Bellingham, on the mainland.

Although Matia might well be the loveliest of these jewel-like northern isles, it is often passed over by visiting boaters because it has limited overnight space. The exposed walls of the coves are naturally sculpted masterpieces.

Hollowed and smoothed by wind and waves, the stony banks are accentuated by banded patterns of layered conglomerate.

Only 5 acres, facing Rolfe Cove on the west side of the island, are open to camping; the remainder of the island is designated as national wildlife refuge and wilderness area. The U.S. Fish and Wildlife Service permits use of this small part of the island as a state park, in hopes that such limited use of the land will be compatible with wildlife preservation. If the presence of the public on Matia ever becomes a threat to the birds and mammals living there or on nearby Puffin Island, all human intruders will be asked to pull up their tent stakes and anchors and go elsewhere.

Rolfe Cove holds a dock with a 45-foot float and two mooring buoys, with room for only a few more boats to drop a hook. Hovering at the mouth of the cove, a rocky islet gives some protection from northerly wind, but it also causes peculiar current flows that disrupt confident anchoring. The bottom of Rolfe Cove is deep and quite rocky; in a strong blow it might be difficult to secure a safe anchorage.

On the bank at the head of the cove are picnic tables, six campsites, and a composting toilet. A sign tells you all you ever wanted to know about composting toilets—and then some. Drinking water once was available from a nearby pump; it was capped because of problems with adequate purification, so bring your own.

For day excursions, small boats can be beached in any of several coves on the island; camping is allowed only on state park land. ✦ Boats also might anchor in a long, narrow bay on the southeast end of the island;

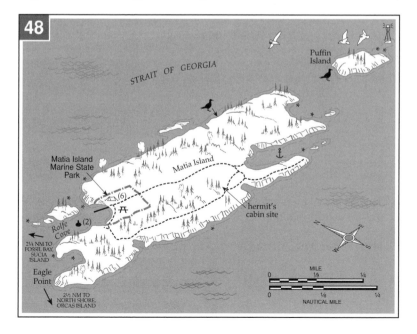

however, the end of the bay is extremely shoal at low water. Several rocks lying in the entrance are an additional hazard. Going ashore is permitted at the head of the bay. The north shore and south shores are posted as wildlife refuges.

"Matia" has undoubtedly the most varied and disputed pronunciation of any San Juan Island. The Spanish pronunciation of the word, meaning "no protection," is MAH-tee-ah. The name is often corrupted as MAY-shuh, MAY-tee, or MAT-ty.

Near the head of the southeast bay, a faint spur trail heads out along the finger of land framing the south side of the bay. Here are terrific views west over a tiny cove and south to Orcas Island and Mount Constitution. In about $1/4$ mile is a sign reading "Wilderness Area." End your hike here.

The main loop trail turns north, passes the head of the southeast bay, and then bends west for its return to Rolfe Cove. A sign at the east end of

The Hermit of Matia

In early years, this island was the longtime home of one of the San Juans' most interesting characters, known as the "Hermit of Matia." His name was Elvin Smith, and even though local newspapers of the day referred to him as a hermit, in truth he was not antisocial, for every week, in all but the foulest of weather, he rowed his skiff to North Beach on Orcas Island. From there he hiked a 2-mile trail to Eastsound Village to collect his mail, buy supplies, and gossip with his cronies.

The pioneer recluse had gained a reputation as a mystic and a mail-order faith healer. His weekly mail included dozens of letters, and sometimes money, from supplicants all over the country seeking his assistance. At home, on the retreat of his island, Smith claimed to spend many hours each day in prayer on behalf of his correspondents.

Smith lived for nearly thirty years in this briny paradise. From time to time other pioneers showed interest in the land, but one occupant on a 150-acre island was considered quite crowded enough for the time, so they settled elsewhere. One stormy February, in 1921, Smith (who was then eighty-six) and a visiting friend, their boat heavily laden with supplies, cast off from Orcas Island for a return trip to Matia. They were never seen again. Stones marking two vacant graves in an Orcas Island cemetery commemorate their lives.

A wilderness loop trail on the island passes the location of Smith's early settlement. Pets are not allowed on the trail because this is a wildlife refuge. A wide path leaves the dock at Rolfe Cove and heads south near the edge of the cove. After reaching a marshy area on the south side of the island, the path continues eastward, shaded by second-growth maple and Douglas-fir.

Look sharply along this section of trail to spot faint skeletons of ancient fences. Although Smith was a vegetarian, he kept sheep for wool and chickens for eggs. And rabbits? Perhaps for companionship.

At Matia Island Marine State Park, the dock sits in protected Rolfe Cove.

the loop trail indicates that the remainder of the island is closed to public access; respect it. As the trail heads west, the nature of the forest changes to huge old-growth trees, predominately cedar but with a sprinkling of hemlock, Douglas-fir, and alder.

Puffin Island • Puffin Island sits just a stone's throw offshore from the east end of Matia. This steep, rocky island, topped with a scraggly pompadour of trees and grass, is one of the islands of the San Juan Islands Wilderness Area; going ashore is prohibited. Seals and sea lions can often be seen lolling about in the warmth of the sun, and, with binoculars, squawking, gossipy seabirds can be identified: ungainly murres and auklets, and shy pigeon guillemots.

From mid-March to mid-September these birds gather in colonies and lay their eggs in rock clefts, tending them until the downy chicks feather out and are able to fly. During this nesting time, any close approach by boats or people is disturbing to the families; if the birds become alarmed by your presence, you are too close.

Early day Lummi Indians from the Bellingham region paddled dugout canoes to Matia and Puffin Islands to collect eggs, which they packed in cool, moist leaves of sea lettuce to safeguard against spoilage and breakage. The sea lettuce, too, was later eaten or dried for winter use. Today, visitors can sample the green, tissuey seaweed if they gather it from the water or nearby shores. However, Uncle Sam protects Puffin Island and its eggs.

249

Clark Island Marine State Park   Map 49

Boating • Paddling • Camping • Picnicking • Clam Digging • Beach Walking • Scuba Diving • Fishing • Tidepools • Birdwatching

Facilities: 2 campsites, picnic tables, fire rings, toilets, 9 mooring buoys; *no drinking water, no garbage collection*

Park area: 55 acres, 11,292 feet of shoreline on the Strait of Georgia

Clark Island is 6½ nautical miles southeast of Fossil Bay on Sucia Island. Although it is located less than 2 miles from the shores of Orcas Island, the nearest boat launching area is 5 nautical miles to the west, at Bartwood Lodge, at North Beach. Launch ramps at Bellingham, on the mainland, are approximately 14 nautical miles distant.

Swept by the waters of the Strait of Georgia, shadowed by the mountains of Orcas Island, a group of rocks and islands cluster together like a family. On the southwest, the smaller, barren rocks are known as The Sisters, with the southernmost wedge-shaped rock named Little Sister Island.

The largest of the rocks once sported a single pine tree, prompting the name Lone Tree Island, but the tree has long since surrendered to the sea, leaving the islet to some tenacious grass and hundreds of nesting birds. The rock is now marked by a navigational light.

Kayakers enjoy a campsite near the beach at Clark Island.

The Sisters and Little Sister Island are included in the San Juan Islands Wilderness Area. In spring and summer, cormorants, pigeon guillemots, glaucous-winged gulls, and other pelagic birds nest here. At other times of the year gulls gather on the rocks, occasionally in enormous numbers, for reasons known only to them—perhaps for an afternoon coffee (or herring) klatch. Whatever the reason, the cacophony of their conversation at such times is overwhelming, even on the shores of Clark Island.

Barnes Island, second in size of the island group, lies on the west. The uplands of Barnes are private, but the surrounding tidelands below the mean high water level are public. Do not stray above the driftwood level onto private property.

Less than ½ mile east of Barnes is the largest of the island family, 55-acre Clark Island, a marine state park. The distance from populated areas, the lack of drinking water for campers, and the lack of protected anchorages make this one of the less frequented of the San Juan Islands marine state parks. The slender island is a mile in length, but scarcely 300 yards across at its widest point. Its southern end hooks sharply eastward to form a small, broad bay; here six mooring buoys offer easy, although exposed, anchorages. ✿ Skippers approaching this bay should use care, as several rocks lie just beneath the surface along its east side; boats have been known to run aground. Refer to a good navigational chart for location of hazards. A slight indentation on the opposite side of the island holds three additional mooring buoys, sheltered from the west by Barnes Island and from the southeast by the end of Clark.

Timber and impenetrable brush cover most of the island. Along the edges, graceful red-barked madronas lean over the ever-eroding banks. Near the toilets, a single trail crosses the island. Waves ate through a protective berm

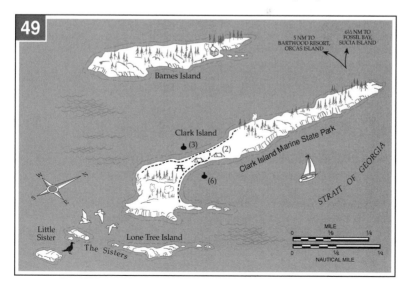

Harbor seals forage the water near Clark Island.

on the east side of the island, and the entire beach, running some 20 feet back, has been lost. Violent winter storms in 1989 and 1990 began the damage, and serious erosion has continued since then. All six of the campsites that were here were swept away. They will not be replaced until alternative sites can be found that allow for protection of wildlife and habitat.

Campers may pitch tents in the two remaining campsites found in the trees along the cross-island trail connecting the two anchorages. One of these inland sites is large enough to hold several tents for a group gathering. The west beach, with a warm, inviting sand strip above a gradually tapering gravel beach, is a day-use picnic area. Camping or building fires on the beach is prohibited in order to keep it as natural as possible. A fire circle, surrounded by rough-hewn log benches, is on the west side, above the beach.

Clark Island has some of the most varied beaches of any of these northern island marine state parks. Sand and mud flats to the south, exposed at low tide, are good for clamming and summertime wading; mussels cling to protruding rocks. The steeper, rocky northern beaches, inaccessible from land, hold an array of marine life—purple starfish, pastel sea anemones, barnacles, sea squirts, purple and green urchins, and more—to be admired by scuba divers and tidepool explorers. Trails that once skirted the south end of the island have been removed to protect nesting bald eagles and seabirds.

Mountains rising on the British Columbia mainland are visible from anchorages on the east side of the island. Monstrous oil tankers occasionally sail by in the distance, delivering their cargo from Alaskan oil fields to the refinery at Cherry Point. At night the lights of the refinery glimmer across the water—a reminder of civilization so near the marine treasure.

San Juan Islands Wildlife

MAMMALS

Many land mammal species have reached the various islands by swimming, drifting on floating debris, or hitchhiking on boats, especially in the case of rodents. Not all species listed here are found on all islands. Black bear and elk once were native to the islands but have been extirpated.

The asterisk identifies non–native species that have been introduced. At one time European ferrets were introduced to control rabbits, but it is believed they have died out. Exotic species such as sika deer, which were introduced on Spieden Island, are particular to that locale and are not listed.

LO = Lopez Island, SH = Shaw Island, OR = Orcas Island, SJ = San Juan Island

HABITAT	POPULAR SITES	SPECIES
Forests, meadows	Odlin County Park (LO), Moran State Park (OR), Jakle's Lagoon (SJ)	Vagrant shrew, meadow vole
Caves, buildings; seen swooping overhead at night	Throughout the islands	Bat (numerous species, especially little brown bat)
Brush, meadows; seen in campgrounds	Spencer Spit State Park (LO), Odlin County Park (LO), Moran State Park (OR), San Juan Island National Historical Park (SJ)	Rabbit*
Forests, gardens	Spencer Spit State Park (LO), Shark Reef (LO), Odlin County Park (LO), Moran State Park (OR), English Camp (SJ), American Camp (SJ)	Douglas squirrel (chicka-ree)*, Eastern fox squirrel, Eastern gray squirrel*, Townsend's chipmunk*
Ponds, marshes, lakes	Moran State Park (OR)	Beaver, muskrat*
Meadows, brush, woodlands	Moran State Park (OR), English Camp (SJ), Jakle's Lagoon (SJ)	Deer mouse, Norway rat*
Towns, buildings	(LO, SH, OR, SJ)	Black rat, house mouse
Wooded areas, brushlands	American Camp (SJ)	Red fox*
Forests, especially near water; seen in campgrounds	James Island, Spencer Spit State Park (LO), Shark Reef (LO), Odlin County Park (LO), Moran State Park (OR), James Island, English Camp (SJ), American Camp (SJ)	Raccoon

HABITAT	POPULAR SITES	SPECIES
Conifer forests, especially near water	SJ	Marten, fisher, weasel, mink
Beaches, protected bays	Throughout the islands	River otter
Roadsides, pastures, orchards	(LO, OR, SH, SJ), Jones Island	Black-tailed deer (mule deer)
Seen hauled out on offshore rocks and reefs and foraging in kelp beds and tide rips	Shark Reef (near SJ), Parker Reef (near OR), Clements Reef (near Sucia Island), rocks and islets of San Juan Islands National Wildlife Refuge	California sea lion, northern elephant seal, northern sea lion, Pacific harbor seal, Stellar sea lion
Seen in deep, wide channels	Haro Strait, San Juan Channel, President Channel, Spieden Channel, Rosario Strait, Strait of Georgia, Strait of Juan de Fuca	Dall's porpoise, gray whale, harbor porpoise, humpback whale, minke whale, orca whale, Pacific white–sided dolphin

A curious young raccoon checks out hikers at Turn Island.

BIRDS

The San Juan Islands' wide range of habitats, along with its location on the Pacific Flyway, makes it prime birdwatching territory. This table includes birds most commonly seen in particular San Juan habitats. Many are not resident and can be sighted primarily during migratory or nesting season. Popular birdwatching areas are listed; however, many of the habitats are found throughout the islands.

Note: The list is by no means inclusive of all the species that might be seen, and not all birds are seen at the sites listed; for example, blue grouse have been spotted only on Orcas Island. Some species are named under more than one habitat. Groups and species are listed in the order they are usually found in bird identification guides.

LO = Lopez Island, SH = Shaw Island, OR = Orcas Island, SJ = San Juan Island

HABITAT	POPULAR SITES	GROUP, SPECIES
Docks and pilings	Ferry landings, marinas (LO, SH, OR, SJ), marine state parks	CORMORANTS: Double-crested Cormorant, Brandt's Cormorant, Pelagic Cormorant; GULLS, TERNS: Heerman's Gull, Bonaparte's Gull, Mew Gull, Thayer's Gull, California Gull, Glaucous-winged Gull, Western Gull, Common Tern; KINGFISHERS: Belted Kingfisher
Open saltwater	Seen from boats and ferries throughout the islands	GULLS, TERNS: Heerman's Gull, Bonaparte's Gull, Mew Gull, Thayer's Gull, California Gull, Glaucous-winged Gull, Western Gull, Common Tern; MURRES, AUKS: Common Murre, Pigeon Guillemot, Rhinoceros Auklet
Offshore rocks	Richardson (LO), Point Colville (LO), Shark Reef (LO),San Juan Channel, President Channel	SHOREBIRDS: Black Oystercatcher, Ruddy Turnstone, Black Turnstone, Surfbird; GULLS, TERNS: Heerman's Gull, Bonaparte's Gull, Mew Gull, Thayer's Gull, California Gull, Glaucous-winged Gull, Western Gull, Common Tern; MURRES, AUKS: Common Murre, Pigeon Guillemot, Rhinoceros Auklet
Rocky cliffs	Point Colville (LO), Moran State Park (OR), Waldron Island, Stuart Island, Willow Island	MURRES, AUKS: Common Murre, Pigeon Guillemot; NIGHTJARS, SWIFTS: Common Nighthawk, Black Swift; SWALLOWS: Cliff Swallow
Glacial till bluffs	American Camp (SJ), Westside Road (SJ)	MURRES, AUKS: Common Murre, Rhinoceros Auklet; SWIFTS: Black Swift; KINGFISHERS: Belted Kingfisher; SWALLOWS: Northern Rough-winged Swallow
Sandy, gravelly shores	Odlin County Park (LO), West Beach (OR), Jackson Beach (SJ), Cattle Point (SJ), False Bay (SJ), Fossil Bay (Sucia Island)	SHOREBIRDS: Black Oystercatcher, Semipalmated Plover, Black-bellied Plover, Greater Yellowlegs, Common Sandpiper, Ruddy Turnstone, Black Turnstone, Surfbird, Dunlin; JAYS, CROWS, ALLIES: American Crow, Common Raven

HABITAT	POPULAR SITES	GROUP, SPECIES
Protected shores, saltwater bays, salt marshes, lagoons	Spencer Spit (LO), Fisherman Bay (LO), Squaw Bay (SH), Massacre Bay (OR), Buck Bay (OR), Crescent Bay (OR), Jackson Beach (SJ), False Bay (SJ), Shallow Bay (Sucia Island)	**Loons, Grebes:** Pacific Loon, Common Loon, Western Grebe, Horned Grebe, Pied-billed Grebe; **Wading Birds:** American Bittern, Black-crowned Night-heron, Great Blue Heron; **Waterfowl:** Brant, American Wigeon, Canvasback, Greater Scaup, Lesser Scaup, Surf Scoter, Harlequin Duck, Oldsquaw, Barrow's Goldeneye, Common Goldeneye, Bufflehead, Common Merganser, Hooded Merganser; **Shorebirds:** Greater Yellowlegs, Short-billed Dowitcher, Long-billed Dowitcher; **Wrens:** Marsh Wren
Mudflats	Fisherman Bay (LO), Crescent Beach (OR), Buck Bay (OR), False Bay (SJ)	**Wading Birds:** Black-crowned Night-heron, Great Blue Heron; **Shorebirds:** Semipalmated Plover, Black-bellied Plover, Short-billed Dowitcher, Long-billed Dowitcher, Dunlin
Tree snags	Upright Head (LO), Moran State Park (OR), Westside Road (SJ)	**Gulls, Terns:** Glaucous-winged Gull; **Raptors:** Turkey Vulture, Golden Eagle, Bald Eagle, Osprey
Conifer forests	Spencer Spit State Park (LO), Shark Reef (LO), Moran State Park (OR), Obstruction Pass Campground (OR), English Camp (SJ), James Island, Jones Island, Stuart Island, Sucia Island, Matia Island	**Diurnal Raptors:** American Kestral; **Gamebirds:** Blue Grouse; **Hummingbirds:** Anna's Hummingbird, Rufous Hummingbird; **Woodpeckers:** Northern Flicker, Red-breasted Sapsucker, Yellow-bellied Sapsucker, Downy Woodpecker, Hairy Woodpecker, Pileated Woodpecker; **Flycatchers, Larks, Swallows:** Western Wood-pewee, Hammond's Flycatcher; **Jays, Crows, Allies:** Steller's Jay, Gray Jay, Clark's Nutcracker; **Chickadees, Nuthatches:** Chestnut-backed Chickadee, Brown Creeper, Red-breasted Nuthatch; **Wrens:** Winter Wren, Bewick's Wren; **Thrushes, Kinglets, Allies:** Golden-crowned Kinglet, Ruby-crowned Kinglet, Hermit Thrush, Varied Thrush, Northern Shrike; **Waxwings, Starlings:** Cedar Waxwing; **Warblers, Sparrows:** Audubon's (Yellow-rumped) Warbler, Townsend's Warbler; **Blackbirds, Allies:** Western Tanager; **Finches:** Pine Siskin, Red Crossbill, Pine Grosbeak
Open meadows, grasslands, open rocky slopes	Center Road (LO), Crow Valley (OR), Mount Finlayson (SJ), Beaverton Valley (SJ)	**Shorebirds:** Killdeer; **Diurnal Raptors:** Peregrine Falcon; **Gamebirds:** California Quail, Ring-necked Pheasant; **Pigeons, Doves:** Band-tailed Pigeon, Rock Dove; **Owls:** Snowy Owl; **Flycatchers, Larks, Swallows:** Eurasian Skylark, Violet-green Swallow, Purple Martin, Barn Swallow; **Pipits:** Red-throated Pipit, Water Pipit; **Warblers, Sparrows:** Lapland Longspur, Snow Bunting; **Blackbirds, Allies:** Brown-headed Cowbird
Wet pastures	Center Road (LO), Crow Valley (OR), Beaverton Valley (SJ)	**Waterfowl:** Tundra Swan, Trumpeter Swan, Canada Goose; **Shorebirds:** Semipalmated Plover, Black-bellied Plover, Dunlin; **Owls:** Snowy Owl; **Warblers, Sparrows:** Common Yellowthroat

HABITAT	POPULAR SITES	GROUP, SPECIES
Riparian woodland	Hummel Lake (LO), Killebrew Lake (OR), Cascade Lake (OR), Mountain Lake (OR), Sportsman and Egg Lakes (SJ), Lakedale Campground (SJ), Jakle's Lagoon (SJ)	OWLS: Barn Owl, Short-eared Owl, Great Horned Owl, Western Screech-owl; HUMMINGBIRDS: Anna's Hum-mingbird, Rufous Hummingbird; Woodpeckers: Northern Flicker, Downy Woodpecker, Hairy Woodpecker, Pileated Woodpecker; FLYCATCHERS, LARKS, SWALLOWS: Olive-sided Flycatcher, Willow (Traill's) Flycatcher, Western Flycatcher, Tree Swallow; VIREOS: Solitary Vireo, Red-eyed Vireo, Warbling Vireo; CHICKADEES, NUTHATCHES: Black-capped Chickadee, Chestnut-backed Chickadee, Brown Creeper, Red-breasted Nuthatch; WRENS: Winter Wren; THRUSHES, KINGLETS, ALLIES: American Dipper, Golden-crowned Kinglet, Swainson's Thrush; WARBLERS, SPARROWS: Orange-crowned Warbler, Yellow Warbler, Wilson's Warbler, Evening Grosbeak, Rufous-sided Towhee, Dark-eyed (Oregon) Junco; BLACKBIRDS, ALLIES: Brown-headed Cowbird, Western Tanager; FINCHES: Pine Siskin, Pine Grosbeak, Purple Finch
Brush and thickets	Ferry Road (LO), Mud Bay Road (LO), Center Road (LO), Blind Bay Road (SH), Hoffman Cove Road (SH), Orcas Road (OR), Crow Valley (OR), Cattle Point Road (SJ), Beaverton Valley Road (SJ), Yellow Island	GAMEBIRDS: California Quail, Ring-necked Pheasant, Wild Turkey; FLYCATCHERS, LARKS, SWALLOWS: Olive-sided Flycatcher, Willow (Traill's) Flycatcher, Western Flycatcher; BUSHTITS: Bushtit; WRENS: House Wren, Bewick's Wren; WAXWINGS, STARLINGS: Cedar Waxwing; WARBLERS, SPARROWS: Orange-crowned Warbler, Audubon's (Yellow-rumped) Warbler, Yellow Warbler, MacGillivray's Warbler, Rufous-sided Towhee, Savannah Sparrow, Song Sparrow, Chipping Sparrow, White-crowned Sparrow, Golden-crowned Sparrow, Fox Sparrow; BLACKBIRDS, ALLIES: Brewer's Blackbird; FINCHES: American Goldfinch
Towns and gardens	Lopez Village (LO), East Sound (OR), Deer Harbor (OR), Orcas Landing (OR), Olga (OR), Westsound Village (OR), Rosario Resort (OR), Friday Harbor (SJ), Roche Harbor Resort (SJ)	PIGEONS, DOVES: Band-tailed Pigeon, Rock Dove; HUMMINGBIRDS: Rufous Hummingbird; FLYCATCHERS, LARKS, SWALLOWS: Violet-green Swallow, Purple Martin, Barn Swallow; JAYS, CROWS, ALLIES: Steller's Jay, American Crow; CHICKADEES, NUTHATCHES: Black-capped Chickadee, Red-breasted Nuthatch; WRENS: House Wren; THRUSHES, KINGLETS, ALLIES: American Robin; WAXWINGS, STARLINGS: European Starling; WARBLERS, SPARROWS: Evening Grosbeak, Rufous-sided Towhee, Savannah Sparrow, Song Sparrow, Golden-crowned Sparrow; FINCHES: House Sparrow, Purple Finch, House Finch
Fresh-water lakes	Hummel Lake (LO), Cascade Lake (OR), Mountain Lake (OR), Sportsman and Egg Lakes (SJ), Lakedale Campground (SJ)	LOONS, GREBES: Pied-billed Grebe; WATERFOWL: Trumpeter Swan, Canada Goose, Mallard, American Wigeon, Northern Pintail, Northern Shoveler, Blue-winged Teal, Wood Duck, Greater Scaup, Lesser Scaup, Common Merganser, Hooded Merganser; RAILS, COOTS: American Coot; FLYCATCHERS, LARKS, SWALLOWS: Willow (Traill's) Flycatcher; BLACKBIRDS, ALLIES: Red-winged Blackbird

HABITAT	POPULAR SITES	GROUP, SPECIES
Fresh-water marshes	Point Colville (LO), Frank Richardson Wildlife Preserve (OR), Sportsman and Egg Lakes (SJ), West Valley Road (SJ), Beaverton Valley Road (SJ)	**Wading Birds:** American Bittern, Black-crowned Night-heron, Great Blue Heron; **Waterfowl:** Blue-winged Teal, Cinnamon Teal; **Rails, Coots:** Virginia Rail, Sora, American Coot; **Shorebirds:** Common Sandpiper, Long-billed Dowitcher, Western Sandpiper; **Wrens:** Marsh Wren; **Pipits:** Red-throated Pipit, Water Pipit; **Warblers, Sparrows:** Common Yellowthroat; **Blackbirds, Allies:** Red-winged Blackbird
Soaring overhead	All islands and waterways	**Gulls, Terns:** Heerman's Gull, Bonaparte's Gull, Mew Gull, Thayer's Gull, California Gull, Glaucous-winged Gull, Western Gull, Common Tern; **Diurnal Raptors:** Turkey Vulture, Golden Eagle, Bald Eagle, Northern Harrier, Sharp-shinned Hawk, Cooper's Hawk, Red-tailed Hawk, Rough-legged Hawk, Osprey, American Kestral, Merlin, Peregrine Falcon; **Jays, Crows, Allies:** American Crow, Common Raven
Darting overhead	All islands and waterways	**Nightjars, Swifts:** Common Nighthawk, Black Swift; **Flycatchers, Larks, Swallows:** Violet-green Swallow, Purple Martin, Cliff Swallow, Barn Swallow
Telephone poles and fences	(LO, SH, OR, SJ) Waldron Island, Stuart Island	**Diurnal Raptors:** Northern Harrier, Red-tailed Hawk, Rough-legged Hawk, Merlin; **Flycatchers, Larks, Swallows:** Violet-green Swallow, Purple Martin
Roadsides	Center Road (LO) Crow Valley Road (OR), Moran State Park (OR), Roche Harbor Road (SJ)	**Gamebirds:** California Quail, Ring-necked Pheasant, Wild Turkey; **Warblers, Sparrows:** Rufous-sided Towhee, Song Sparrow; **Blackbirds, Allies:** Brewer's Blackbird; **Finches:** House Sparrow

SAN JUAN ISLANDS BIRDING CHECKLIST

Loons, Grebes
- ❏ Pacific Loon
- ❏ Common Loon
- ❏ Western Grebe
- ❏ Horned Grebe
- ❏ Pied-billed Grebe

Cormorants
- ❏ Double-crested Cormorant
- ❏ Brandt's Cormorant
- ❏ Pelagic Cormorant

Wading Birds
- ❏ American Bittern
- ❏ Black-crowned Night-heron
- ❏ Great Blue Heron

Waterfowl
- ❏ Tundra Swan
- ❏ Trumpeter Swan
- ❏ Canada Goose
- ❏ Brant
- ❏ Mallard
- ❏ American Wigeon
- ❏ Northern Pintail
- ❏ Northern Shoveler
- ❏ Blue-winged Teal
- ❏ Cinnamon Teal
- ❏ Wood Duck
- ❏ Canvasback
- ❏ Greater Scaup
- ❏ Lesser Scaup

- ❏ White-winged Scoter
- ❏ Surf Scoter
- ❏ Harlequin Duck
- ❏ Oldsquaw
- ❏ Barrow's Goldeneye
- ❏ Common Goldeneye
- ❏ Bufflehead
- ❏ Common Merganser
- ❏ Hooded Merganser

Rails, Coots
- ❏ Virginia Rail
- ❏ Sora
- ❏ American Coot

Shorebirds
- ❏ Black Oystercatcher

- ❏ Semipalmated Plover
- ❏ Killdeer
- ❏ Black-bellied Plover
- ❏ Greater Yellowlegs
- ❏ Common Sandpiper
- ❏ Short-billed Dowitcher
- ❏ Long-billed Dowitcher
- ❏ Ruddy Turnstone
- ❏ Black Turnstone
- ❏ Surfbird
- ❏ Dunlin
- ❏ Western Sandpiper

Gulls, Terns
- ❏ Heerman's Gull
- ❏ Bonaparte's Gull
- ❏ Mew Gull
- ❏ Thayer's Gull
- ❏ California Gull
- ❏ Glaucous-winged Gull
- ❏ Western Gull
- ❏ Common Tern

Murres, Auks
- ❏ Common Murre
- ❏ Pigeon Guillemot
- ❏ Rhinoceros Auklet

Diurnal Raptors
- ❏ Turkey Vulture
- ❏ Golden Eagle
- ❏ Bald Eagle
- ❏ Northern Harrier
- ❏ Sharp-shinned Hawk
- ❏ Cooper's Hawk
- ❏ Red-tailed Hawk
- ❏ Rough-legged Hawk
- ❏ Osprey
- ❏ American Kestral
- ❏ Merlin
- ❏ Peregrine Falcon

Gamebirds
- ❏ Blue Grouse
- ❏ California Quail
- ❏ Ring-necked Pheasant
- ❏ Wild Turkey
- ❏ Pigeons, Doves
- ❏ Band-tailed Pigeon
- ❏ Rock Dove

Owls
- ❏ Barn Owl
- ❏ Short-eared Owl
- ❏ Great Horned Owl

- ❏ Snowy Owl
- ❏ Western Screech-owl

Nightjars, Swifts
- ❏ Common Nighthawk
- ❏ Black Swift

Hummingbirds
- ❏ Anna's Hummingbird
- ❏ Rufous Hummingbird

Kingfishers
- ❏ Belted Kingfisher

Woodpeckers
- ❏ Northern Flicker
- ❏ Red-breasted Sapsucker
- ❏ Yellow-bellied Sapsucker
- ❏ Downy Woodpecker
- ❏ Hairy Woodpecker
- ❏ Pileated Woodpecker

Flycatchers, Larks, Swallows
- ❏ Olive-sided Flycatcher
- ❏ Western Wood-pewee
- ❏ Hammond's Flycatcher
- ❏ Willow (Traill's) Flycatcher
- ❏ Western Flycatcher
- ❏ Eurasian Skylark
- ❏ Tree Swallow
- ❏ Violet-green Swallow
- ❏ Purple Martin
- ❏ Cliff Swallow
- ❏ Northern Rough-winged Swallow
- ❏ Barn Swallow

Vireos
- ❏ Solitary Vireo
- ❏ Red-eyed Vireo
- ❏ Warbling Vireo

Jays, Crows, Allies
- ❏ Steller's Jay
- ❏ Gray Jay
- ❏ Clark's Nutcracker
- ❏ American Crow
- ❏ Common Raven

Chickadees, Nuthatches
- ❏ Black-capped Chickadee
- ❏ Chestnut-backed Chickadee
- ❏ Brown Creeper
- ❏ Red-breasted Nuthatch

Wrens
- ❏ House Wren
- ❏ Winter Wren

- ❏ Bewick's Wren
- ❏ Marsh Wren

Thrushes, Kinglets, Allies
- ❏ American Dipper
- ❏ Golden-crowned Kinglet
- ❏ Ruby-crowned Kinglet
- ❏ Swainson's Thrush
- ❏ Hermit Thrush
- ❏ Varied Thrush
- ❏ American Robin
- ❏ Northern Shrike

Pipits
- ❏ Red-throated Pipit
- ❏ Water Pipit

Waxwings, Starlings
- ❏ Cedar Waxwing
- ❏ European Starling

Warblers, Sparrows
- ❏ Orange-crowned Warbler
- ❏ Audubon's (Yellow-rumped) Warbler
- ❏ Townsend's Warbler
- ❏ Yellow Warbler
- ❏ MacGillivray's Warbler
- ❏ Wilson's Warbler
- ❏ Common Yellowthroat
- ❏ Evening Grosbeak
- ❏ Rufous-sided Towhee
- ❏ Savannah Sparrow
- ❏ Song Sparrow
- ❏ Chipping Sparrow
- ❏ Dark-eyed (Oregon) Junco
- ❏ White-crowned Sparrow
- ❏ Golden-crowned Sparrow
- ❏ Fox Sparrow
- ❏ Lapland Longspur
- ❏ Snow bunting

Blackbirds, Allies
- ❏ Red-winged Blackbird
- ❏ Brewer's Blackbird
- ❏ Brown-headed Cowbird
- ❏ Western Tanager

Finches
- ❏ House Sparrow
- ❏ Pine Siskin
- ❏ American Goldfinch
- ❏ Red Crossbill
- ❏ Pine Grosbeak
- ❏ Purple Finch
- ❏ House Finch

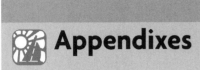 **Appendixes**

A. Emergency Phone Numbers and List of Contacts
The local area code in the San Juan region is 360.

Fire (Alarms Only)
Blakely, Lopez, Orcas, San Juan, and Shaw Islands: 911
For fires on remote islands, call the Department of Natural Resources:
(800) 562-6010. If calling by radio, notify the U.S. Coast Guard.

Medical Emergencies
Blakely, Lopez, Orcas, San Juan, and Shaw Islands: 911
Poison Information Center: (800) 732-6985

Sheriff
Emergencies on all islands: 911
Lopez and Shaw Islands: (360) 468-2333
Orcas Island: (360) 376-2207
San Juan and all other islands: (360) 378-4151

U.S. Coast Guard
Marine and Air Emergency: (206) 286-5400

Toll-free Hotlines
Red Tide/Marine Biotoxins Hotline: (800) 562-5632
Whale Hotline: (800) 562-8832

Radio Contacts
Marine V.H.F., Coast Guard distress and hailing: channel 16
Marine V.H.F., Coast Guard liaison: channel 22A
Marine V.H.F., Victoria, B.C.: channel 26 and 84
Citizens Band, Distress: channel 9
To contact a boat via the marine telephone system: (800) 955-9025

U.S. Customs
Friday Harbor and Roche Harbor: (360) 378-2080; after hours: (800) 562-5943

Washington State Ferries
Information: (800) 843-3779 (automated, no human attendant available);
    (888) 808-7977 (also automated, but does provide access to an attendant)
Seattle: (206) 464-6400
Anacortes terminal: (360) 293-8166
Lopez terminal: (360) 468-2252
Orcas terminal: (360) 376-2134
Friday Harbor terminal: (360) 378-4777
Shaw terminal: (360) 468-2142
Internet ferry information: *www.wsdot.wa.gov/ferries*

Parks
San Juan Island National Historical Park, P.O. Box 429, Friday Harbor, WA
    98250; (360) 378-2240; *www.nps.gov/sajh/index.htm*
Washington State Parks and Recreation Commission, 1111 Israel Road SW,
    Olympia, WA 98504-2650; (360) 902-8844; *www.parks.wa.gov*
Spencer Spit State Park, 521A Bakerview Road, Lopez, WA 98261;
    (360) 468-2251
Moran State Park, 3572 Olga Road, Olga, WA 98279;
    (360) 376-2326
Lime Kiln Point State Park, 1567 Westside Road, Friday Harbor, WA 98250;
    (360) 378-2044
All other San Juan State Parks: Star Route, Box 177, Olga, WA 98279;
    (360) 376-2073
San Juan County Park, 50 San Juan Park, Friday Harbor, WA 98250; (360)
    378-2992
Odlin County Park, 148 Odlin Park Road, Lopez, WA 98286; (360) 468-2496

Museums
Lopez Island Historical Museum, P.O. Box 163, Lopez, WA 98261;
    (360) 468-2049; *http://lopezmuseum.org*
Orcas Island Historical Museum, 181 North Beach Road, Eastsound
    Village, WA 98245; (360) 376-4849; *http://orcasmuseum.org*
San Juan Island Historical Museum, 405 Price Street, Friday Harbor, WA
    98250; (360) 378-3949; *http://sjmuseum.org*
Shaw Island Historical Museum: (360) 468-2637
The Whale Museum, 62 First Street North, Friday Harbor, WA 98250; (360)
    378-4710; *www.whale-museum.org/index*

Marinas and Businesses with Some Marine Facilities
Bartwood Lodge; 178 Fossil Bay Drive; Eastsound, WA 98245;
    (360) 376-2242
Beach Haven Resort: 684 Beach Haven Road; Eastsound, WA 98245;
    (360) 376-2288

Blakely Island General Store and Marina; Blakely Island, WA 98222;
(360) 375-6121
Deer Harbor Marina; P.O. Box 344; Deer Harbor, WA 98243; (360) 376-3037
Island Petroleum Services; Orcas Landing; Orcas, WA 98280;
(360) 376-3883
Islander Lopez Resort and Marina; P.O. Box 459; Lopez Island, WA 98261;
(360) 468-2233
Islands Marine Center; P.O. Box 88; Lopez Island, WA 98261;
(360) 468-3377
Port of Friday Harbor; P.O. Box 889; Friday Harbor, WA; (360) 378-2688
Roche Harbor Resort; P.O. Box 4001; Roche Harbor, WA 98250;
(360) 378-2155
Rosario Resort; 1400 Rosario Road; Eastsound, WA 98245; (800) 562-8820
Snug Harbor Marina Resort; 1997 Mitchell Bay Road; Friday Harbor, WA
98250; (360) 378-4762
West Sound Marina; P.O. Box 119; Orcas Island, WA 98280; (360) 376-2314

B. Nautical Charts and Maps

Sketch maps for this book are intended for general orientation only. When traveling by boat on any of the San Juan waters, it is imperative that the appropriate nautical charts be used. The following charts cover the area included in this book. They can be purchased at map stores or many marine supply centers.

NOAA Chart 18423: Bellingham to Everett, including the San Juan Islands
(scale 1: 80,000; folio of charts including some detailed insets)
NOAA Chart 18421: Strait of Juan de Fuca to Strait of Georgia (scale 1:
80,000; covers all areas included in this book)
NOAA Chart 18429: Rosario Strait: southern part (scale 1: 25,000)
NOAA Chart 18430: Rosario Strait: northern part (scale 1: 25,000)
NOAA Chart 18431: Rosario Strait to Cherry Point (scale 1: 25,000)
NOAA Chart 18432: Boundary Pass (scale 1: 25,000)
NOAA Chart 18433: Haro Strait: Middle Bank to Stuart Island (scale 1:
25,000)
NOAA Chart 18434: San Juan Channel (scale 1: 25,000)

Although it would be difficult to get seriously lost on any of the islands,
the USGS topographic maps listed below are useful and interesting.
7.5' series maps: Mount Constitution, Blakely Island, Lopez Pass, Lummi
Island, Eastsound Village, Shaw Island, Richardson, Waldron Island,
Friday Harbor, False Bay, Sucia Island, Stuart Island, Roche Harbor.

C. Selected Reading

Bicycling
Kirkendall, Tom, and Vicky Spring. *Bicycling the Pacific Coast,* 3d ed. Seattle: The Mountaineers, 1998.

Woods, Erin, and Bill Woods. *Bicycling the Backroads Around Puget Sound,* 4th ed. Seattle: The Mountaineers, 1997.

Boating, Paddling
Evergreen Pacific San Juan Cruising Atlas. Shoreline, WA: Evergreen Pacific Publishing, Ltd., 2000.

McGee, Peter, ed. *Kayak Routes of the Pacific Northwest Coast.* Vancouver, B.C., and Seattle: Greystone Books and The Mountaineers, 1998.

U.S. Department of Commerce. *United States Coast Pilot: 7 (Pacific Coast: California, Oregon, Washington and Hawaii).* Washington D.C.: U.S. Department of Commerce, published annually.

Washburn, Randel, and Carey Gersten, ed. *Kayaking Puget Sound, the San Juans, and the Gulf Islands,* 2d ed. Seattle: The Mountaineers, 1999.

Western Marine Enterprises, Inc. *Pacific Boating Almanac: Pacific Northwest and Alaska.* Ventura, CA: Western Marine Enterprises, Inc., published annually.

Fishing and Shellfish
Evergreen Pacific Fishing Guide. Seattle: Evergreen Pacific Publishing, Ltd., 1998.

Hagen, Scott. *Recreational Dungeness Crabbing.* Portland, OR: Frank Amato Publications, 2003.

Wade, J. D. *Evergreen Pacific Shellfish Guide.* Shoreline, WA: Evergreen Publications, Ltd., 2000.

White, Charlie. *How to Catch Crabs: A Pacific Coast Guide,* 2d ed. Surrey, B.C.: Heritage House Publishing, Ltd., 1998.

White, Charlie. *How to Catch Salmon: Basic Fundamentals,* 13th printing. Surrey, B.C.: Heritage House Publishing, Ltd., 1993.

White, Charlie. *How to Catch Shellfish along the Pacific Coast,* 2d ed. Surrey, B.C.: Heritage House Publishing, Ltd., 1998.

General
Diamond, Lynnell, and Marge Mueller. *Let's Discover the San Juan Islands.* Seattle: The Mountaineers, 1989.

Mueller, Marge, and Ted Mueller. *The Essential San Juan Islands Guide,* 4th ed. Medina, WA: JASI, 2004.

Hiking
Sterling, E. M. *Best Short Hikes in Washington's North Cascades and San Juan Islands,* 2d ed. Seattle: The Mountaineers, 2002.

History

Glidden, Helene. *The Light on the Island.* Woodinville, WA: San Juan Publishing, 2001.

Richardson, David. *Pig War Islands: The San Juans of Northwest Washington,* 2d ed. Friday Harbor, WA: Orcas Publishing Company, 1990.

Vouri, Michael. *The Pig War: Standoff at Griffin Bay.* Friday Harbor, WA: Griffin Bay Bookstore, 1999.

Nature

Adams, Evelyn. *San Juan Islands Wildlife: A Handbook for Exploring Nature.* Seattle: The Mountaineers and The San Juan Preservation Trust, 1995.

Alden, Peter, and Dennis Paulson. *National Audubon Society Field Guide to the Pacific Northwest.* New York: Chanticleer Press, 1998.

Atkinson, Scott, and Fred A. Sharpe. *Wild Plants of the San Juan Islands.* Seattle: The Mountaineers, 1993.

Lewis, Mark G., and Fred A. Sharpe. *Birding in the San Juan Islands.* Seattle: The Mountaineers, 1987.

Paulson, Dennis, and Jim Erckmann. *Shorebirds of the Pacific Northwest.* Seattle: University of Washington Press, 2003.

Yates, Steve. *Marine Wildlife From Puget Sound Through the Inside Passage.* Seattle: Sasquatch Press, 1998.

Scuba Diving

Fischnaller, Steve. *Northwest Shore Dives,* 3d ed. Edmonds, WA: Bio-Marine Images, 2000.

Index

ABOUT THE AUTHORS

Photo: Heidi Mueller

Marge and Ted Mueller are outdoor enthusiasts and environmentalists who have explored Washington State's waterways, mountains, forests, and deserts for more than forty years. Ted has taught classes on cruising in Northwest waters, and both Marge and Ted have instructed mountain climbing through the University of Washington. They are members of The Mountaineers and The Nature Conservancy. They are the authors of twelve regional guidebooks.

THE MOUNTAINEERS, founded in 1906, is a nonprofit outdoor activity and conservation club, whose mission is "to explore, study, preserve, and enjoy the natural beauty of the outdoors.... " Based in Seattle, Washington, the club is now one of the largest such organizations in the United States, with seven branches throughout Washington State.

The Mountaineers sponsors both classes and year–round outdoor activities in the Pacific Northwest, which include hiking, mountain climbing, ski–touring, snowshoeing, bicycling, camping, kayaking and canoeing, nature study, sailing, and adventure travel. The club's conservation division supports environmental causes through educational activities, sponsoring legislation, and presenting informational programs. All club activities are led by skilled, experienced volunteers, who are dedicated to promoting safe and responsible enjoyment and preservation of the outdoors.

If you would like to participate in these organized outdoor activities or the club's programs, consider a membership in The Mountaineers. For information and an application, write or call The Mountaineers, Club Headquarters, 7700 Sand Point Way NE, Seattle, WA 98115; (206) 521–6001.

The Mountaineers Books, an active, nonprofit publishing program of the club, produces guidebooks, instructional texts, historical works, natural history guides, and works on environmental conservation. All books produced by The Mountaineers Books fulfill the club's mission.

Send or call for our catalog of more than 500 outdoor titles:

The Mountaineers Books
1001 SW Klickitat Way, Suite 201
Seattle, WA 98134
(800) 553–4453
mbooks@mountaineersbooks.org
www.mountaineersbooks.org

The Mountaineers Books is proud to be a corporate sponsor of Leave No Trace, whose mission is to promote and inspire responsible outdoor recreation through education, research, and partnerships. The Leave No Trace program is focused specifically on human–powered (nonmotorized) recreation.

Leave No Trace strives to educate visitors about the nature of their recreational impacts, as well as offer techniques to prevent and minimize such impacts. Leave No Trace is best understood as an educational and ethical program, not as a set of rules and regulations.

For more information, visit *www.LNT.org,* or call (800) 332–4100.

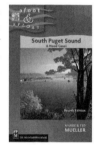

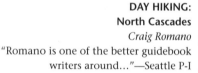
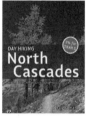